Reynard, Renart, Reinaert

Reynard, Renart, Reinaert

and Other Foxes in Medieval England:
the Iconographic Evidence

A Study of the Illustrating of Fox Lore and Reynard the Fox Stories in England during the Middle Ages

followed by a brief survey of their fortunes in post-medieval times

Kenneth Varty

Amsterdam University Press

Cover illustration: A mitred, robed fox preaches to geese from a pulpit. Byfield, Holy Cross, now housed in the Stained Glass Museum in Ely Cathedral, glass roundel, late 14th C. The Royal Commission on the Historical Monuments of England.

Cover design: Kok Korpershoek, Amsterdam
Lay-out: BEELDVORM, Leidschendam

ISBN 90 5356 375 x

For Hety

who shared in so much of the seeking and the finding

with me when, in 1959, we came upon the Nantwich fox
with me when, in 1999, we handed this text over in Amsterdam

Contents

List of Illustrations

17 A fox tries to steal a goose from the goodwife's basket. Tuttington Parish Church, bench end finial; 15th C. E.L. Jones.

18 A fox with a cock flung over its back is closely chased by a woman wielding her distaff. Cley-next-the-Sea, St Margaret, porch roof boss; 15th c. Kenneth Varty.

19 A drawing of this sculpture based on the photograph. E. de la Mare Norris.

20 A woman leaves her house in pursuit of a fox fleeing with its victim. Foxes at their lessons in either supporter. Manchester Cathedral, misericord; 1508. J.C.D. Smith.

21 A woman runs from her house in pursuit of a fox fleeing with its victim past honking geese. Foxes plot on the left supporter while one holds its victim down on the right supporter. Beverley Minster, misericord; 1520. D.R. Maxted.

22 A fox looks up at a cock perched on a tree branch. Worcester Cathedral, stone spandrel; 13th C. Kenneth Varty.

23 A fox runs off with a cock watched by a woman with a distaff. The Bodleian Library, MS Ashmole 1504, f.34, early 16th C.

24 A mitred fox preaches to birds. A fox with a goose is pursued by a distaff-wielding woman. The British Library, MS Roy. 10 E. IV, f.48; c.1335.

25 A woman attacks a seated fox with her distaff. The seated fox, holding a crozier, listens to another fox preaching from a pulpit. The Burrell Collection, Glasgow. A wooden doorframe spandrel in Burrell's reconstructed Hall. English late 15th C. Kenneth Varty.

26 A fox preaches from a pulpit to four geese. The Burrell Collection, Glasgow. A tapestry cushion cover. Swiss, 1450-75.

27 A fox preaches at a lectern to three geese. Leicester Cathedral, etching made for a study by J. Nichol in 1815 based on a late medieval piece of stained glass, now lost.

28 A fox leans forward on a staff to preach to three relaxed geese. Wells Cathedral, misericord; 1330. D.R. Maxted.

29 A fox makes off with a goose slung over his back. Wells Cathedral, misericord; 1330. D.R. Maxted.

30 A robed fox religious leads a cock, hen and duck. Beverley Minster, stone spandrel, early 14th C. Kenneth Varty.

31 A robed fox preaches from a pulpit to numerous birds. Lincoln Cathedral, wooden quatrefoil in choir-stalls; late 14th C. National Buildings Record.

32 An enthroned fox-bishop attended by a cock and an ass. Boston, St Botolph, misericord; late 14th C. D.R. Maxted.

33 A robed fox preaches from a pulpit to a kneeling woman. St Austell, Holy Trinity, pew end fixed to tower wall; late 14th C. (?). National Buildings Record.

34 A mitred fox preaches to birds. The British Library, MS Roy. 2. B. VII, f.157v; early 14th C.

35 An upright fox with crozier faces a cock. The Bodleian Library, MS Asmole 1504, f.22v; early 16th C.

36 A mitred, robed fox preaches to geese from a pulpit. Byfield, Holy Cross, now housed in the Stained Glass Museum in Ely Cathedral, glass roundel, late 14th C. The Royal Commission on the Historical Monuments of England.

Acknowledgments

For information

Concerning the whereabouts of representations of the fox, especially in medieval England, as well as abroad.

First, there is that numerous band which formed chiefly as a result of an appeal I made through letters published in 1959 by the Editors of the *Sunday Times* and the *Observer*. Of them I am especially grateful to J. Cameron Alexander, A.E. Blackburn, Sidney Blackmore, Canon G.E. Britten, Lady Mary D. Cox, V. Curzon, John Flinn, Sir Barry Jackson, D.R. Maxted, E. de la Mare Norris, F.E. O'Donnel, J.C.D. Smith, Stanley Stewart, N. Stone, Lewis Thorpe, E.R. Waterhouse, A. Wegener and Dean Christopher Woodforde.

Secondly, there are those who have joined me in the hunt since the publication in 1967 of my Leicester University Press book, *Reynard the Fox: a Study of the Fox in Medieval English Art*, or have given me precious advice. Of them I am particularly pleased to thank Norman Blake, editor, leading critic and historian of Reynardian texts published in English; Elaine Block, who has seen and photographed almost every extant historiated misericord and most of the creatures which inhabit the stallwork surrounding them; Wilfried Grauwells and Hubertus Menke, each of whom has an outstanding private library of Reynardian texts, and has made them available to me; Malcolm Jones, whose knowledge of the folklore, legends and myths behind historiated matter in churches and in early prints is unsurpassed; Jill and Brian Lucas who have spent years photographing the animals, birds and insects depicted in any shape or form in English churches; David Ross whose review of my 1967 book was most helpful, and led to a long and fruitful collaboration; E. Clive Rouse, restorer and conserver par excellence of wall paintings in England; Brian Spencer, expert in medieval pilgrim (and other) pewter badges and souvenirs. Important information and help has also been given to me by R. Bosanquet, Jean Duffy, Valerie Hamilton, Mary Hobbs, Jill Mann, and Kerstin Rodin.

For the illustrations

I am most grateful to all those people named in the preceding List of Illustrations for giving me permission to reproduce their copyright photographs, drawings, or other illustrative matter in rare books owned by them: E. Block, F.H. Crossley, B. Dewar, L.H. Felton, W. Grauwels, P.P. Howells, M. Friend, E.L. Jones, J. Knowles, J. V.Lee, J. & B. Lucas, D.R. Maxted, H. Menke, G. Percy, J.C.D. Smith, and P.S. Spokes.

I gratefully acknowledge the permission given to me by the Directors, Trustees, Curators and Librarians of several institutes, museums, art galleries, and libraries to photograph the pictures here reproduced, and for permission to reproduce them. In particular: Abington Manor near Northampton; the Bodleian Library of the University of Oxford, and the Fellow Librarian of All Souls College, Oxford; the Courtauld Institute of Art; the City of Glasgow Art Galleries, and the staff of the Burrell Collection; the British Library; the Editor of the *Kent and Sussex Courier*; Moyses Hall Museum in Bury St Edmunds; the Museum of London; the former National Buildings Record, now the National Monuments Record; the Royal Commission on Historical Monuments for England; the St Annan Museum in Lübeck; the Salisbury and South Wiltshire Museum; the Stained Glass Museum in Ely Cathedral; the Stichtung Behoud Cultuurbezit in Amsterdam; and the Walters Art Gallery in Baltimore.

For permission to photograph, I am grateful to the Dean and Chapter of the Cathedrals of Blackburn, Bristol, Carlisle, Chester, Chichester, Ely, Gloucester, Hereford, Lincoln, Manchester, Norwich, Peterborough, Ripon, Salisbury, Wells, and Worcester; to the authorities at Beverley Minster, Christchurch Priory, St George's Chapel Windsor, Westminster Abbey and York Minster; also to the vicars and priests in charge of the medieval parish churches of Alne in Yorkshire, Barfreston, Beverley St Mary, Bloxham, Boston, Bovey Tracey, Brent Knoll, Bury St Edmund's, St Mary Byfield, Castle Hedingham, Cley-next-the-Sea, Etchingham, Gresford, Holt in Worcestershire, Knowle, Ludlow, Melbourne, Minster-in-Thanet, Nantwich, Oakham, Padstow, Poughill, Swavesey, Tilton-on-the-Hill, Tuttington, West Keal, and Whalley.

Introduction

A lively literature centred on the fox we call Reynard has flourished in Flanders since about 1150, and it still flourishes there. These days, and for quite a long time, most folk in Britain know little about Reynard. They may know the name, and know it as the name sometimes given to the fox just as Bruin is given to the bear and Polly to the parrot, but few know anything about his roles in literature. People who do know the fox, Mr Fox, most probably know him as the trickster in short stories in illustrated children's books, and would be surprised to learn that he was once the leading character in a book meant for adults which became a best-seller in the late fifteenth century and remained popular for more than two hundred years, a book characterized by violence, murder, adultery, rape and corruption in high places. At first sight, it looks as if Reynard may have been as little known to most people in medieval England as he seems to be nowadays, for only two tales of any literary quality running to less than a thousand lines of verse between them have come down to us from those distant times, before William Caxton's 1481 *Historye of Reynart the Foxe* inaugurated more than two centuries of fame for the fox in England, chiefly in adult circles.

Contrast this with the situation across the Channel. To many people who live in Flanders, Reinaert is well known as a very special fox, the villainous hero of some of the most engaging tales ever told in Dutch or, for that matter, in any other language. And very many tales were told (and are still told) in other languages, notably French and German. At different stages in the Middle Ages, a Reynardian literature flourished from Normandy and Picardy in what is now northern France, eastwards through Belgium, Holland, and northern Germany as far as Schleswig-Holstein. It also spread southwards, through the regions dominated by Paris, through Alsace, and as far as northern Italy. In most of these countries a rich post-medieval Reynardian literature has developed, especially in Dutch- and German-speaking lands. Goethe's *Reineke Fuchs* (1794) is one of Germany's brightest literary gems, and Michel Rodange's *Renert* (1872) is one of Luxemburg's outstanding narrative poems.

It was as Reinardus that Reynard the Fox made his literary début in one of the finest masterpieces of all time, the *Ysengrimus*, a Latin verse epic of over six and a half thousand lines, composed in 1148-49, in a clerical milieu in Ghent. The narrative focuses on a strong but not-so-bright wolf named Ysengrimus. His main opponent and tormenter is a cunning little fox, his nephew, Reinardus. It is also here that, for the first time in a literary work of art, the antagonism between wolf and fox bcomes the animating force which drives a story from beginning to end.

The *Ysengrimus*'s fox (Reinardus vulpes) becomes Renart le Goupil in the forty-odd tales which make up the twenty-six branches and nearly thirty thousand lines of the French *Roman de Renart*. They were composed as separate, only loosely linked narrative poems, over a period of about seventy years, beginning in the 1170s. At one point in the *Ysengrimus* the fox rapes the wolf's wife. It is this more than any other crime or insult which lies at the root of their unending enmity, and it is this which seems to have inspired a Frenchman, called Pierre de Saint Cloud, to compose and put together the first group of narrative poems in French centred on the fox. Since the publication of the first scholarly edition of the *Roman de Renart* in the 1870s, this bears the branch number II and tells of Renart's brushes with a cock called Chantecler, an unnamed titmouse (both based on episodes in the *Ysengrimus*), a crow called Tiécelin (based on the Aesopian fable of the fox and the crow), and a cat called Tibert before climaxing with an account of his adultery with, then rape of Hersent, the wife of Isengrin the Wolf. The author of this exceptionally entertaining, artistically splendid earliest branch (or group of little branches) was careful not to resolve the quarrel between the fox and the wolf, and to leave the situation open so that their story might be continued. And continued it was! First by the branch known as 'Reynard's Solemn Oath' (*Le Serment*, Va) in which Isengrin complains to the king chiefly about Reynard's criminal violation of his wife, and the fox is brought to court to answer the charges made against him. This is the first of several of his court appearances. At all of them, he wins the day by verbal dexterity, trickery and lying. Within the next few years and probably by 1180 this first *Roman de Renart* quickly attracted seven or eight more individual or little groups of tales: 'Reynard, Isengrin and the Side of Ham' (based on the first episode in the *Ysengrimus*) together with 'Reynard and the Cricket' (Branch V); 'Reynard, Tibert and the Chitterling' together with 'Tibert and the Two Priests' (Branch XV); 'Reynard and the Theft of Eels' together with 'The Tonsuring of Isengrin' and 'Isengrin Goes Fishing With His Tail' (the last two being inspired by episodes in the *Ysengrimus*) (Branch III); 'Reynard and Tibert in a Farmer's Cellar' together with 'Reynard and the Wolf Primaut' (Branch XIV); 'Reynard and Isengrin in the Well' (Branch IV); 'Reynard's Trial' (Branch I); 'The Siege of Reynard's Castle' (Branch Ia); 'Reynard and the Dyer' together with 'Reynard the Minstrel' (Branch Ib); 'Reynard Tricks Roenel the Dog and Brichemer the Stag' together with 'Reynard the Physician' (the latter inspired by an episode in the *Ysengrimus*) (Branch X). Easily the most successful and artistically accomplished of this early group of branches is 'Reynard's Trial' (Branch I) which, though composed after several others, was to be placed first in most of the extensive medieval French anthologies of Reynardian tales (hence its being numbered I) and was to inspire the composition of other branches as well as long narrative poems, Beast Epics in their own right, in other languages and cultures.

This relatively quickly composed group of branches, which often exploited material found in the *Ysengrimus*, was followed by a second group which has long been thought to have been composed between approximately 1190 and 1205. This consists of 'Reynard's Duel With Isengrin' (Branch VI); 'Reynard's Pilgrimage' (inspired by an episode in the *Ysengrimus*) (Branch VIII); 'Reynard and Tibert in Church' (Branch XII); 'Reynard Eats His Confessor, Hubert the Kite' (Branch VII); 'Reynard the Emperor' together with (and preceded by) 'Reynard's Friendship with Isengrin', 'Reynard and the Blackberries', 'Reynard and Roenel', and 'Reynard and the Kites' (Branch XI); 'Reynard, Bruin and Farmer Liétart' (Branch IX); 'Reynard and Farmer Bertaut' together with 'The Division of Booty' (Branch XVI); and finally 'Reynard's Death and Funeral Procession' (Branch XVII). Clearly the author of this last branch felt it was about time to bring the series to an end. Even so, he had Reynard die only a feigned death, making it easy for later storytellers to resurrect the fox if they so desired. And they did.

The third and last group of branches are generally assigned to the period c.1205-c.1250, and they include 'Reynard Dyed Black' together with (and preceded by) 'The Fox Skins', 'Reynard and the Rook', and 'Reynard and the Ferryman' (Branch XIII); 'Reynard the Magician and the Lion's Marriage' (Branch XXIII); 'The Creation of Reynard and Isengrin' together with 'Reynard's Early Days' (Branch XXIV); 'Reynard and Pinçon the Heron' followed by 'Reynard and the Ferryman' (quite different from the story with the same title in Branch XIII) (Branch XXV); 'Tibert Plays Hopscotch for a Chitterling' (Branch XXVI); 'Isengrin, Patous the Bear, the Farmer, and his Wife Show Their Bottoms' (Branch XXI); 'Isengrin and Martin the Priest' (Branch XVIII); 'Isengrin and Rainsant the Mare' (Branch XIX); and, finally, 'Isengrin and the Two Rams' (Branch XX). Some of these branches are quite short while others are long and exceed two thousand lines of octosyllabic verse. They are mostly of inferior quality and imitate episodes or whole branches from the first or second group.

The renown of Renart was such that, very soon after the composition of the last of the branches in the first group, he made his first appearance in a foreign masterpiece. Called Reinhart, he repeats many a crime and commits many a new one in the 2260-odd lines of the German Alsatian Heinrich der Glichesaere's *Reinhart Fuchs*, probably composed around 1191. Heinrich selected much of his material from those first French branches, added new material and moulded it all into a well-unified whole. His poem is one of the great works of medieval German literature, one of the finest of the Beast Epics.

The fox's next known appearance in another foreign literature is as Reinaert in the thirteenth-century 3500-line Flemish Beast Epic entitled *Van den Vos Reynaerde*, better known as *Reinaert de Vos*, though one guesses that an earlier Reinaert closely related to the fox of the *Ysengrimus* prowled in the forests and the countryside around Ghent for the six or seven decades between these two compositions. Be that as it may, this masterpiece, which owes much to 'Reynard's Trial' (Branch I), was to become (in a modified form, of which more later) the best known and most admired of all the Beast Epics.

It was also in the early thirteenth century that the fox crossed the Alps to play the major part in an Italian mini-epic poem, just over eight hundred lines long, *Rainaldo e Lesengrino*, which is also based on 'Reynard's Trial'. This highly entertaining, mock-heroic tale of animal barons sitting in judgment on one of their rebellious peers obviously created a great impression on medieval audiences wherever they heard it.

Back in France, numerous works in which Renart and other well-known characters of the *Roman de Renart* took part began to appear during the thirteenth century. The earliest of these is perhaps the most curious. It is by Philippe de Novare who composed a history of the wars fought from 1228 to 1243 in the eastern Mediterranean between Emperor Frederick II and Jean d'Ibelin, Lord of Cyprus and Beyrouth. Philippe took part in these wars on the side of Jean d'Ibelin, and he composed some satirical songs (1229-33) in which he gave the names and characteristics of various protagonists in the *Roman de Renart* to his enemies. When the wars were over he wrote his *Mémoires* (1258). These contain a long satirical tale modelled on the branches of the *Roman de Renart*. In it he casts his lord, Jean d'Ibelin, in the role of Isengrin, and himself as Chantecler the Cock. Other leaders on the side of Ibelin were cast as Brun the Bear and Tibert the Cat. Frederick's lieutenents in Cyprus were cast as Renart, Grimbert the Badger and Cointereau the Monkey. In this grouping of allies and enemies, and in many other ways, Philippe de Novare reveals a thorough knowledge of the *Roman de Renart*, and clearly also expected his readers to know it well. At the same time his work shows quite plainly that Renart was fast becoming, or had even become, a powerful symbol for falsehood and treachery.

In the lyric and satiric poet Rutebeuf's *Renart le Bestourné* (162 lines), composed in the early 1260s, the fox is little more than a symbol of religious hypocrisy. This is a brief and bitter attack on the mendicant orders which are represented chiefly by Renart, but also by other protagonists of the *Roman de Renart* such as the wolf, the dog and the ass (Isengrin, Roenel and Bernart). Between 1263 and 1270 there appeared, anonymously, the *Couronnement de Renart*, a 3300-line-long narrative poem which describes how Renart succeeds Noble the Lion, on his death, to the throne of the animal kingdom, thereby inaugurating a reign of injustice, pride and envy. Here Renart is little more than the symbol of successful hypocrisy and wickedness. Much the same 'moral' is pointed by Jacquemart Gielée's *Renart le Nouvel* (1288-89), an 8000-line allegorical poem which tells of the unsuccessful war waged by Noble, representing Virtue, against Renart, representing Vice.

The last long French poem (over forty thousand lines) about Renart belongs to the early fourteenth century. *Renart le Contrefait* was composed by a discontented merchant who had been in minor holy orders. Through Renart, severe criticism of the political and religious institutions of the day are loudly voiced. Minor French poems and fables featuring Renart in one or other of his symbolic roles appear in the later fourteenth, the fifteenth and sixteenth centuries, but there is scarcely anything worth mentioning here except, perhaps, for a prose version of *Renart le Nouvel* which was entitled *Le Livre de Maistre Regnard et de Dame Hersent sa femme*, made in 1466 and printed several times, perhaps first towards the end of the fifteenth century, then several times in the sixteenth century. Copies dated 1516 (Michel le Noir, Paris); 1534 (Philippe le Noir, Paris); 1550 (Robert and Jehan Dugort, Rouen), and 1551 (Nicolas Buffet) are known, and bear witness to the relatively late popularity of the medieval Renart in France.

It is also important to take into account that manuscript 'editions' of the *Roman de Renart* continued to be made throughout the Middle Ages in France. Of the fourteen extensive anthologies of branches to come down to us, two date from the end of the thirteenth century, eight from the fourteenth century, three from either the late fourteenth or the early fifteenth century, and one definitely from the fifteenth century. The nineteen fragments or partial manuscript editions repeat much the same story.

Alongside these later medieval tellings and retellings of Renart's adventures in French-speaking regions, something similar was happening in Dutch-speaking lands. *Van den Vos Reynaerde* survives in two complete manuscripts, the Comburg manuscript and the Dyck manuscript, both of which were copied in the fourteenth century. Later in the century, or early in the fifteenth century, a new version of this epic was made chiefly by the addition of a substantial new ending which sometimes incorporates non-*Roman-de-Renart* material and sometimes repeats material already present in the earlier part. This longer rehandling of the epic is entitled *Reynaerts Historie* while the earlier one is often called *Reynaert de Vos*. (For simplicity, scholars sometimes refer to the first as *Reinaert I* and the second as *Reinaert II*). It is possible, even probable, that a prose version of *Reynaerts Historie* was made in the early fifteenth century.

It is a fact, and an important fact for this study, that Gheraert Leeu published in Gouda in 1479 a prose version of *Reynaerts Historie* which he called *Die Hystorie van Reynaert die Vos,* for this is the text which William Caxton translated into English in 1481. Leeu also published another, illustrated edition in Antwerp between 1487 and 1490, and it was the illustrations in this edition which Wynkyn de Worde's illustrator imitated in his c.1495 edition of the Caxton translation.

So we return to pre-Caxton times in England and the only two narrative poems we know which feature the fox. They are the *The Fox and the Wolf* (anonymous, 295 lines, c.1260) and *The Nun's Priest's Tale of the Cok and the Fox* (Chaucer, 680 lines, c.1390). The first tells how the fox got trapped in a well and managed to get the wolf to exchange places with him; the second how the fox managed to trap the cock by flattery, but then lost him through his own vanity. Both are related, one way or another, and perhaps remotely, to branches of the *Roman de Renart*; the first to Branch IV, Reynard and Ysengrin in the Well (*Renart et Ysengrin dans le puits*); the second to the part of Branch II called *Renart et Chantecler*. In the first, the fox tells the wolf that his name is Reneuard. The wolf is called Sigrim, and the cock is twice referred to as Chaunticler, all of which are obvious echoes of proper names in Pierre de Saint Cloud's poem. In Chaucer's poem, only the cock's name, Chantecler, has a familiar echo. The fox is daun Russell, the cock's wife is Pertelote (Pinte in Pierre de Saint Cloud's poem), but there is other evidence, neatly summarized by Kenneth Sisam in the introduction to his Clarendon Press edition of the *Nun's Priest's Tale,* to show that Chaucer almost certainly had a French model in mind, later than Pierre's poem, but probably a reworking of it. For example, Pinte shouts out *'Avoi !'* in the *Roman de Renart* when Chantecler says he is frightened by his dream, and *'Avoy !'* shouts Pertelote at exactly the same place in Chaucer's poem, using a word he uses nowhere else in his works. Curiously, Chaucer does know the name Renard, for he uses it in *The Legend of Good Women* (line 2448) as does another fourteenth-century English poet, the author of *Sir Gawain and the Green Knight*. He calls the fox Renaud (line 1898), Renaude (line 1916), and Reynarde (line 1920). These are a few (but very few) indications that Renart and some of his companions in the *Roman de Renart* or in its French continuations were probably known in medieval England.

One more thing before we look at the iconographic evidence, especially where the French tradition and the *Roman de Renart* are concerned. There is some new documentary evidence to be taken into account, and some literary evidence which I did not bring to bear in my 1967 Leicester University Press book. Firstly, it is clear that the *Roman de Renart* was available in fourteenth-century England. In J. Vale's *Edward III and Chivalry: Chivalric Society and its Context 1270-1350* we read (p.50) that John Fleet issued, on 5 March 1327, to the Queen Mother, Isabella, wife of Edward II, mother of Edward III, from the Library in the Tower of London, 'unus liber romanc de Renart', that is, a copy of the *Roman de Renart*. This is recorded in the British Library's manuscript Add 60 584 m., 27v. Then, in L. Douet-d'Arcq's *Comptes de l'argenterie des rois de France au XIVe siècle*, published in 1851, (p.223), we are told that a servant of the King of France, a certain Tassin, went from Somerton (where the king was being held prisoner) to Lincoln in December 1359 to buy goods for the king. He returned with some rolls of cloth, furs and a copy of the *Roman de Renart*. (Jean II, called *le Bon*, was defeated at the

Battle of Poitiers by the Black Prince, and taken prisoner to England. One of the places he was held was called Somerton, in Norfolk.) Then there is the evidence provided by Guillaume le Clerc de Normandie in his account of the fox in his *Bestiaire divin*, a book he composed in England in 1210-1211. At the beginning of that account he writes: 'You have heard enough about the way Renart would steal hens from my lord Constant des Noues...', the clearest of allusions to the beginning of the first tale in the earliest branch of the *Roman de Renart*, the tale of *Renart et Chantecler*. For those who could understand French, at least the beginning of the *Roman de Renart* was well known in England into the thirteenth century, and the whole of it was available well into the fourteenth. I did mention, in my 1967 book, the Renardian proper names used in the fable collections of two 'English' fabulists, Odo of Cheriton and Nicholas Bozon, the former writing in Latin, the latter in Anglo-Norman. Odo was born between 1180 and 1190, only a decade or so after the beginning of the *Roman de Renart*. He belonged to the aristocracy, to a family which came to England from Normandy at the Conquest, and lived in or very near to Folkestone. He studied in Paris and travelled through France and Spain. He inherited a sizeable domain in 1232-33, and died in 1246-47. He published sermons, theological works and fables. These fables seem to have been composed after 1225, and they must have been very popular judging by the many manuscripts which survive all over Europe. They were often used by priests in their sermons as exempla. Although they are in Latin, there can be little doubt that they were retold in English because, from time to time, English expressions or proverbs interrupt the Latin text. In three of his fables he writes of a fox called Reinardus or Renaldus who encounters a cock called Chantecler, a cat called Tebergus and a wolf called Ysengrimus. These proper names, especially that of the cock, point to a knowledge of Pierre de Saint Cloud's branch. In fact, eight of Odo's fables which feature animals with proper names similar to or indeed identical with those used in the *Roman de Renart* also correspond to branches in the French Beast Epic. Nicholas Bozon, a Franciscan, lived in the first half of the fourteenth century, probably near Nottingham. In his *Literature and Pulpit in Mediaeval England*, G. R. Owst says that he 'is the English preacher on whom the mantle of Odo of Cheriton seems to have fallen... ' He retells, much modified, many of the fables formerly told by Odo. If both these fabulists used proper names made familiar by the *Roman de Renart*, we may surely presume that not only they but also their readers and audiences were acquainted with the French epic or some of its continuations, and that they liked to identify the fox of these fables with Reynard. Many fox fables were, however, drawn into the mainstream of the *Roman de Renart* from quite early on, and in this way they lived a double life.

Although there is little pre-Caxton fox literature in English, and although literary references to what seems to be the French Renart are few, a lot of visual representations (carvings in wood and stone, paintings on wood and walls, drawings and paintings in manuscripts and on glass) of the fox and other animals prominent in the *Roman de Renart* and its French continuations do survive from pre-Caxton times. Here is another area to explore for evidence of a knowledge of that villainous hero, his allies and his enemies. After all, only relatively rarely were stories set down on parchment, at considerable cost, for the library of a monastery or wealthy, landed lord who could afford to own them. As most people were illiterate, good stories were passed on by word of mouth, and images assumed enormous importance. Just as key events in the life of

Christ, the prophets and saints were depicted in churches in so many of the graphic and plastic arts, so were some of the most popular and vividly remembered episodes of 'secular' stories, both in castles and churches, especially if they could be given or justified by a moral. So, even when we find visual representations of the fox, it is often difficult if not impossible to prove they had anything to do with the Beast Epic, especially since moralizing fables about the fox were told long before the creation of Reynard, and continued to be told during his and his relations' lifetime, even incorporated into his story, into the Beast Epic. Sometimes the foxes we find are just foxes, sometimes they are symbols, sometimes characters from Aesopian fables, sometimes from the Beast Epic, and sometimes perhaps a curious mixture of them all.

It was in the late 1950s that I began to collect and analyse graphic and plastic representations of the fox in medieval and Renaissance English art. The specialist in medieval and Renaissance French literature in me hoped to show that, in spite of the dearth of literary evidence, iconographic material would bear witness to the existence of more fox literature than has survived, and prove that continental fox tales, and especially French ones, were known before Caxton introduced the Flemish-Dutch Reinaert to this island. My first (and so far only) book to present the evidence I had collected with these aims in view was published by Leicester University Press in 1967. Though well received on the whole, some scepticism was aired by several reviewers. Apparently sceptical about my arguments concerning the possible or probable influence of the *Roman de Renart*, Heinz Bergner (while complimenting me on the book in general) said in his 1973 article '*The Fox and the Wolf* und die Gattung des Tierepos in der Mittelenglischen Literatur', that not a single piece of iconographic evidence contained in it proved beyond any reasonable doubt the existence of an *English* (my italics) Beast Epic. This made me re-think and revise what I had written, look for more evidence (which I have found) and re-present my findings with as much objectivity as I could muster, bearing in mind the Flemish-Dutch tradition as well as the French. After all, there were political, commercial and cultural links with Flanders over a long period of time (especially with London and the South-East, East Anglia and Humberside). And a court which spoke Anglo-Norman ruled (and was entertained) well into the thirteenth century, and there were close links with France and French-speaking territories (even if not always friendly ones) throughout the Middle Ages. In both these rich cultures, the French and the Flemish, Renart-Reinaert was especially well known. He was carved and painted in their churches and castles, too, and wherever he was seen, it is likely that his French- or Dutch-speaking spectators would have named him (at least mentally) with his proper name. What, one wonders, would they have thought and said when they came to England and saw the English foxes? And what of the English when they saw French or Flemish foxes? For there was quite a lot of coming and going, especially between aristocrats, merchants, scholars and members of religious communities in England, France and Flanders.

Among the iconographic material to which I refer will be found, here and there, drawings, carvings and artefacts from other countries and other ages. This is chiefly to show something of the similarities and differences between what is English and what is not, and between what is medieval and what is modern. In the process, I draw attention to a few remarkable, indeed unique, foreign manifestations of Reynardian matter housed in England, as well as to some that is English but housed abroad. The focus, nevertheless, is firmly on English matter, though this is sometimes open to question for craftsmen, especially experts in woodcarving and in the making of stained glass (particularly from Flanders), often crossed national frontiers and cultural boundaries; and pattern books used by native English craftsmen sometimes came from abroad.

Notes

REYNARDIAN LITERARY HISTORY

The standard literary history is Flinn 1963. This contains summaries, critical analyses and details of all editions of all the Beast Epics and related literature referred to in this Introduction except for the *Ysengrimus*. For this, see Mann 1987. More modern editions of the primary texts cited by Flinn are as follows:
For the latest editions (as well as translations and adaptations) of branches of the *Roman de Renart* published since Flinn 1963, see Varty 1998, items 2-7, 10, 12 and 15; and for the titles and numbers of all the branches, see Varty 1988, pp. 7-12.
Other relevant post-Flinn 1963 publications are: a translation into English of Rutebeuf's *Renart le Bestourné*, Owen 1994, pp. 256-260. *Le Livre de Maistre Regnart*, Suomela-Härmä 1998. Heinrich der Glichesâre's *Reinhart Fuchs des Elsässers Heinrich*, Düwel 1984; and for a translation of it into French, Buschinger and Pastré 1984. *Van den Vos Reynaerde*, Lulofs 1983; also Van Daele 1989, pp. 85-145. *Reinaerts Historie*, Goossens 1983. *Rainaldo e Lesengrino*, Lomazzi 1972. *The Fox and the Wolf*, Bennett and Smithers 1968, pp. 65-76. Guillaume le Clerc de Normandie's *Bestiaire divin*, Reinsch 1967; (also Druce 1936). Odo of Cheriton's fables, Jacobs 1985. For the Luxembourgish *Renert*, see Rodange 1975.

CRITICAL STUDIES AND SUPPORTING INFORMATION

The comment to which I refer in Bergner 1973 is on pp. 282-83.
I gladly acknowledge that it was Dr Malcolm Jones who drew my attention to the published references which revealed something of the availability of the *Roman de Renart* in fourteenth-century England.

CHAPTER ONE

The Fox and the Cock

One of the earliest branches of the *Roman de Renart* (perhaps the very first branch), almost certainly composed by a certain Pierre de Saint Cloud in the 1170s, tells a tale about Renart the Fox and Chantecler the Cock, and there can be no doubt that this tale was retold *in French* in the south of England early in the thirteenth century. At the beginning of the entry on the fox (*du goupil*) in his *Bestiaire divin* (Sacred Bestiary) composed in England in either 1210 or 1211, Guillaume le Clerc de Normandie writes (in Norman French): 'You have heard tell quite enough about the way in which Renart stole more often than not hens from Constant des Noues... ' This is a clear reference to that episode in the *Roman de Renart* about Renart and Chantecler (for it is in the wealthy farmer Constant des Noues' farmyard that Renart seizes Chantecler and is chased by the farmer and his wife), and it suggests that Guillaume's listeners (who were, presumably, French-speaking Normans and Anglo-Normans) had heard it many times during the years preceding the composition of his Bestiary.

Here, part translated, part paraphrased and abbreviated, is that story of which, in one form or another, some scenes seem to be represented in medieval English art well before the earliest surviving *English* narrative featuring these protagonists:

It happened that Reynard, ever guileful, came to a woodland farm. It abounded in poultry, and a rich farmer called Constant des Noues lived there. He had plenty of hens, capons, salted meat and bacon... Reynard went there to amuse himself. The yard was well fenced in with oaken stakes and a hawthorn hedge. Master Constant kept his hens in this fortress. Reynard approached it but, resourceful as he was, the powerful thorns turned him aside... Eventually he found a broken stake in the palisade and managed to creep through. The farmer had planted red cabbages there, and Reynard took shelter among them, but the hens saw him and took flight. Sir Chantecler the Cock, who had retired to a dung-heap, came proudly forward and asked them why they had run homewards. Pinte the Hen, who knew most and laid the biggest eggs, said: 'We were frightened.' 'Why? What did you see?' 'Some sort of wild beast who might easily have done us harm if we hadn't sought shelter.' 'Don't be frightened,' said the Cock. 'You are perfectly safe here.' 'But I saw it myself,' said Pinte, 'I do assure you.' 'And how did you see it?' 'How? I saw the palisade shake, and the cabbage leaves tremble.' 'Pinte, there is nothing there; on my honour, no fox or polecat would dare come into the yard. Go back again.' And he returned to his dung-heap.

He began to doze, and as he dozed he had a dream. He dreamt that a Thing came into the yard carrying a red fur coat with a collar of bone. The Thing forced this collar on to his back, and he became very distressed. The collar was so tight... He trembled because of his dream, and was much frightened... At last he came to his senses and awakening cried out 'Holy Spirit, keep my body out of prison and guard me!' He hurried over to his hens who were under the hawthorns, and called to Pinte. 'Pinte, I'm in dreadful trouble. I'm greatly afraid of being betrayed by some wild beast or bird.' 'Come now,' said Pinte, 'my dear sir, you must not say such things. You frighten us all! Tell me what is wrong.' 'You don't know what a strange dream I've had! It was an evil vision, that's why I am so pale. I'll tell you all about it. Do you think you could advise me what to do? While I was asleep, it seemed to me that a strange creature came and forced a red fur coat on me. It had a bone collar, very tight. You see why I tremble so! Do you know what it means?' 'Please God your dream will not turn out to be true!' she answered, 'but I can tell you what it means. It's about the fox. You can tell that from the red fur coat. The bone collar must be his teeth. The fox will get you by the neck. No money can save you. If you don't believe me, turn round. He's there, in those bushes, waiting to betray you.' When he heard this answer, he said: 'Pinte, you're a silly old fool. I simply will not believe any ill can come to me from this dream.' And he went back to his dung-heap where he began to doze.

When the subtle Reynard, master of so many cunning tricks, saw this, he padded softly towards him. But Chantecler saw him and hopped to the top of the dung-heap. 'Don't be frightened, Chantecler,' said Reynard. 'We are closely related to each other; we're cousins, you know.' Chantecler, reassured, began to crow. 'Do you remember your excellent father, Chanteclin?' Reynard continued. 'There never was a cock who could sing like him. How well he took the top notes, and what a long breath he had! He used to shut both eyes when he crowed, and you could hear him a mile off!' 'You wouldn't play a trick on me, would you, cousin Reynard?' 'Certainly not, cousin Chantecler! But do shut your eyes and sing. You and I are of the same flesh and blood. I'd rather lose a hand than see you come to any harm.' 'I don't quite believe you. Stand a bit further back, and I'll sing a song for you.' Chantecler, with one eye closed and the other open, threw off a note, still distrustful of Reynard. 'That was nothing,' said Reynard. 'Chanteclin sang quite differently. On a long note he would shut his eyes. You would hear him twenty fields away.' Chantecler at last believed he was telling the truth, shut his eyes and crowed with gusto. From under a red cabbage Reynard made a grab, caught his prey by the neck and fled in high spirits. Pinte, who saw Chantecler carried off, lamented in her distress. 'Sir, I told you this would happen, and you thought I was a silly fool. Alas I shall die of grief! If I lose my lord I lose my honour for ever!'

Just then, the good woman of the house opened her door for it was evening and she wanted to have her hens under cover. She called for Bise and Rosette, but neither came and she wondered what on earth they were up to. She called for her cock at the top of her voice, and then she saw Reynard running off with him. She started to run, too, but when she realised she could not catch up with him she shouted 'Hey there!' as loud as she could. The farmhands, who were playing a ball game, came running to find out what was the matter. She answered 'Alas, what misfortune!' 'What is?' 'I've lost my cock. The fox has got him.' 'You stinking old baggage,' said Constant. 'What a fat lot of good you were not to catch him.' 'By all the saints in Heaven, I couldn't. He went too fast for me.' 'Why didn't you hit him?' 'With what?' 'This stick.' 'But I couldn't. He went so fast that two hounds couldn't have caught him.' 'Which way did he go?' 'This way, straight ahead.' All the farmhands ran off shouting 'After him! After him!' Reynard, far ahead, heard them and began to run faster. They all began to shout 'Kill him! Kill him!' Constant cried out, 'Quick, get him!', and he called for his mastiff Mauvoisin. 'Bardolph! Travers! Humbart! Rebors! Run after Reynard!' he shouted.

Chantecler would have been in real danger then if he hadn't used his wits. 'Sir Reynard,' he said, 'can't you hear the shameful things those peasants are shouting at you? When Constant says "Now Reynard's got him" why don't you retort "Yes, in spite of anything you can do!"?' There's none so wise he never makes a fool of himself just once. Reynard who tricks everybody was himself tricked this time. He opened his jaws to taunt Constant. When he did so, Chantecler beat his wings, took flight, and landed in an apple-tree. Reynard, standing beneath, was furious at the cock's escape. Chantecler laughed down at him. 'Well, what do you think of that?' 'Damn the mouth that opens when it ought to keep shut,' said the fox. 'And damn the eye that closes when it ought to stay open,' said the cock. 'To Hell with your cousining!'

This tale developed out of earlier fables. Its most obvious ancestor is a fable about a wolf and a cock told in Latin by Alcuin of York (d. 804). Another ancestor is the fable of the fox and the partridge, also told in Latin, by Adhemar (d. 1034), a monk of St Martial's Abbey at Limoges. Its immediate source is an episode in the *Ysengrimus*. At the end of its fourth book, the poet tells a tale about Reinardus (the fox) and Sprotinus (the cock). Sprotinus is the lord of a dozen hens, and proud of his crowing. The fox comes to him in the guise of a pilgrim, and though Sprotinus is suspicious, he is induced by taunts to follow the alleged example of his father and crow, first standing on one leg with one eye shut, then with both eyes shut. The fox grabs him. Rustics give chase. Sprotinus persuades the fox to shout back defiance, then escapes from his opened jaws, and leaves him to curse his foolish mouth. More or less contemporary with Pierre de Saint Cloud's version of this tale is a fable by Marie de France who lived and composed her fables at the court of England's Henry II. Her fable contains much the same narrative elements. With this we enter Anglo-Norman England ahead of Guillaume le Clerc whose comment, quoted at the beginning of this chapter, merely confirms how well-known this tale was in French, in that country, in these clerical and courtly milieux, in the late twelfth and early thirteenth centuries. According to one manuscript of Marie's fables, she claims to have translated them from the English of King Alfred. If Alfred ever wrote fables, no trace of them survives. But if Marie were telling the truth, it would establish her form of the tale as of at least equal antiquity with that of the eighth-century model of Adhemar's fable of the fox and the partridge, and root it firmly in England.

The first known telling of this tale in English is by Chaucer in his *Nun's Priest's Tale*, c. 1390. This begins with a description of a poor widow and her household. Her humble roof supplies the perch for the more brilliant household of a prince among cocks. There follows a description of Chanticleer and his wives, the chief of whom is Pertelote. Chanticleer has a dream which includes a miniature portrait of Russell the Fox. The cock tells his wife about it, and Pertelote warms to the subject of dreams and medical explanations and theories about them. Chanticleer refutes the views she advances with two lengthy accounts of dreams told originally by Cicero, and with other examples of dreams by St Kenelm, Scipio, Daniel, Joseph, Pharaoh, Crœsus and Andromache. Dawn puts an end to his discourse, and Chanticleer flies down from his perch. At this point the fox gets into the poultry yard. Chaucer comments ironically on the cock's unsuspecting joy and the sorrow to come. He digresses on predestination and the folly of taking a woman's advice. Russell approaches Chanticleer, flattering him with honeyed words about his and his father's ability to sing with both eyes tightly closed. Chanticleer falls for the trick and is captured. After digressing on destiny and love, Chaucer completes his tale with a magnificent description of the farmyard in turmoil. As Kenneth Sisam writes: 'The great scene in the tale of [Chaucer's] Cock and the Fox...is the scurrying chase that turns a peaceful farmyard into pandemonium, and he deliberately holds back this scene, approaching it as slowly and indirectly as his audience will permit. For he is both entertaining them and teasing them with suspense and irrelevance: he keeps an eye on them all the time, gauging to a nicety how far he can go without spoiling their pleasure, cajoling them with a promise or muffling a protest by protesting first. But when once the chase is started, his burst of pace is all the more effective by contrast. A score of verses are crowded with noise and action, and nothing is allowed to drag afterwards: even the moral, which at an earlier stage might have given rise to a long discussion, is dispatched in two business-like lines.'

Here, in Nevil Coghill's modernized rendering of the scene, is Chaucer's account of the catastrophe:

This Chanticleer stood high upon his toes,
He stetched his neck, his eyes began to close,
His beak to open; with his eyes shut tight
He then began to sing with all his might.
Sir Russel Fox then leapt to the attack,
Grabbing his gorge he flung him o'er his back.
And off he bore him to the woods, the brute,
And for the moment there was no pursuit...
This blessed widow and her daughters two
Heard all these hens in clamour and halloo
And, rushing to the door at all this shrieking,
They saw the fox towards the covert streaking
And, on his shoulder, Chanticleer stretched flat.
'Look, look!' they cried, 'O mercy, look at that!
Ha! Ha! the Fox!' and after him they ran,
And stick in hand ran many a serving man,
Ran Coll our dog, ran Talbot, Bran and Shaggy,
And with a distaff in her hand ran Maggie,
Ran cow and calf and ran the very hogs,
In terror at the barking of the dogs;
The men and women shouted, ran and cursed,
They ran so hard they thought their hearts would burst,
They yelled like fiends in Hell, ducks left the water
Quacking and flapping as on the point of slaughter,

Up flew the geese in terror over the trees,
Out of the hive came forth the swarm of bees,
So hideous was the noise...
They grabbed up trumpets made of brass and box,
Of horn and bone, on which they blew and pooped,
And therewithal they shouted and they whooped
So that it seemed the very heavens would fall.

There is then, a considerable gap in the known history of the composing of the French and the English versions of this story in England, a gap of about two hundred years. On the Continent this gap was bridged by numerous imitations and adaptations of Pierre de Saint Cloud's poem. For example, in about 1190 there was the Alsatian, Heinrich der Glichezaere's *Reinhart Fuchs* which begins with the story of Reynard and Chantecler, and it is retold in the first half of the fourteenth century in the French *Renart le Contrefait*, which may be where Chaucer became acquainted with it, though he may also have known it through an oral tradition, partly French, partly English, which had its beginnings in Pierre de Saint Cloud's poem, and was both continued and contaminated by popular countryside, farmyard versions (i.e. folklore) for which there is some evidence in both popular lyrics, carvings and drawings.

Two anonymous poems are relevant to this argument, but they date from the fifteenth century so, unless they had earlier forms, they are less relevant than they might have been. The first of these goes by the title *The False Fox* and contains the following lines:

The fals fox came unto our cowpe,
And ther he made our gese to stowpe,
He toke a gose fast by the nek,
And the goose thoo began to quek.
The good-wyfe came out in her smok,
And at the fox she threw hir rok.
The good-man came out with his flayle,
And smote the fox upon the tayle.
He threw a gose upon his back,
And furth he went thoo with his pak...
The fals fox went into his denne
And ther he was full mery thenne.
He came ayene yet the next weke,
And toke awey both henne and cheke...

The other poem goes like this:

'Pax vobis,' quod the ffox,

'for I am comyn to toowne.'

It fell ageyns the next nyght
the fox yede to with all his myghte,
with-outen cole or candlelight,
whan that he cam unto the toowne.

Whan he cam all in the yarde,
soore te geys wer ill a-ferde;
'I shall macke some of yow lerde,
or that I goo from the toowne!'

Whan he cam all in the croofte,
there he stalkyd wundirfull soofte;
'for here have I be frayed full ofte
when that I have come to toowne.'

He hente a goos all by the heye,
faste the goos began to creye!
oowte yede men as they myght heye,
and seyde, 'fals fox, ley it doowne!'

'Nay,' he saide, 'soo mot I the,
sche shall goo unto the wode with me;
sche and I unther a tre'
e-mange the beryis browne.

I have a wyf, and sche lyeth seke;
many smale whelppis sche have to eke;
many bonys they muste pike
will they ley a-downe.'

The main evidence for an oral tradition linking late twelfth-century Anglo-Norman-speaking to late fourteenth-century English-speaking England is to be found in carvings and drawings from this period, and from their successors in later times. The earliest of these is a carving on a capital in Wells Cathedral [1] which may be dated c.1190; that is, some fifteen years after Pierre de Saint Cloud composed his poem. This carving depicts a man with a mallet over his shoulder and a ball clasped to his chest as he watches a fox making off with a goose. Here literary and folklore traditions seem to have fused. The literary tradition is clearly indicated by the mallet and ball. In Pierre's poem we are told that when the farmer's wife sees the fox disappearing with her cock, she shouts at the top of her voice. This brings to her side the farmhands who were playing a ball game

1 *A fox seizes a goose watched by a peasant shouldering a mallet. Wells Cathedral, capital; c.1190. L. Herbert Felton.*

which was probably a bit like croquet, played with mallets and large wooden balls. The Wells sculptor shows us one of the farmhands who had been playing this game. The popular tradition is indicated by the fox's victim which is a goose and not a cock. We find that this substitution of a goose for a cock is often made in medieval English representations of this scene, yet the cock is vital to the literary versions of it. Nobody can observe a cock for long without imputing to it a vain and pompous character. The poet-storyteller needed such a character, and the cock met this need so much more readily than the goose, duck or hen. The goose was particularly unsuitable because, in the Middle Ages, it was considered either clever or, mostly, very silly: clever (and foreseeing) because its ancestors who inhabited the Capitol in Rome had warned the Romans of the approach of their enemy. If it were clever, it would have seen through the fox and there would have been no story; if it were very silly, there would have been no need for the fox to exercise his wiles, and again there would have been no story. But there is a good reason why graphic and especially plastic artists should prefer the goose to the cock. For them, the long, slender neck of the goose had an attractive line which considerably enhances a composition, just as it does at Wells. Conversely, the shorter neck of the cock, hen or duck can make for confused outlines when it comes to depicting a fox

2 *A fox seizes a cock pursued by a woman wielding a distaff. Ely Cathedral, misericord; early 14th C. Kenneth Varty.*

seizing a bird by its neck. Different media (especially stone and wood as opposed to parchment and glass) as well as parallel literary and folklore traditions no doubt account for some of the differences between the literary and visual representations of this and other fox scenes.

Another carving which may have been inspired by Pierre de Saint Cloud's poem or one of its variants is in Ely Cathedral [2]. Here, on an early fourteenth-century misericord, the victim is a cock. The fox has it by the body between his jaws. Towering over the fox is the good-wife wielding her distaff. On the right supporter with a mallet or stake over his shoulder stands a man who may be Constant or one of his farmhands. To judge by their fierce expressions and open mouths, both man and woman are shouting loudly after the fox. The distaff is a particularly interesting detail. It is not mentioned in Pierre's poem, though it is in Chaucer's, and in the first of the two anonymous lyrics quoted above ('hir rok'). (Although Pierre does not name the distaff, he does have Constant refer to a *baston* [stick] held most probably by the good-wife. [When he asks her why she did not hit the fox, she asks 'what with?', and he replies, perhaps pointing to her distaff, 'with that stick.']. There is much iconographic evidence to prove that wherever the farmer's wife went, she took her distaff with her and, if needed, used it as a weapon. There is, for example, in the Luttrell Psalter a drawing which shows that, when she went to feed the poultry, she took her distaff with her; and another drawing in this psalter [representative of many more like it] shows a woman beating her man with a distaff). The fact is, the good-wife's distaff features in most representations of this episode including, most important of all, the miniature illustrating this branch in a fourteenth-century manuscript of the *Roman de Renart* [3].

3 *A fox chased by a woman and a man. The Bodleian Library, MS Douce 360, f.21; 1338.*

This Ely misericord, dated 1338, is about fifty years earlier than Chaucer's *Nun's Priest's Tale*, and there are several other pre-Chaucerian representations of this scene. One of the earliest is a late thirteenth- or early fourteenth-century drawing in the Ormesby Psalter [4]. Here the farmer's wife, depicted at the foot of the page, displays alarm and hesitation as she sees the fox making off with her cock which is very neatly drawn, held by the neck in the fox's jaws and almost thrown across his back. We await her shouting and the arrival of Constant and the farmhands who will reprimand her for not giving chase and striking the intruder with her distaff. In Oakham parish church there is an early fourteenth-century carved capital where one sees a woman's head then, moving eastwards around the pillar, her hands clasped around the base of an outstretched distaff [5]. On either side of the distaff is a goose or a duck. Continuing around the pillar are two more

4 *A woman holding a distaff watches a fox seizing a cock. The Bodleian Library, MS Douce 366, f.71v.; c.1300.*

5 *A distaff-wielding woman pursues a fox pursued by ducks. Oakham Parish Church, capital; c.1325. Kenneth Varty.*

6 *Ducks attack the hind quarters of a fox which seizes a bird. A chained monkey leads this procession. Oakham Parish Church; capital; c.1325. Kenneth Varty.*

web-footed birds. One tugs at the fox's brush while the other snaps at his rump [6]. The fox has one of them by the throat, half-slung over his back. Other birds scurry before the fox. Also early in the fourteenth century, in York Minster, in the lower margin of the great window in the north aisle depicting St Peter at its centre, is a woman with an outstretched distaff chasing an impudent fox which has a goose's neck between his jaws and the goose's body half-over his back [7]. Behind the woman is a palatial building which is surely far too grand to be Constant's farmhouse, although Pierre did say he was rich. On the left is a man fetching a horse from the stables, presumably to give chase. As there is no suggestion of pursuing Reynard on horseback in any extant version of the story, this may well represent a lost variant of it.

Several mid-fourteenth-century drawings also belong to this group of pre-Chaucerian representations of the episode. Two are to be found in the Queen Mary Psalter [8 & 9]. (Perhaps, since these two drawings face each other, and the fox's pose is almost identical, this is the same fox-with-victim being chased by both the woman and the two men). Two more are in the Smithfield Decretals [10 & 24]. There is also an interesting mid-fourteenth-century drawing added to the lower margin of a page in the splendid thirteenth-century Amesbury Psalter which was made for a nunnery, probably in Salisbury [175]. In all these drawings the fox's victim is a goose or a duck, which might suggest that the artists were influenced more by the popular tradition represented by the lyrics quoted above rather than the literary tradition of the *Roman de Renart*, but the Amesbury Psalter drawing is linked to one of the fox attending a

7 *A fox with a goose is chased by a woman with a distaff while a man prepares to mount a horse. York Minster, stained glass; c.1325. Drawing by J. Knowles.*

8 *A woman with a distaff pursues a fox with prey. The British Library, MS Roy. 2. B. VII, f.157v; early 14th C.*

9 *Two men pursue a fox making off with a goose. The British Library, MS Roy. 2. B. VII, f.158; early 14th C.*

10 *A woman wielding a distaff pursues a fox with a goose flung over its back. The British Library, MS. 10. E. IV, f.175; c.1335.*

sick lion, a crowned sick lion, and this makes one think of Noble, king of the animals in the Beast Epic.

Probably contemporary with Chaucer is a sculptured frieze on the east side of the tower of St Mary's, Bloxham [11], in which one sees a fox running off with a goose over his back and the farmer's wife wielding her distaff in hot pursuit. Close behind her is Constant or a farm-hand who threateningly waves a curious weapon, more like a washing-beetle than a mallet. A much livelier carving contemporary with Chaucer is to be found on a misericord in St Botolph's, Boston [12]. Here the farmer's wife chases the fox with tremendous determination as he makes off with a bird that could be a cock. The good-wife's expression is ferocious as she lunges out with an enormous distaff. Something of the commotion in the literary accounts of this episode is conveyed by the scurrying duck in the foreground and by another one which dashes ahead of the fox in complete bewilderment. The proportioning of the woman, her distaff and the fox is so cleverly done that we have the impression that the fox is rapidly approaching us: quite the reverse of the Ely misercord [2].

A number of fifteenth-century carvings appear to depict an interesting variant of this episode. They are characterized by the portrayal of a seated woman and/or the representation of a

11 *A man and a woman chase a fox with a goose. Bloxham, St Mary, tower frieze; 14th C. Kenneth Varty.*

12 *A woman with distaff chases a fox with prey. Boston, St Botolph, misericord; later 14th C. D.R. Maxted.*

13 *A seated inattentive woman allows a fox to make off with a goose flung over its back. Whalley, St Mary and All Saints, misericord; 1435. J.C.D. Smith.*

kitchen interior. This variant may have told how the farmer's wife fell asleep in her kitchen into which the fox stealthily penetrated. There he found a goose which had been killed and lay waiting to be plucked and prepared for a meal. The fox seized this goose and made off with it, but the woman was awoken by the barking of her dog, and when she saw what was happening, she grabbed her distaff and pursued the fox. A misericord in St Mary and All Saints, Whalley, [13] shows the woman sitting down, asleep. Her cat cringes behind her, but her dog stands his ground in front of her and barks after the fleeing fox who has a goose flung over his back. He nears his hole from which peer two foxes. In St Mary's, Minster-in-Thanet [14], the woman is sitting down and clearly awake. Beside her are a cat and a dog. Neither shows any inclination to pursue the fox who makes off with a goose. In Ripon Cathedral [15] the woman is still seated, but she has in effect shouldered arms, and the dog is in hot pursuit. There is no sign of a cat here. In Norwich Cathedral [16] the farmer's wife has also joined in the pursuit. Here is much evidence of a kitchen interior. These particular misericord carvings are, of course, post-Chaucerian, and his influence may be recognized in them. The interior scene is perhaps inspired by his description:

> Sooty her hall, her kitchen melancholy,
> And there she ate fully many a slender meal...

The tall pot at her knee may contain milk, and the open sack may hold flour:

> She drank no wine, nor white nor red had got.
> Her board was mostly served with white and black,
> Milk and brown bread, in which she found no lack...

In the top right corner of this Norwich Cathedral carving are two birds, apparently in flight and making for some trees. Are they inspired by the line

> Up flew the geese in terror over the trees...?

14 *Between an alert dog and cat sits (centre) an inattentive woman; to the left a fox makes off with its victim flung over its back. Minster-in-Thanet, St Mary, misericord; 1410. National Buildings Record.*

15 *A fox seizes a goose (centre), to the left sits a sleeping (?) woman; to the right a dog growls at the fox. Ripon Cathedral, misericord; 1490. D.R. Maxted.*

16 *The goodwife leaves her kitchen in hot pursuit of the fox which has seized a duck. Norwich Cathedral, misericord; 1480. J.C.D. Smith.*

17 *A fox tries to steal a goose from the goodwife's basket. Tuttington Parish Church, bench end finial; 15th C. E.L. Jones.*

The artistic merits of this carving are considerable. It is full of life and action, and the fox seems to stream through the air at break-neck speed. The dog pounds the earth behind him, and the woman's face is full of venomous determination. A fine bench-end finial in the parish church of Tuttington near Norwich [17] gives us what may be a glimpse of another variant of this fifteenth-century version of the tale, for here the fox is shown trying to take a wide-eyed goose from a basket, just as its owner, a hefty woman, lands a blow with her distaff on the fox's back. One wonders if this happened as she was about to set out for market, or on her return home from market. (Another bench-end finial at Tuttington shows a fox making off with a goose, so the pick-basket marauder may have succeeded in his aim in spite of being thumped on the back!). There are other fifteenth-century representations of the fox chased by a distaff-wielding woman of the more usual variety. The best of these is on a roof boss in the south porch of St Margaret's, Cley-next-the-Sea [18 & 19]. Although the stone has been eroded, it is not too difficult to make out a fox running off with a cock held firmly by the neck and yet thrown over his captor's back. There is the vaguest hint of a wood in the background. No doubt the confined space in which the sculptor worked would force him to reject what he considered to be superfluous details in the story.

It is not until we come to the sixteenth century that we detect with near-certainty Chaucer's influence on carvings of this particular scene. In Manchester Cathedral a misericord dated 1508 shows a woman who could be Dame Malkyn about to bring down her (now broken-off) distaff on the rump of the fleeing Don Russell [20]. Just behind her we see a house and a little girl - one of the two daughters mentioned by Chaucer? The girl stands at the entrance to the house, just inside the doorway, and holds her arms out in evident consternation. Mother and child witness the fox making off with a goose slung over his back. In Beverley Minster the scene (dated 1520) is very similarly depicted [21]. It has, however, one more detail which seems to confirm the Chaucerian influence. Here we see four ducks in the background, and they appear to be quacking loudly in fear:

...ducks left the water
Quacking and flapping as on the point of slaughter.

At Beverley, the victim could be a duck or a goose, but not a cock, for it clearly has webbed feet. If these two carvings, at Manchester and Beverley, are in part influenced by the climactic incident in Chaucer's *Nun's Priest's Tale*, one could argue that, in a long and roudabout way, Pierre de Saint Cloud's version of the episode has reached even this far in time and space. There is a further suggestion of some knowledge of the spirit of the Beast Epic in the supporters of both misericords. At Manchester, on the left, are two little foxes who seem to be learning a lesson in school under the supervision of a fox-teacher armed with a fearful birch. On the right supporter is another adult fox absorbed in a book. The schooling of Reynard's children is not told in the *Roman de Renart*, but he is the only clever and relatively lettered animal in Noble's kingdom. At Beverley, on the left supporter, are two foxes in an attitude which suggests they are planning mischief together. Reynard and his wife Hermeline? On the right, a fox is shown after having made his escape with his victim. He looks back to make sure the coast is clear, and pins his victim down, forepaws firmly planted on its neck.

18 *A fox with a cock flung over its back is closely chased by a woman wielding her distaff. Cley-next-the-Sea, St Margaret, porch roof boss; 15th c. Kenneth Varty.*

19 *A drawing of this sculpture based on the photograph. E. de la Mare Norris.*

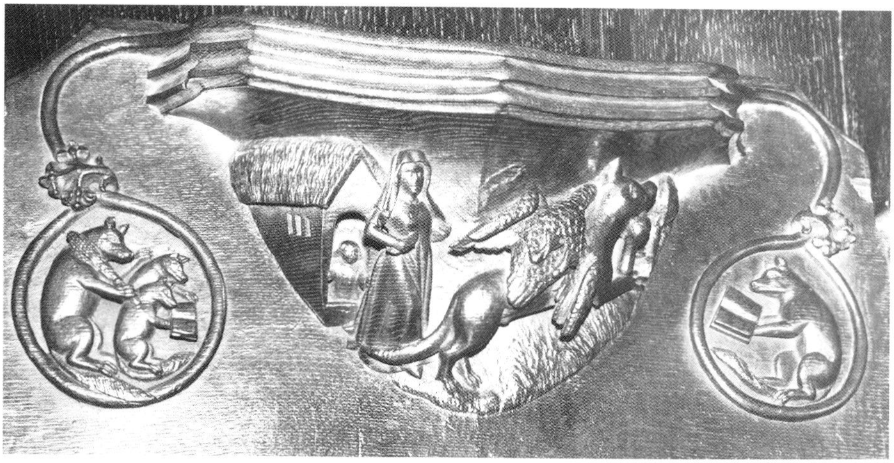

20 *A woman leaves her house in pursuit of a fox fleeing with its victim. Foxes at their lessons in either supporter. Manchester Cathedral, misericord; 1508. J.C.D. Smith.*

21 *A woman runs from her house in pursuit of a fox fleeing with its victim past honking geese. Foxes plot on the left supporter while one holds its victim down on the right supporter. Beverley Minster, misericord; 1520. D.R. Maxted.*

Pierre tells us that the fox took the cock by the neck and then ran for it. Chaucer tells us that the fox took the cock by the neck and then flung the bird over his back. The author of *The False Fox* more or less repeats Chaucer, and tells us 'he threw a gose upon his back'. If we examine the carvings and the drawings of this scene, we discover that although there is a twelfth-century carving in Bristol Cathedral's Lady Chapel showing the fox in the process of throwing a goose over his back, it is chiefly from the fourteenth century and later that he is shown (and then not always) with his victim thrown over his back a bit like the way a man might carry a sack full of goods. How realistic is this?

It may be objected that a goose is far too big a bird for a fox to throw over his back, and that is undoubtedly true of a fully grown goose nowadays; but was it so in the Middle Ages? The medieval goose was probably at least a half, perhaps a third the size of a modern goose which, in common with most farmyard animals, has increased at least twofold in size since the Agricultural Revolution, whereas the fox remains as small as ever he was. Perhaps it is worth recalling Queen Elizabeth I's supposed description of a goose as a disappointing bird, too big for one and too little for two.

I once made extensive enquiries into the way the fox runs off with his victims and found some evidence to support the argument that he could and indeed did throw it over his back. A rector's daughter wrote to me to tell me that when a fox raided her father's poultry-yard, she actually saw the fox take a hen off the doorstep: 'he flung her jauntily on to his back and set off down the path, with the family in hot pursuit'. She added that her mother, the rector's wife, 'touched the fox's brush before he dropped the bird which recovered after a time'. Another correspondent writes: 'when walking in Surrey many years ago I saw a fox emerge from a spinney some fifty yards away carrying a hen pheasant slung like a sack across its shoulder'. And a newspaper reported in 1809 that a fox, in the middle of the day, seized a goose in the farmyard at Writtle Park, Essex, and, 'but for a cow with her calf meeting Reynard with his prize thrown over his back, would have carried it off: the cow pursuing him, and his load being heavy, he dropped it and escaped'. Against this kind of evidence, more than one zoologist has told me that a fox's muscles are simply not strong enough to do this, and another correspondent wrote: 'Some years ago I was living in Sudbrooke Park near Lincoln. I was fattening a few geese up for Christmas. One morning about four o'clock I heard sounds of great confusion coming from my geese. I dashed down in my pyjamas, put on a pair of gum-boots, grabbed a torch, picked up a bucket and ran out into the foggy night. The cries of one of my geese were receding into the distance. Then, strangely enough, the cries became louder, and I realized that the fox was heading in my direction. In a few moments the fox actually ran into my legs. I yelled for all I was worth, swung my bucket and gave the fox a heavy blow and shouted "Drop it!" The fox obligingly did so. I then flung my torch after the fox, which disappeared into the gloom. Although the goose's neck was badly lacerated, it was very much alive. The fox was dragging the goose by its neck, alongside it. One of the goose's wings looked as if it was over the fox's back, but it probably got there by accident. The fox did not have the bird slung over its back.' (I had writen to *Country Life* asking readers to tell me what they thought of Chaucer's description, hence the detailed observations on the way the fox carried off its victim). I am inclined to think that this last correspondent's observation about the accidental way a victim's wing might fall over the fox's back is at least in part the explanation for the way artists and

22 *A fox looks up at a cock perched on a tree branch. Worcester Cathedral, stone spandrel; 13th C. Kenneth Varty.*

poets have depicted the fox making off with it. But only partly. This last correspondent's goose was a modern one, and being fattened! And then, there could be, in our medieval poets' and artists' work, a parodic, anthropomorphic element. Some hunters will have carried their quarry slung over their back, just as the fox carries a monk in the world-upside-down image carved on the misericord supporter in St Nicholas's, Castle Hedingham [48]. And there could have been a reflection of the artist's intention (be he literary artist, graphic artist or sculptor) to reflect elegant, cultured ways of doing things, as Richard Trachsler has convincingly argued in a recent study which takes as its starting point Chrétien de Troyes' description in his courtly romance, *Yvain* (from round about the middle of the last quarter of the twelfth century) of a lion carrying off a stag which he flung over his shoulder.

Two other carvings may illustrate quite different moments in this tale. One is an early fourteenth-century misericord in Winchester Cathedral showing a fox emerging from behind a large stylized leaf which may represent the red cabbage under which Reynard tried to hide at the beginning of the tale; the other is a thirteenth-century stone sculpture in Worcester Cathedral [22] which shows a cock perched on a tree-top and a fox slinking below another nearby tree. At the end of the tale we are told that, as soon as Chantecler escaped, he flew up into an apple-tree while Reynard stood, disconsolate, below a nearby pear-tree. In this way, these creatures are in their positions for the final scene in both the the relevant branch of the *Roman de Renart* and the *Nun's Priest's Tale*.

23 *A fox runs off with a cock watched by a woman with a distaff. The Bodleian Library, MS Ashmole 1504, f.34, early 16th C.*

The popularity of this tale and the impact of its culminating scene right up to the time of Caxton's *Historye of Reynart the Foxe* are attested by a little drawing in a pattern book kept in the Bodleian Library. This is MS Ashmole 1504 dated early sixteenth century. Folio 34 depicts an elephant in the top half of the page and a fox in the bottom half [23]. Between these two animals the author-artist has inserted the picture of a fox running off with a cock in his jaws. Behind the fleeing fox is a woman holding her distaff upright in her right hand while, with her left hand, she pulls up the hem of her long dress and takes the first step in the chase. The action of drawing a natural fox obviously reminded the artist of what must have been one of the best-known fox tales of his time and, it would seem, one that was suitable for a young person.

To sum up, one could say that Pierre de Saint Cloud's influence is probably discernible in the carvings in Wells and Ely; Chaucer's in those in Manchester and Beverley. In between there is a long tradition into which everyday reality, folklore, symbolism and preaching play their part, especially preaching.

Notes

BASIC TEXTS

For the *Ysengrimus*, see Bibliography, Mann 1987. For a careful translation into English of Pierre de Saint Cloud's *Renart et Chantecler*, see Owen 1994, pp. 53-59. For Chaucer's *Nun's Priest's Tale*, see Coghill and Tolkien 1959. For a translation into modern English, see Coghill 1959, pp. 238-55. For translations of the text of the fables by Alcuin, the monk of St Martial's Abbey, Marie de France and other relevant texts, see Sisam 1927, pp. viii -xxiii; also Varty 1967, pp. 33-34.

CRITICAL STUDIES

On the *Roman de Renart* and all other Beast Epics listed here, see Flinn 1963. For Guillaume le Clerc's *Bestiaire Divin*, see Bianciotto 1980, pp.67-116. This contains comments on the knowledge of Pierre de Saint Cloud's poem in England on pp.67-69 and p. 90. For more on the way the fox carries off his victim, see Trachsler 1994.

SUPPORTING INFORMATION

For details of the Amesbury Psalter, the Ormesby Psalter, the Queen Mary Psalter and the Smithfield Decretals, see the Indexes of Proper Names and of Subject Matter. My first letters to *Country Life* (published by George Newnes, London, weekly on Thursdays) and replies were published on October 15 & 29, November 5 & 12, and December 10, 1959.

CHAPTER TWO

The Fox-Preacher and Religious

Images of the fox preaching, more often than not to birds of one kind or another, abound in medieval art in England as well as in continental countries, especially in churches and monastic buildings and in many a manuscript decorated by clerics in their scriptoria. Their symbolic, sermonizing, moralizing purpose is certain. Some of them are linked to the carvings and drawings of the fox making off with a cock or goose in his jaws followed by a distaff-wielding woman. The earliest representation I have been able to trace of these two scenes is on the 1338 Ely Cathedral misericord referred to in Chapter One [2]. Next to the scene of the chase, on the left supporter, we see an upright fox wearing a gown and cowl. The cowl falls loosely down his back. With his left hand he holds a crozier, and from the point where his right hand rests on the crozier flows a scarf-like band separating a cock (below) from two hens (above), or are they ducks? This band was almost certainly meant to be inscribed with the first words of the fox's sermon, perhaps 'Pax vobiscum', or his text for the day. There is however no evidence of an erased or eroded inscription. The cock is the most prominent member of the fox's congregation and, in the central chase scene, it is the cock which the fox has grabbed. The implication is that these two scenes are part of the same moralizing tale: a fox disguises himself as a priest and manages to get sufficiently close to the members of his unwary congregation to be able to grab one of them and make off. The resulting commotion alerts the farmer's wife (the true guardian of the flock who, for one reason or another, let her guard slip for a moment) and she gives determined chase. But for those of us familiar with Pierre de Saint Cloud's and Chaucer's tales, the prominence of the cock makes us think of the climactic episode in their compositions even if neither of them has the fox make his approach to the cock in a religious disguise.

Before we pursue this any further, we should note that there are other drawings and carvings which link the preacher with the chase. One of the earliest of these is in the Smithfield Decretals of about 1330-40 [24]. Here, to the left of a decorated lower-margin sequence we see the fox assuming one of his more grandiose disguises for he wears a mitre and carries a crozier. In the front row of his congregation are two hens and a cock; behind them, a long necked-goose (easily the most prominent of all the birds depicted here); behind it, three ducks (one more interested in something on the ground than the sermon); and, drawing up the rear, a stork. Over to the right we see the fox heading for his hole in a hillside, the goose's neck firmly between his jaws and its body flung over his back. Close behind him the farmer's wife swings a distaff at his belly.

In Glasgow's Burrell Collection there is a curiously abbreviated, almost jumbled version of these linked scenes. It is a wood carving, said to be from the late fifteenth century, in the top

24 *A mitred fox preaches to birds. A fox with a goose is pursued by a distaff-wielding woman. The British Library, MS Roy. 10 E. IV, f.48; c.1335.*

25 *A woman attacks a seated fox with her distaff. The seated fox, holding a crozier, listens to another fox preaching from a pulpit. The Burrell Collection, Glasgow. A wooden doorframe spandrel in Burrell's reconstructed Hall. English late 15th C. Kenneth Varty.*

right corner of an oak panel above the north exit door from Burrell's reconstructed Hall [25]. It shows (from right to left) a group of four geese peering up at a devilish-looking fox in a slender, egg-cup-shaped pulpit. To the left of the pulpit is a seated, devilish-looking fox (the little stool on which he sits is scarcely visible), legs crossed. He holds a crozier and also looks up at the preacher. Dangling from his neck by, it seems, its neck (as if it had become rope), is a goose. (Usually, as we will see, the victim has been put inside a cowl, and it is this which hangs down the fox's back). And then, still further to the left, are the head and shoulders only of the farmer's wife who is caught in the act of bringing her distaff down on the shoulders of the seated fox-bishop. (The distaff handle has been broken off). There is in fact still more to this series of carvings for, in the corresponding left corner panel we see the face or mask of a devil from which a rope-like design reaches across the top of the door to join the length of cloth which streams in the wind from the farmer's wife's headgear, confirmation perhaps that the fox bishop is a devil in disguise on the look-out for unwary souls? Behind this, and therefore perhaps behind all or most of the scenes of the woman with her distaff who chases the fox with either a cock or a goose, is both the story with a moral as told by both Pierre de Saint Cloud and Chaucer and a well-known and widespread proverb: 'when the fox preaches, beware your geese.'

In 1983, Kerstin Rodin made a detailed study of this proverb, and in particular of its iconography: *Räven predikar för Gässen* (The Fox Preaches to the Geese). She traced it in several languages and in several countries (e.g., in what are now England, Holland, Belgium, France, Spain, Germany, Switzerland, Austria, Norway and Sweden); and from the thirteenth century to modern times (though she concentrated on the Middle Ages, and most of her examples are from the fifteenth and sixteenth centuries). Curiously, one of the most interesting of the continental examples is housed at Glasgow's Burrell Collection [26]. It is also rather unusual chiefly because it is in the form of a small tapestry (54.6 x 59 cm), and partly because the text on which the fox bases his sermon is given in a banderole. It is of Swiss origin and dated 1450-75. The fox is shown preaching from a lattice-work pulpit, an open book in his left hand, and two bewildered geese looking out of his cowl which, thrown back, resembles a large sack. The four geese which form his congregation have rosaries dangling from their bills, and they are being approached by a prowling red fox at the foot of the pulpit, no doubt the preacher himself at the conclusion of his sermon. The text of the banderole is difficult to read, because of wear and tear. It seems to read: 'Listdickheit. han. (*or* hau.) ich. wol. do. mit. fuill. ich. min. K...gen (= Kragen?). gar. foll.' This may be translated: 'I am well provided with cunning, enough to fill my stomach.' That this little tapestry may have been a cushion-cover is suggested not only by its size and shape and the way it is worn, but also by the information provided by Johannes Wolf's *Lectionum memorabilium...* where there is a woodcut illustration reproducing the design of a cushion-cover similar to this one, a cushion-cover which, in 1580, was on the seat of the Provost of the Kollegiatstift St Michael at Pforzheim and which bore on a banderole the words: 'Ich wil euch wol viel fabeln sagn Biss fülle allen meinen kragn', which may be translated: 'I will tell you many stories until I fill my stomach well full.'

26 *A fox preaches from a pulpit to four geese. The Burrell Collection, Glasgow. A tapestry cushion cover. Swiss, 1450-75.*

The proverb to which Rodin refers appears in a number of similar forms, several of which she quotes from late medieval literary texts and from early proverb collections. The earliest examples she gives are from morality and mystery plays: 'whanne the fox prechyth, kepe well yore gees' cries the Malus Angelus sarcastically in the *Castle of Perseverance* (c.1425). From the Towneley Plays (c.1460): 'let furth youre geyse, the fox will preche'; from *The Glasse of Government* (1575): 'the fox can preach sometimes, but then beware your geese'; from a collection of proverbs dated 1562: 'For though this appeere a proper pulpet peece / Yet whan the fox preacheth then beware your geese'; from *Euphues and his England* (1580): 'It is a mad Hare yat wil be caught with a Taber, and a foolish bird that staieth the laying salt on her taile, and a blinde Goose that commeth to the Foxes sermon.'

This proverb will almost certainly have been in the minds of most people, especially the unlettered and humble folk when they looked at carvings or other representations of the preaching fox. The lettered and the aristocratic of both Church and State may also have recalled the named fox of the Beast Epic or fable, for he too played the preacher, as he does even in the Chantecler branch of a fourteenth-century French version of the Epic, *Renart le Contrefait*

(Renart the Imitator). Here Pierre de Saint Cloud's poem is expanded from about 450 to some 2000 lines of octosyllabic verse.

It begins in a similar way to Pierre's, with Reynard arriving in the neighbourhood of a farm. The hens flee at his approach, but Chantecler reassures them, then goes to sleep. He dreams that he is captured by some terrible creature. When he wakes up he asks his wife, Pinte, to interpret his dream. She takes the opportunity to argue that men should not always despise women's advice as did Hector, the victim of Achilles, and the Count of Bar who died at Athens in 1337. Pinte makes Chantecler feel quite ashamed of being so stupid. Then he sees Reynard and tells him to be off. Reynard replies: 'I don't want to upset you. Please don't go away till I have prayed for peace, love and charity, for as long as Christianity shall last, I will go about preaching the Gospel. As the Lord said at the time of His Ascension "predicate euvangelium!" I belong to the Order of the Repented, and I have been converted because of a sign I have had...' Reynard goes on to assert that Chantecler's father had even commended his children to him; the cock should therefore have confidence in him. Reynard illustrates his arguments with a lengthy story about a peasant and his ass. Then he tells Chantecler that he is not only converted, but is also an excellent preacher, so good that he can make nuns and worthy men sleep when he preaches! 'I am a poor man and a beggar; I make no attempt to hide this from you. I could have been quite rich, but my conscience struggled with me, and commanded me to preach Holy Scripture. Less than three days have passed since I was made so weary by the crowds who gathered round me as I preached for a whole day. God! Many a tear was shed there, and many a prayer recited...Many a nun slept and snored because of the good sermon they heard. Many a worthy man slept too. He who knows how to deliver a sermon makes men sleep, for those who sleep the best will come nearest to God...'

Chantecler says he has confidence only in God, and digresses to tell a story about two blind men in Rome, and another about two clerks and their lord. With numerous quotations from impressive sources, Reynard asks Chantecler to be his friend. There then follows a diatribe against the Dominicans. The fox weeps and repents, saying: 'In my youth I was called Reynard, but now I am called Brother Bernard.' He recalls the repentance of St Paul and St Mary the Egyptian, whose stories he retells. God will have mercy on him, so why not Chantecler?

The cock now asks Reynard how he came to repent and be converted. The fox replies that it is because, ever since he heard the story of St Urban, he has been able to hear the music of Paradise and the groans of Hell. Chantecler says he would like to share this experience. Reynard tells him he must first confess. 'I cannot', says Chantecler, 'since there is no priest here'. 'But', replies Reynard, 'I am a priest. I may hear confession.' Chantecler insists on saying only his prayers. At this, Reynard announces he will first let Chantecler hear the groans of Hell, but as one ought not to see or hear two things at the same time (remember Lot's wife, whose story he tells), he orders the cock to glue one eye to the ground (since Hell is down below) and to close the other. Chantecler obeys. Reynard seizes the cock and makes off with him...

It is possible, then, that this particular version of the story of the cock and the fox, or one like it, was known in England at some time between the arrival of Pierre de Saint Cloud's tale and the composition of Chaucer's, and that the carvings and drawings which show the fox preaching to poultry in close physical proximity to the distaff chase are evidence of this, not to

27 *A fox preaches at a lectern to three geese. Leicester Cathedral, etching made for a study by J. Nichol in 1815 based on a late medieval piece of stained glass, now lost.*

mention those buildings and manuscripts in which both may be seen, but at a distance from each other (e.g. Beverley Minster, Canterbury Cathedral, and the Smithfield Decretals). And it is possible, even likely, that viewers of different cultural levels saw one or other or even several references or meanings in them.

It so happens that within this particular area of fox-religious images we have one that demonstrates very clearly the artist's ability to appeal to viewers with different levels of learning and culture. The painted glass of the great window of the north transept of St Martin's Cathedral in Leicester used to depict a fox preaching to a group of three geese and addressing them from a lectern on which lay an open book, presumably a Bible. This glass has long been lost, but in his *History and Antiquities of the County of Leicester* J. Nichol has left us with a clear drawing of the scene [27]. The fox is without disguise, a natural, upright fox. One of the geese pays attention, but the other two have turned their bodies away from the preacher as if to make off. Even so, their heads look back at him. Above them is a lengthy banderole in the shape of a large horseshoe on which Nichol tells us were painted the words 'Testis est mihi Deus, quam cupiam vos omnes visceribus meis.' The lettered and learned viewer would know that this meant 'God is my witness how I desire you all in my bowels,' and it would make him smile, especially if he were familiar with parallel scenes in other places where the preacher makes similar remarks such as those made by the fox on the Provost's cushion cover in Pforzheim ('I will tell you many stories until I fill my stomach well full'). The viewer who knew his Bible really well would recognize a misquotation or parody of the words of St Paul to the Philippians: 'God can testify how I long for all of you with the affection of Jesus Christ' (Philippians, 1, 8) and have an additional reason to smile. The unlettered majority who would normally be in this part of the church would most probably think of the proverb: 'when the fox preaches beware your geese.' The lord of the manor and other local aristocrats, as well as the bishop and some of the high-ranking clergy, might just be familiar with tales like those possibly reflected in the Ely misericord [2], the Smithfield Decretals drawing [24], and the Burrell Collection carved panel [25], or in other versions of the fox and cock story like the one in *Renart le Contrefait*.

It is perhaps worth recalling here that Reynard's earliest literary appearance to the cock in the guise of a holy man goes back to about 1150, to the *Ysengrimus*, where he is called Reinardus and the cock is Sprotinus. He also presents himself as a holy man to the cock in the early thirteenth-century Flemish *Reinaert de Vos*. In this epic poem Chantecler reports to Noble that he was once walking with fifteen of his children in a beautiful park when Reynard tried to take some of them by trickery. At first he failed, but one day he returned in clerical garb and bearing a letter sealed with the royal seal and addressed to the cock. He said it informed the cock that Noble had proclamed a general peace throughout his kingdom: animals and birds no longer had anything to fear from each other. Reynard also claimed that he had repented of his crimes and had become a hermit. As proof he showed Chantecler his pilgrim's staff and clothing. 'My lord Chantecler,' he said, 'you can now live without fear. I have solemnly declared my intention never to eat flesh. I am old, and I intend to think only of the good of my soul. I commend you to God. Now I must attend to my duty for I still have to say all my prayers for today.' The new hermit goes off reciting his creed. Full of joy, Chantecler leads his family beyond the enclosure wall. Meanwhile Reynard has hidden under a hedge and is waiting for his chance. He soon takes most of Chantecler's children, one after the other, so that only four of the original fifteen remain. Slightly modified, this episode reappears in the later fourteenth-century *Reinaerts Historie*, and in Caxton's 1481 *Historye of Reynart the Foxe*. And in the next chapter we will pause over the woodcut Wynkyn de Worde's artist made for it [62]. The fame of the holy preacher-fox lasted for centuries. In the last chapter we will read of his appearance in the seventeenth-century *Shifts of Reynardine...* where, after a few days in a monastery, he decided to abscond: 'being extremely pinched with Hunger, he resolved to take the opportunity of that time to make his escape. Accordingly, searching a Compass about, he purposed to run to the further side of an Hill, which stood right against the Monastery Gate, where being come, he espied many Geese sporting themselves in a large Pond at the foot of the Hill on that side. Before the Fox would go near them, he sought out a retiring place for himself, which being there ready, and therefore by him quickly found, he walked softly towards the Pond, seeming devoutly to read all the way he went, but when he was come near, he read louder, that they might hear him. The Geese seeing his Religious Habit, and hearing him read so devoutly, fearing nothing, came all out of the Pond, and became his Auditors, among whom two of the eldest (tho not the wisest) would needs thrust their heads even into his Mouth, to look upon his Book. The Fox seeing this, immediately kills them both: and then the others in great fear fled into the Water again, sounding an alarm all the way they went...' As we will see in an illustration made for this episode in the *Shifts* [248], the fox is depicted preaching to geese as they swim on the pond,

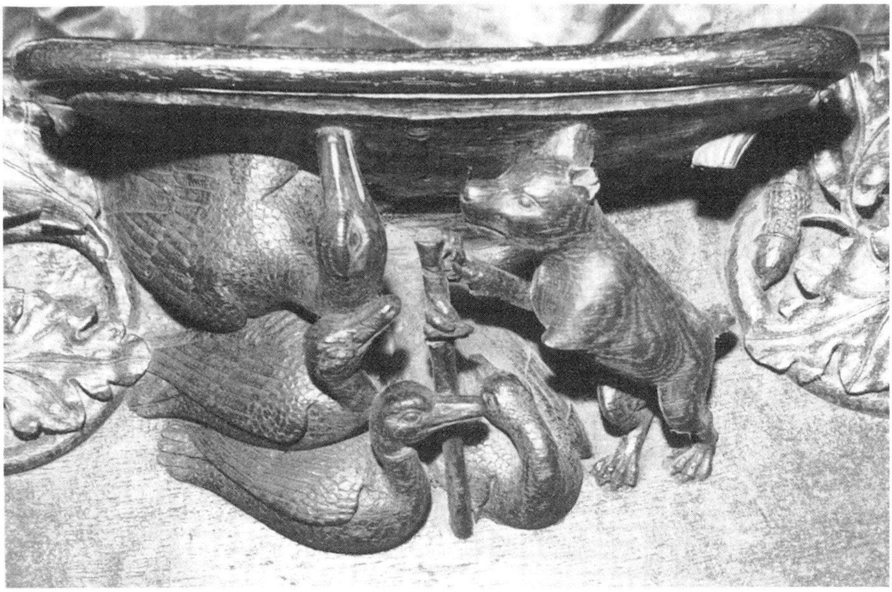

28 *A fox leans forward on a staff to preach to three relaxed geese. Wells Cathedral, misericord; 1330. D.R. Maxted.*

29 *A fox makes off with a goose slung over his back. Wells Cathedral, misericord; 1330. D.R. Maxted.*

30 *A robed fox religious leads a cock, hen and duck. Beverley Minster, stone spandrel, early 14th C. Kenneth Varty.*

not reading to them. Obviously, the iconographic tradition was so present to the artist that it, rather than the text, determined how he depicted this particular incident.

The earliest carvings I have been able to find of the holy (and, most often, preaching) fox are dated about 1330 and are to be seen on two misericords in Wells Cathedral. Beautifully carved, the first [28] shows the fox leaning forward on his staff and addressing a group of four seated ducks, one of which, right underneath him, has fallen asleep (one thinks of Reynard's boast in *Renart le Contrefait* that he could preach so well that he put some of his congregation to sleep!). On another misericord, [29] on the opposite side of the stalls, a fox runs off with a duck thrown over his back, perhaps the one that fell asleep. In the first of these carvings, only staff and gesture reveal the religious pose. Most representations of the preaching fox will show him wearing religious habit and, in particular, a cowl thrown back in which some of his victims are stored. Next in date is the misericord supporter scene in Ely Cathedral where, as we have seen [2] the fox has a cock and two hens in his congregation. Also belonging to the first half of the fourteenth century is a stone carving in Beverley Minster [30] where, unusually, the fox does

31 *A robed fox preaches from a pulpit to numerous birds. Lincoln Cathedral, wooden quatrefoil in choir-stalls; late 14th C. National Buildings Record.*

32 *An enthroned fox-bishop attended by a cock and an ass. Boston, St Botolph, misericord; late 14th C. D.R. Maxted.*

not face his intended victims (here a cock, a hen and a duck or goose), but seems instead to be leaving them behind or leading them somewhere. He carries a crooked staff and wears a gown. Might this be Reynard in his pose as a hermit-pilgrim leaving Chantecler after delivering the news about the king's peace and his conversion to a holy way of life? In Lincoln Cathedral a robed fox of about 1370 stands in a pulpit and preaches to geese [31]. The fate of the unwary is depicted in the lower left corner where the fox is shown seizing one of the geese by the neck. This is the earliest sculpture I have found of a fox in a pulpit. In St Botolph's, Boston, a much-worn, late fourteenth-century misericord depicts an enthroned fox-bishop wearing his mitre and flowing, ornate robes [32]. In his left hand he holds a crozier, in his right the neck of a cock behind which crouches a hen. The fox is served to his left by a grinning ass which wears priestly garments and holds an open book. Might the lettered spectator have thought of Bernard the Ass, the animals' archbishop in the French Beast Epic, and at one point Reynard's companion on a pilgrimage to Rome which ends in an assault on Ysengrin the Wolf's home and person? In Holy Trinity at St Austell, a late fourteenth-century bench-end carving [33], now fixed to the tower wall, shows a fox in his pulpit preaching to a fashionably dressed woman who kneels before him. Perhaps the ridicule of fashion, quite commonly found in

33 *A robed fox preaches from a pulpit to a kneeling woman. St Austell, Holy Trinity, pew end fixed to tower wall; late 14th C. (?). National Buildings Record.*

medieval literature, is part of the artist's aim here. This is the earliest English representation I have discovered of the fox preaching to a human being.

Before turning to manuscript drawings of this subject, there is one important wood carving to consider. Probably from the mid- to late fourteenth century, it is part of an isolated desk-end kept in Haddon Hall, in Derbyshire. It is the double-sided shouldered top of this panel that is of special interest, for it depicts relevant subject-matter on both sides of the shoulder. On the outer face we see the fox preaching to birds, while on the inner face they are shown in the process of hanging him. In their detailed study of these carvings, Malcolm Jones and Charles Tracy describe the fox as a bishop who 'stands in a pulpit wearing a clearly delineated mitre and cowled vestment and preaches to a congregation of birds (probably intended to be geese) who stand on the ground before him in the shade of a tree...surmounted by a cockerel. A banderole (apparently blank) issues from the cock's beak and another, still legibly inscribed, issues from the mouth of the fox-bishop. Behind the preaching fox, at the foot of another similar tree (despite the damage which has rendered both animals headless) the highly significant figure of a (young?) fox running off with a goose in its jaws is still visible; clearly this detail pre-figures the eventual, and indeed, proverbial fate of any goose silly enough to listen to the fox's sermon. One of the important features of this desk-end is that the fox-bishop's banderole reads 'Pes be here In' by way of episcopal greeting, not, importantly, the 'Pax Vobiscum' in liturgical Latin, but 'Peace be herein' in the Middle English vernacular...The fox preaching to birds *as bishop* would appear to be a peculiarly English iconographical development: of the nine examples known, only one is not English and, while early, is not the earliest representation, which honour goes to that in the Rutland Psalter. The three woodwork instances date from about 1400, but all the other manuscript depictions belong to the first half of the fourteenth century, so that it would seem (from the surviving evidence at least) that the iconography here follows that of the manuscript illuminators, and our desk-end represents the earliest example of the motif in woodwork. This peculiarly English iconography of the fox as bishop is perhaps open to a wider, political, interpretation. Although...the commonest representation of the fox is in a friar's habit (an image which could quite safely appear inside a parish church without risk of offence to the incumbent), to represent the fox unequivocally as a bishop may perhaps hint at proto-Lollard sympathies and anticipate Wycliffe's attacks on episcopal privileges later in the century... Turning now to a more detailed consideration of the scene carved on the inner face of the desk-end: despite having sustained relatively more damage than the other side, the main components are still clear. The fox hangs from a rope cast over a beam lodged between two trees, thus forming a make-shift gallows, the other end of which is being pulled by two geese with their beaks. A cockerel...perches on the gallows-beam and is provided with a semi-circular banderole: sadly the inscription is by no means as legible as that of the outer scene.' Nevertheless, Jones and Tracy think they can make out the words 'dra no to is damagat' which they think can be modernized as 'draw now to his damage' (or, as there is some doubt as to the termination of the final word, 'damnation'). This may be interpreted as the cock's encouragement to the geese-hangmen to pull hard on the rope. The authors continue: 'It is perhaps further worth noting that if the inscription is correctly transcribed, it forms an acceptable metrical line which is both rhythmical and alliterates on 'd'. It is perhaps going further than such uncertainly estab-

34 *A mitred fox preaches to birds. The British Library, MS Roy. 2. B. VII, f.157v; early 14th C.*

lished evidence will permit, to argue from this apparently alliterative line for the existence of a fourteenth-century poem which included this Death of Reynard scene.'

Some of the earliest drawings of the preaching fox date from the end of the thirteenth century and the beginning of the fourteenth. Typical examples are to be found in the Gorleston Psalter. On ff.47., 49v., 128. and 143v., enveloped in religious habit, he wears a mitre, holds a crozier and preaches to quacking geese. On f.143v. he is seated on a bishop's throne. His perfidiousness is often apparent. For example, on f.47 he holds a crozier in one hand and a duck (by the neck) in the other; on f.49v. he has the crozier tucked under his left arm while a duck dangles from his hand. (Very different is the drawing on f.152v. of a fox in religious habit seated side-saddle on an enormous goat, usually a symbol of evil and lechery.) Relatively early and mid-fourteenth-century drawings also bear witness to Brother Fox's preaching. We have already met him disguised as a bishop in the Smithfield Decretals [24] preaching to the cock and several other birds. He does much the same in the Queen Mary Psalter [34], but here his congregation consists of a goose, a bird, a mallard and a stork. The goose (in the front row) and the stork (at the back) are clearly standing on the ground, but the bird and the mallard appear to be airborne and coming in to land by the side of the others. (The cock and the hen reappear before the fox-bishop in a delightful drawing in the sixteenth-century MS. Ashmole 1504 kept in the Bodleian Library [35]. The fox holds a most elegant crozier, but wears no mitre, only a rather inadequate robe. Cock and hen seem spellbound. From behind the fox a large stork prances to join the congregation.) A mid fourteenth-century Bodleian manuscript (MS Auc. D 2.2, f.22v.) presents an interesting variation on this theme. Here the fox leans on a crutch before two hens who look up enquiringly at him. The fox says: 'Pax vobis.' Presumably, he

35 *An upright fox with crozier faces a cock. The Bodleian Library, MS Asmole 1504, f.22v; early 16th C.*

36 *A mitred, robed fox preaches to geese from a pulpit. Byfield, Holy Cross, now housed in the Stained Glass Museum in Ely Cathedral, glass roundel, late 14th C. The Royal Commission on the Historical Monuments of England.*

37 *An ornately robed fox preaches from a pulpit. Kirby Wharfe Parish Church, panel of stained glass; late 16th C.(?). Jill and Brian Lucas.*

hopes to dupe these hens not only by his holy manner, but also by feigning some serious physical disability. (In the Ormesby Psalter a cowled fox leaning on a crutch tries out a similar trick on a hare.) Perhaps the single most interesting scene from this period is a late fourteenth-century stained glass roundel [36] depicting a fox-monk-bishop preaching from a bright yellow pupit set outdoors on a flower-bedecked, grassy mound and against stylized trees. That this is a monk-bishop is clear from the brown cassock and hood (thrown back) and the yellow and white mitre. A quacking goose approaches from behind the fox, and another, facing him, begins to turn its head away, possibly to rest it on its back and go to sleep. In his left hand the fox holds a goose by the neck, and he has another one peeping out of his cowl. This roundel, about 12 cm in diameter, was in Holy Cross Church, Byfield, but is now housed on loan to the Stained Glass Museum in Ely Cathedral. It is one of only two preaching foxes on stained glass that I have been able to trace in England. The other, in the parish church of Kirby Wharfe, Yorkshire, either late fifteenth or sixteenth century, is set in a diamond-shaped quarry in the cusp of a small nave window [37]. The yellow fox is robed in white and stands in a white pulpit on three panels of which are painted robed human figures. The fox's tongue projects from his jaws. He holds a goose by the throat in his right hand, and its body dangles down the front of the pulpit.

38 *A fox preaches from a pulpit to a goose and a cock. Ripon Cathedral, misericord; 1490. J.C.D. Smith.*

39 *A robed fox preaches from a pulpit to a cock with hens, and to geese. Gresford, All Saints, misericord; 15th C.(?). D.R. Maxted.*

The list of fifteenth- and sixteenth-century religious foxes is a long one. Mention is therefore made of only a few of the more interesting ones.

We have seen that the preaching fox of the fourteenth century is sometimes a bishop, sometimes an itinerant friar preaching by the wayside. In the fifteenth and sixteenth centuries we find him more often indoors, preaching from a pulpit. In Ripon Cathedral [38] he preaches to a magnificent cock and a beautiful duck (or goose). Both birds hang upon his every word as he preaches with, it seems, great earnestness. In All Saints, Gresford, a much inferior carving [39] shows a similar division, cock (with hens) on one side, geese on the other. It is as if the artists were conscious of the two main sources of inspiration, the literary one in which the cock plays the chief role, and the folklore one in which the goose is more prominent. In St Petroc's, Padstow, a magnificent bench-end carving, now part of the sedilia in the south aisle chapel [40] shows the fox preaching to a group of ducks or geese, one of which has turned its back on the

40 *A robed fox preaches from a pulpit to geese. Padstow, St Petroc, bench end (sedelia, south aisle chapel); 15th C.(?). J.C.D. Smith.*

41 *A robed fox preaches from a pulpit to geese. Bristol Cathedral, misericord; c.1520. D.R. Maxted.*

42 *A mitred, well-robed fox preaches from a pulpit to birds. Ludlow, St Lawrence, misericord; c.1435. D.R. Maxted.*

preacher and seems to be about to go to sleep. The fox wears an ample cowl which is thrown back and from which lolls a dead goose's head. In Bristol Cathedral [41] the fox preaches to geese, nearly all of which have lost their heads through wear and tear. One which has not is clearly asleep. This carving shows two scenes in one for, from behind the pulpit, we see a fox (or possibly an ape) emerging with a staff held in a threatening manner. This is almost certainly meant to show our preacher (or an associate) a few minutes later attacking the sleepy goose. In St Lawrence's, Ludlow [42], a much damaged misericord depicts a very piggy fox wearing a bishop's mitre and robes (perhaps a satirical comment on the greediness of bishops) preaching to geese and other birds (mostly lost through wear and tear), while a couple of people (probably women) to the left gossip instead of listening to the sermon. A self-satisfied smugness oozes from the features of the giant fox who preaches in Christchurch Priory [43]. Here the cock is separated from his wives, and stands behind the fox's pulpit on a little bench all to himself. The hens stand below the fox and seem to be looking for juicy worms rather than

43 *A cowled fox preaches from a pulpit, birds below and before him, a cock on a stool behind him. Christchurch Priory, below elbow rest separating stall seats; c.1515. D.R. Maxted (from the east); Elaine Block (from the west).*

listening to his sermon. In St Mary's, Beverley, there is a fine early sixteenth-century roof boss depicting a cock as the victim in the fox's cowl [44], although his congregation consists entirely of geese, one of which approaches the fox with a large coin in its bill and which it foolishly offers to him. Also in St Mary's is a misericord carving depicting the fox preaching from his pulpit to a friar and a nun [45]. He wears a large cowl around his neck and which flows down his back. His wide-open jaws and gesticulating paws give the impression that he preaches with passion. Both the friar and the nun hold lengthy scrolls in their hands, as do two seated foxes (or apes ?) at each lower corner of the carving. They were probably meant to have inscribed upon them the text around which the fox preached, but no signs of inscription remain. The artist was most probably aiming a satirical shaft (similar to many in *Renart le Contrefait*) at friars and nuns, in particular at those in the Franciscan Order, for the knotted cord dangling from the man's waist shows him to be a Franciscan; and he is probably suggesting that they are subject to the vices so often represented by the villainous hero of fifteenth-century versions of the Beast Epic: hypocrisy, vanity, gluttony, lust, and so on. A similar satiric purpose may be behind another misericord carving in this same church [46] where a Franciscan friar addresses two foxes, each of whom carries a crozier and wears a cowl out of which lolls a dead goose. Hypocrisy is probably the main vice targetted here. An unusual way of depicting the fox's hypocrisy is to be seen in the right supporter of a misericord in Worcester Cathedral [47] where he kneels at an altar with his paws laid, as if in blessing, on the amputated head of some small animal placed on the altar just where one would expect the chalice to be. It is

44 *A robed fox preaches from a pulpit to geese, a cock in his cowl. Beverley, St Mary, roof boss; c.1520-25. Leicester University Press.*

45 *A robed fox preaches from a pulpit to a friar and a nun. Beverley, St Mary, misericord; c.1445. D.R. Maxted.*

46 *A Franciscan friar preaches to two robed foxes with croziers, geese in their cowls. Beverley, St Mary, misericord; c.1445. D.R Maxted.*

47 *A fox-priest kneels before an altar, paw laid upon an animal's head. Worcester Cathedral, misericord supporter; 1397. Elaine Block.*

48 *A fox carries off a man from a stake over his shoulder; another fox blows a trumpet. Castle Hedingham, St Nicholas, misericord; 15th C.(?). Kenneth Varty.*

49 *A cowled, robed fox stands between fleeing geese. Etchingham, St Nicholas, misericord; 15th C. The Kent and Sussex Courier.*

unlikely to be the head of the poor hare whose fate is told in Caxton's epic (and in its Dutch predecessors) and illustrated by Wynkyn de Worde's artist [209, 210 & 211], but it calls that animal's fate to mind. A satiric purpose no doubt inspired a roof boss carving in Winchester Cathdral where a fox in religious habit stands between two monks reciting their prayers. The fox lays a paw on an open book from which the monks read or chant. The extent to which some monks were subject to hypocrisy is suggested in a rather unusual way by the centrepiece of a misericord in St Nicholas's, Castle Hedingham [48]. Here an erect fox carries off a monk hanging upside down from a staff slung over the fox's shoulder. The fate of these hypocrites is predicted by a choir desk-front carving in St George's Chapel, Windsor, where three monks and a fox with a goose in his jaws are piled into a wheelbarrow and pushed by the Devil towards Hell's mouth. Normally, Brother Fox is shown to be quite successful in approaching his intended victims. A rare exception is in St Nicholas's, Etchingham [49], where all the geese flee from him. Even so, the fox (wearing a Franciscan's knotted cord-belt) holds his hands on his tummy in a gesture usually associated with a feeling of satisfaction and repletion.

The fox-religious is found in many parts of the church, but chiefly in the choir stalls, on misericords, elbow rests, bench fronts, bench ends and poppyheads. He is also to be found, appropriately, on pulpits. He runs round capitals, peers down from roof bosses, peeps up from tiles and paving stones, parades on friezes, high and low. He ornaments all kinds of church

50 *A robed fox preaches from a pulpit to geese. Abington Manor, Northampton, wooden panel in panelled room; late 15th or early 16th C. Kenneth Varty.*

furniture. On rare occasions he penetrates into secular surroundings and may be seen on the panelling of a great hall [50] or even on the outside timberwork of an inn [51]. The fox-religious is usually portrayed with those he means to dupe, but from time to time, he stands alone, fixing his pseudo-saintly eye on the passer-by. He is most commonly seen preaching in nondescript religious garments, but occasionally may be recognized as a pilgrim, priest, friar, monk, bishop or abbot. In the *Roman de Renart* and its French descendants he plays all these roles at one time or another, but it seems that his role as bishop is one he plays more in medieval English art than anywhere else.

51 *A robed fox preaches to geese from a pulpit, then seizes one of them by the neck. Ipswich, former Old Half Moon Inn, external corner post; probably early 16th C. National Buildings Record.*

One of the literary Reynard's earliest and often-repeated roles is that of pilgrim. The summary of the first parts of Caxton's *Historye* early in the next chapter surveys the events that led to Reynard's being summoned to Noble's court, tried, and pardoned on condition that he went on a pilgrimage, which he did, to the considerable cost of others. This story was particularly well told in Branch I, *Le Jugement,* one of the earliest branches of the *Roman de Renart*, usually dated about 1180, repeated in many a 're-edition' in the thirteenth, fourteenth and fifteenth centuries, and also incorporated, in modified form, in the highly successful Dutch versions of the Beast Epic from which Caxton's text ultimately came. Another branch of the *Roman de Renart*, Branch VIII, composed about 1190, is entirely about Reynard the Pilgrim, and this too reappeared in French many times throughout the Middle Ages.

The artist who sculpted the Beverley Minster fox leading a cock, hen and duck or goose [30] may have cast him in the role of a pilgrim, but one of the few certain fox pilgrims I have found is in the Smithfield Decretals, in the upper margin of f.55, where he is shown wearing a typical pilgrim's hat, smock and scrip, and carries a pilgrim's staff. He reappears with some of these accoutrements in other drawings in this manuscript as, for example, when he is approached by the hare on f.53 v [167].

52 *A robed (and plumed?) fox preaches from a pulpit to geese. Salisbury and South Wiltshire Museum, pewter badge, 14th or 15th C. Courtesy of The Salisbury and South Wiltshire Museum.*

This brings us to the particularly intriguing appearance of the fox on badges usually catalogued, described and exhibited among pilgrim badges, that is, badges said to have been worn by pilgrims as they returned from their pilgrimage. In his Introduction to a catalogue of *Pilgrim Souvenirs and Secular Badges* Brian Spencer writes: 'Going on a pilgrimage was one of the most popular ways by which medieval men and women actively sought the path to salvation. Yet by the fourteenth century, instead of being a purely religious or penitential exercise, pilgrimage had for most people become something of a social occasion that combined an element of tourism with religion... All pilgrims wanted to carry home visible proof of their travels...usually in the form of metal badges...normally worn on the hat...' In relatively recent years many of these badges, mostly of a tin-lead alloy, have been excavated from river beds, studied, catalogued and put on exhibition. The Salisbury and South Wiltshire Museum has over three hundred of them, mostly found in the bed of the river Avon or the Millstream at Salisbury

53 *Geese on the side panels of a pulpit in which probably stood a fox. Museum of London, fragment of a pewter badge; 14th or 15th C. Courtesy of the Museum of London.*

between 1975 and 1987. One of these shows, appropriately enough (illustration 303 in the Museum's catalogue) [52] a fox preaching from a pulpit to geese. The description in the catalogue reads: 'Badge: a fox preaching to geese. The fox stands in a polygonal pulpit (modelled in relatively high relief) and leans on a staff. Geese stand around the pulpit, two looking up at the fox in rapt attention, while two others may even be falling over backwards, lulled to sleep by the sermon. Another goose to the fox's right has either been lured to perch on the top of the pulpit or, when the badge was complete, was perhaps shown to be forcibly held there by the fox, who already has a dead goose tucked under his belt and may have others concealed beneath the bulges of his pseudo-monk's habit. 14th or 15th century. Height 48 mm.' The design of the fox's habit is odd: it looks as if it may be decorated with long feathers, perhaps a camouflage? The position of the captured, dead goose is also most unusual. Perhaps because the fox appears not to have been shown in profile, it was not possible to depict his cowl in which the preacher-fox usually placed his victims, so he uses his belt. Another victim may have been enticed into a position beneath his right forepaw.

There are fragments of two more relevant badges, but these are kept in the Museum of London. They were excavated only in 1980, and are both thought to be from the fourteenth or fifteenth century. The were found on the bed of the Thames at Bull Wharf, Queenhithe, London. The smaller fragment [53], which is about 3 cm square, shows four sides of what was probably an octagonal pulpit, and on each of them is a goose peering upwards, most probably

54 *A fox, standing on the back of another fox, plays a portative organ. Museum of London, fragment of a pewter badge; either 14th or 15th c. Courtesy of the Museum of London.*

55 *A robed fox plays bagpipes. The Bodleian Library, MS Asmole 1504, f.23v; early 16th C.*

at a preaching fox, missing through damage. The other fragment,[54], from which only the head is missing, shows a large upright fox on the back of a small fox on all fours. The upright fox sports two brushes. These foxes' brushes overlap and join with each other. The upright fox clasps a portative organ to his chest. Although a few foxes playing musical instruments are to be seen here and there (and there is a *Roman de Renart* branch [Ib] about a fox minstrel), I know of no other representation like this, in particular the combining of the two animals. Malcolm Jones points out that this kind of organ could represent female genitalia, and it is a fact that the bottom inside corner of the organ rests just where the upright fox's penis would be if it were visible. Other musical instruments could also represent sexual organs, in particular flutes and pipes, especially bagpipes when held by males in a suggestive manner. I know of very few musical foxes, but one of the few I know shows the fox playing bagpipes in combination with other figures which could represent lust [55]. I conclude that this badge also represents that vice. There may well have been quite another meaning if it were (but I doubt it) a pilgrim badge because pilgrim badges were usually sold at the shrine of the saint which the pilgrim had visited. But surely no saint had the fox in any guise or pose as his badge? Perhaps this sort of badge was a kind of parody of the obviously serious ones featuring, for example, the apostles.

These questions become even more interesting when we come to the only other badge I know featuring the fox [56]. This was found in Amsterdam in 1984 and now belongs to the Stichting Behoud Cultuurbezit in Amsterdam's Keizergracht. Nearly 4,5 cm high, of a pewter-lead alloy, it has been dated around 1350-1375 from its archaeological environment. It depicts a fox on pilgrimage. He carries a scrip on his back, and rests his left forepaw on a typical pilgrim's staff or bourdon. With his right forepaw he holds a chain attached to a goose's neck, and the goose appears to be leading him on his pilgrimage, though this may be a different way of showing that it is the fox's captive. To judge by the fox's erect penis, he is for some reason or other sexually excited. Although this is, as far as I know, unique among representations of the fox, other badges depict other animals and even men with large erections, and some badges are composed almost entirely of the shape of human genitalia. An ironic, wry comment on the less holy activities of some pilgrims? A rather vulgar joke? Or are they perhaps intended as protection against the sins they represent: hypocrisy, lust, and so on?

The possibility that the fox may have been used on badges in a parodic manner gains some credence from the variations on badge-like Thomas à Becket objects recently found in the Thames and pointed out to me by Brian Spencer. In a letter he describes 'a tin or pewter finial in the form of a peacock with a fox standing on its back' (in a photostat picture of this object the fox is shown to be only a fraction of the size of the peacock, perhaps about a quarter). 'I say finial because the object, though flattened, was hollow cast and modelled in the round and had a circular aperture and sleeve at the base: furthermore, the sleeves of comparable objects are sometimes pierced with nail holes, as if they had been secured to the end of a rod or staff. To begin to complicate the picture, a similar peacock finial carries a pair of confronted birds on its back. In several other instances, moreover, the peacock supports the figure of an archbishop (presumably Becket) giving his blessing and again modelled back and front. Finally, the peacock, which in these cases begins to look like a cross between a peacock and a cockerel, itself holds either the archbishop's cross-staff or a cross with a banner... I am fairly confident that they are pilgrim souvenirs of the second half of the thirteenth century. They have a good deal

56 *An erect pilgrim fox follows a chained goose. Amsterdam, Stichtung Behoud Cultuurbezeit, pewter badge, c.1350-75. Courtesy of the Stichtung Behoud Cultuurbezit.*

in common with contemporary Canterbury hollow-cast statuettes of Becket, which also bear signs of having been used as finials.' In short, if we review the objects Brian Spencer describes in a different order, we can see how a pilgrim souvenir depicting a saint with a crozier was modified by having the saint replaced by the peacock (representing immortality), replaced by other birds (with other holy symbolic values), by a fox on a bird which begins to recall the cock, thereby slipping into the domain of fable and the world upside down, perhaps with parodic intent.

By the beginning of the fourteenth century, Brother Reynard's reputation in France was such that men enacted some of his roles in the streets of Paris. In 1313, King Philip the Fair (Philippe le Bel) organized a great Pentecostal feast in his capital city, and this included numerous tableaux mounted on wagons (akin to those in many present-day carnival processions) which were drawn through the streets. The metrical chronicle which describes these tableaux (Paris, Bibliothèque Nationale, f.fr. 146, dated 1317) reveals that, mixed up with all kinds of religious tableaux, were several featuring the fox dressed as bishop, archbishop and pope. One of the most distinguished guests of the French king to see these was Edward II, King of England. On this subject Malcolm Jones has written and speculated in a most interesting manner: 'In the metrical chronicle of Geoffroy de Paris...it appears that, at the French king's instructions, an actor was dressed up as Reynard and others as hens and geese. Apparently Philippe had staged this performance more than once, which began with Reynard's entrance as a priest chanting the epistle for the day, but by satirical progression via his donning of the episcopal and then the archiepiscopal mitre, came finally to his assumption of the pontifical tiara, at which point his true nature was suddenly manifested, and he would leap upon the 'hens' and 'geese'. It is a curious fact that only the previous month Edward had managed to prevail upon Pope Boniface VIII to quash the election of the scholar Thomas Cobham to the see of Canterbury, in favour of his favourite, Walter *Reynolds*. Was Philippe's *tableau vivant* merely an unfortunate coincidence that might well have sparked off a diplomatic incident, or was it a deliberate jibe, to present Edward with the spectacle of the voracious Reynard and the fatally weak Pope?'

In the earliest adventures of Reynard the Fox, there is relatively little satire of priests, monks and pilgrims. One has the impression, rather, of joyous parody which may, from time to time, be quite pointed. With the arrival of friars in the thirteenth century, sharp satire does appear, and friars are often the object of it. For example, in *Renart le Nouvel* (1289), one of Reynard's sons becomes head of the Dominicans, and another becomes head of the Franciscans. As this century grows older, the satire grows sharper, and scarcely any religious order, rank or office is spared. Thus, in *Renart le Nouvel*, Reynard is depicted at one stage as the captain of the Ship of Vice, and he tells us that the Pope is his admiral, that his officers are cardinals, and his crew is made up of archbishops, bishops, abbots, monks, friars, priests and clerics. By the fourteenth century, authors of new Beast Epics in France at least, continuators of the *Roman de Renart*, had turned our villainous hero from a living character into a symbol and a figure to tell what they saw as truths about the Church, truths which it might have been dangerous to tell openly. It is in the light of this evolution, and against this background, that one should view and interpret many of the representations of the fox-religious wherever he appears in medieval art.

Notes

CRITICAL STUDIES AND SUPPORTING INFORMATION

For more details about the distribution of the proverb, see Rodin 1983, in particular pp. 28-35. For the etching of the lost Leicester Cathedral stained glass picture of the preaching fox, see Nichol 1815, volume one, part two, plate XLIII, figure one. The lengthy quotation about the Haddon Hall carving of the preaching fox is from Jones and Tracy 1991, pp. 110-112.

Photographs of the carving are to be found in Plate XII. For further information on pilgrim and secular badges, see Bedaux 1989, Spencer 1990, and Jones 1994. Jones writes about the use of the organ as a symbol for female genitalia on pp. 213-214, and about pipes (etc.) as symbols for male genitalia on pp. 216-218. The pilgrim's staff as another symbol for the penis is treated on pp.196-197. For more information about Philippe le Bel's Pentecostal Feast, and in particular the use of Reynardian tableaux, see Regalado 1995, pp. 111-141.

CHAPTER THREE

The Trial of the Fox for Adultery and Rape: *The Tribulations of a Bear, a Cat and a Village Priest*

In the *Roman de Renart*

BRANCH II

The earliest branch of the *Roman de Renart* told how Reynard, after committing crimes against the cock, titmouse, cat and crow, came upon the wolf's den where he found Hersent, the wolf's wife, alone with her four children. Dame Hersent addressed Master Reynard in a friendly, mock-reproachful manner, complaining that he should have come to see her much sooner. Reynard excused himself by saying that he did not want to annoy Isengrin, her husband, who had already accused him publicly of having an adulterous affair with her. Feigning great anger at this news, Hersent exclaimed: 'I have never even had such an evil idea, but if it is said that you and I are having an affair, then I wish it were so... Kiss me, embrace me.' They lie together, and their love-making is witnessed by the wolf cubs over whom Reynard then urinates, so delighted is he by his conquest. He even strikes the cubs, verbally abuses them, and raids the larder. Naturally, when he returns home, the cubs tell their father what has been going on behind his back, and complain about the way they have been treated. Hersent's defence is to claim she was raped.

A few days later husband and wife come upon Reynard by chance. They give chase, set on revenge. Reynard manages to shake off the wolf, but not his wife. She keeps close behind him. He dashes into his hole and Hersent, unthinking, follows only to discover when she is firmly stuck half-way into the hole that it is too narrow for her. He emerges from another hole and returns to find Hersent in no position to resist rape. Isengrin arrives on the scene just in time to witness the assault. His protestations are met with abuse, and Reynard makes off before the wolf can get at him, leaving him the undignified task of pulling his wife out of the hole by her tail. Isengrin is beside himself with rage. Trying to calm him, Hersent suggests they lay a complaint before the king, and have the fox tried for his outrageous conduct.

BRANCH Va

They both testify before Noble who annoys them by showing some sympathy for the fox, but since a complaint has been lodged the law must take its course. The animal peers debate, some taking the fox's side, others the wolf's. The bear and the cat are particularly bitter about Reynard. The cock, titmouse and crow add their complaints to the wolf's. Eventually it is decided that Reynard must appear before the royal court and swear on oath to redress the wrong he has done Isengrin. Roenel the Dog will preside over the ceremony.

Grimbert the Badger is sent to inform Reynard of the court's decision, and to summon him to attend their pleasure. Isengrin feels this is letting the fox off too lightly, so he plans mischief. He gets Roenel to pretend to be dead, and persuades his friends to insist that Reynard should now make his oath over the dog's 'corpse'. The plan is that, when Reynard makes his oath, Roenel shall seize him, whereupon the wolf and his allies present at the ceremony shall then attack and kill the fox. When the time comes, however, Reynard notices that the dog still breathes. He therefore refuses to go forward to make the oath. Indeed, he turns away and flees. He is pursued, even wounded, but eventually reaches the safety of his home. The earliest branches (II together with Va, perhaps the original *Roman de Renart*) end here.

BRANCH I

Just a few years later, perhaps around 1180, another sequel to Reynard's amorous adventures with the wolf's wife made its appearance, more dramatic, more entertaining, and brilliantly told. Called *Le Plaid* or *Le Jugement de Renart* (Reynard's Trial) and traditionally known as Branch I, this tale tells how Noble summoned all the animals before him. All obeyed except Reynard. The fox's enemies, in particular Isengrin, took this opportunity to air their grievances and complaints about him; but his allies, and a sympathetic king, managed to outmanœuvre them. For a moment it seemed that Reynard was to get away once more with his affronts and crimes; but just then Chantecler and his wives arrived in procession with the mutilated and beheaded remains of Coupée, one of the cock's many sisters-in-law. They complained to the king of this and of other murders committed by Reynard in the hen-house. The king, indignant and angry because his peace had been broken, swore to make an example of the fox.

After a state funeral for Coupée, Noble sent Brun the Bear to bring Reynard to court. Brun was seemingly well received by Reynard at Maupertuis, his castle. He pretended to be prepared to accompany the bear to court, but first suggested some refreshment. 'I know where there is honey to be had', says the fox. Brun falls for the trick and is led by Reynard to a half-split log in which the fox says there is honey. Brun puts his head and forepaws into the split whereupon Reynard removes the wedge which kept the split open. The bear is trapped and soon attacked by villagers drawn to him by his roars of pain. Grievously wounded, fiercely taunted by the fox, he escapes and returns to court.

Tibert the Cat is now sent to bring the fox before the royal and terribly angry presence of Noble. He is similarly duped by Reynard who offers him a meal of mice before they set out on their journey. The fox shows him a hole into a priest's barn which, he says, swarms with mice. Reynard knows that the priest has put a snare on the other side of the hole in order to catch him, so the cat, not the fox, gets caught. He too escapes only after being badly beaten, though he inflicts some grievous bodily harm on his chief assailant, the priest.

The third messenger sent to fetch the fox is his cousin and friend Grimbert the Badger. He manages to persuade Reynard that he should appear before the lion, arguing that there is a good chance they will win the day. To prepare himself for the ordeal he forsees, Reynard confesses, perhaps a little too triumphantly, all his sins and is shriven by the badger. After resisting the temptation to raid a nuns' poultry yard on the way to court, Reynard makes a spirited defence against the accusations made by his enemies and is ably supported by Grimbert. Even so, he is found guilty and condemned to death by hanging. Standing before the gallows he makes one last effort. He pleads for mercy and begs for time to repent of his sins. He promises to make a pilgrimage to the Holy Land if he is spared. Grimbert eloquently comes to his aid. Noble is moved to let the fox go free on condition that he journeys to the Holy Land and never returns.

Reynard is then attired as a pilgrim with cross, hood and staff, but no sooner has he left the court than he comes upon Couard the Hare whom he strikes down with his pilgrim's staff and carries off. When he reaches the top of a hill overlooking the valley in which the court remains assembled, he hurls insults to all and sundry, casts off his pilgrim's attire, jumps on it, and throws it into the valley. As he does this, Couard escapes and makes his way back to the assembly. There he reports his ill-treatment to Noble who promptly orders all his barons to pursue the fox. Reynard outstrips them and, on reaching the safety of his castle, is received in grand style.

FROM THE *ROMAN DE RENART* TO CAXTON'S *HISTORYE OF REYNART THE FOXE*

This story proved to be immensely popular over several centuries and in several cultures. It occupied the first place in most medieval French manuscript collections of the *Renart* branches, manuscripts which were copied many times, especially in the fourteenth and fifteenth centuries, and of which two may have been available in fourteenth-century England. Much of it was incorporated into Heinrich's *Reinhart Fuchs* in the late twelfth century; then, almost entire and at the beginning, into the Flemish *Reinhart de Vos* in the early thirteenth, as it was into *Reinaerts Historie* in the later fourteenth, then (from the Dutch) into English with Caxton's late fifteenth-century version. And this, in the hands of Wynkyn de Worde, was illustrated from as early as 1495.

In Caxton's *Historye of Reynart the Foxe*

In its earliest English form, the corresponding part, beginning at the beginning, may be summarized thus:

It was Whitsuntide and Noble had called his annual court gathering to deal with any crimes or complaints which his subjects might wish to bring before him. All had answered his summons except Reynard. In his absence Isegrim complains about the time when, he alleges, Reynard broke into his castle, raped his wife and blinded his children by urinating over them.

Curtois the Hound immediately adds his complaint about the theft of a pudding which Tibert promptly insists was really his. The panther joins in by telling how he had recently rescued Cuwart the Hare from Reynard's jaws. Grimbert speaks up in his uncle's defence, arguing that Isegrim had often offended against the fox. He recalls in particular the time when Isegrim did not wait to share the plaice Reynard had thrown down from a fisherman's cartload of fish, as well as a flitch of bacon the fox had managed to steal for the two of them. One by one he lists the alleged crimes by his uncle's accusers and provides plausible excuses. But then, just as he had made quite a good case in Reynard's defence, Chanticleer the Cock arrives in procession bearing, on a bier, the headless body of a hen, one of his many daughters. This child of his, he tells the assembled court, was treacherously killed by Reynard shortly after he had entered the farmyard dressed as a hermit and carrying what he alleged was a signed and sealed copy of a proclamation made by the king to the effect that henceforward there was to be peace between all his subjects. In any event he, Reynard, had become a peace-loving hermit and a vegetarian. The enraged king declares that Reynard must be brought before him to answer this charge of murder. First, though, Chanticleer's dead daughter is given a proper funeral service and burial. Bruin the Bear is chosen to take the king's summons to Reynard. On his arrival before the fox's castle, Maleperduys, he delivers the summons in a curt and pompous manner. Reynard feigns compliance but speaks of honeycombs on which he has been feasting. Bruin's greed gets the better of him, and instead of making a prompt return to court agrees to follow the fox to a woodcutter's yard where, the fox maintains, honeycombs are to be found in a half-split tree trunk lying on the ground (and kept open by two wedges). If he notices the wedges, Bruin is unconcerned and unsuspicious. In his eagerness to eat, he pushes his head and forepaws well into the crevice. Reynard yanks out the wedges and taunts the stupid bear as he howls in agony. This alarms the woodcutter who alerts his neighbours who descend on the bear with sticks and staves and beat him within an inch of his life. He escapes from the log only by leaving much skin and fur behind; and he gets away from the peasants by creating a diversion when he accidentally knocks the local priest's concubine into the river which flows nearby. As the men rescue her, Bruin jumps into the river and swims away. On his return to court, his sorry state creates much further anger about the fox, and it is decided to send a second envoy to Castle Maleperduys.

The task is given to Tibert. He too is beguiled by the fox and comes to grief through greed. This time Reynard proposes a plentiful meal of fat mice to be had in a nearby village priest's barn. In fact that is where the priest keeps some hens, and only the night before he (the fox) had raided it and taken some poultry. As a result the priest had set up a snare just inside the hole in the wall where Reynard was wont to get in, and the fox is well aware of this. As soon as night has fallen, the cat is led to this hole and, of course, gets caught in the snare. The priest, sleeping with his concubine, is woken by the cat's howling. They jump out of bed, the priest 'all mothernaked' and, well armed, they attack in the darkness what they believe to be the fox. In the ensuing skirmish the cat is blinded in one eye and, in desperation, attacks the priest's genitals. He bites off a testicle which rolls on the ground before the concubine, Dame Julock. On seeing this and realizing that this will curtail the sexual pleasures she might have otherwise looked forward to, she faints. Reynard, from a safe distance taunts them all, including Dame Julock, telling her she should not worry too much for 'there is in this world many a chapel in which is rung but one bell'. This diversion gives Tibert the chance to escape, and escape he does, returning to court as sorry a sight as Bruin was.

Grimbert the Badger is then dispatched to bring Reynard to court. He manages to persuade the fox that it is in his best interests to comply with the king's summons, and they set out together to face the music. In view of the great danger ahead, Reynard decides he ought to confess his sins. Grimbert agrees to shrive him provided he first promises to renounce stealing and plundering. The fox accepts and confesses at length to numerous crimes and vicious attacks, especially upon the wolf. No sooner has Reynard been shriven then he tries to take a fat young hen in a nuns' poultry yard as they pass by their convent on their way to the royal court.

Though full of fear on entering into the king's presence, Reynard makes a bold but vain defence of the way he is alleged to have mistreated his accusers, especially Bruin and Tibert. He is condemned to death by hanging. Tibert urges Bruin and Isegrim to carry out the execution with all possible speed at some nearby gallows, and he leads the fox up the gallows ladder with the very cord which had ensnared him in the priest's barn. From the ladder Reynard begs leave to confess publicly all his sins. Noble grants him this request, and he makes a long speech in which, playing on the royal couple's love of money, he tells how his father had found a great treasure and had conspired with Grimbert, Tibert and Isegrim to murder Noble and replace him with Bruin as king. He deliberately incriminates his late father and his loyal nephew to make his conspiracy story more credible, thus guaranteeing, if believed, the condemnation of Tibert, Isegrim and Bruin as traitors (not to mention poor Grimbert!). He argues that he thwarted the conspiracy by finding out where the treasure was and removing it from its hiding place to a new one known only to himself. His ruse works. Noble agrees to pardon him if he will reveal where the treasure now is and then leave his kingdom to go to Rome to get absolution from the Pope himself before going on to the Holy Land as a pilgrim. From a raised stone platform the king announces to all his subjects that Reynard is pardoned, that he and his whole family are to be well respected, and nobody is to speak against them. Isegrim ignores this command. As a result both he and Bruin are arrested, bound and cast into prison. Furthermore, each of them is made to provide pieces of skin and fur to make boots and a scrip for the pilgrim fox.

At this point the Anglo-Dutch story begins to diverge from the original French version. It tells how Bellin the Ram, priest in the animal kingdom, is made to bless Reynard, his new scrip and staff and, together with Cuwart the Hare, to accompany Reynard on the first part of his journey. They go with him as far as Castle Maleperduys. When they reach the entrance to Reynard's den, the fox tells the ram to remain outside while he goes inside with the hare to say farewell to his wife and children. Once in he murders the hare, and the family feast on his body, leaving aside only the head which the fox then places in his scrip. This he gives to the ram, still waiting outside, telling him it contains important letters for Noble who will be well pleased to receive them. Indeed, he suggests to Bellin that, to ingratiate himself with the king, he should claim part-authorship and responsibility for the scrip's contents. Bellin returns to court and hands over the scrip to the king's secretary. The discovery of the hare's head enrages the lion as he realises just how badly he has been deceived. The wolf and the bear are released from prison, and a great feast is held in their honour. During these festivities Lampreel the Rabbit, wounded in the head and lacking one ear, makes his way to Noble to complain about an attack made upon him by the pilgrim fox. Corbant the Rook follows suit. He tells Noble how the fox had pretended to be dead so that when Sharpbeak his wife laid her ear at Reynard's mouth to find out if he still breathed, he had sprung to life and bitten off her head before going on to eat all of her except for a few feathers which Corbant waves before Noble to make his point. Once more the king vows to bring Reynard to justice.

Illustrating *Reynard's Trial*

From this point on, the Anglo-Dutch version continues on a totally separate course, though often inspired by episodes from other branches of the *Roman de Renart*. With both the early French and the late Dutch accounts of these adventures in mind, we may now survey their iconographies with a view to comparing them with what we find in England, and in particular with the ultimate aim of assessing the possible sources of the Bristol Cathedral misericords and their Englishness.

From the outset it is to be noted that from neither French- nor Dutch-speaking territory do we have any relevant visual material found in medieval buidings: no sculptures, carvings, frescoes, tiles, or stained glass. There are, however, several relevant miniatures in French manuscripts, and three woodcut illustrations in fragments of one late medieval Dutch book.

ROMAN DE RENART MINIATURES

Where the French tradition is concerned, only seven *Roman de Renart* manuscripts are illustrated. Three contain only one picture, a frontispiece. These are manuscripts with the sigla *C* (Paris, Bibliothèque Nationale f fr 1579), *N* (Rome, Vatican, Reg Lat 1699), and *O* (Paris, Bibliothèque Nationale, f fr 12583). Three manuscripts contain a short cycle of miniatures, varying in number from sixteen in *D* (Oxford, Bodleian, Douce 360); thirteen in *E* (London, British Library, Add. MS 15229), though this may have contained one or two more because the first few folios are missing; and ten in *G* (Paris, B.N., f fr 1580), though this also may well have contained more because the first few folios are missing. Lastly, one manuscript, *I* (Paris, B.N., f fr 12584), contains a series of five hundred and thirteen small narrative miniatures.

The most frequently depicted scene relevant to *Reynard's Trial* is the frontispiece picture of Noble presiding over his Whisuntide court at which complaints are made about crimes committed by the fox. This occurs in manuscripts *C*, *D*, and *N* (the latter is in the Vatican, Reg. Lat. 1699) and would probably have been in one of the folios now missing from manuscript *E*, and in one of the blank spaces left in *F* (New York, Pierpont Morgan, MS 932) to receive miniatures. The one in *D*, broadly typical of the others, is reproduced [57] for comparison with what we find as the frontispiece picture in Dutch and English incunabula [58]and, indeed, in a long tradition in printed books well into modern times (e.g. [232, 244, 247, 251, 257 & 263]).

57 *Noble, enthroned, presides over his Whitsuntide court. The Bodleian Library, MS. Douce 360, f.1; 1338.*

The Hystory

hath befallen. I pray & commaund al them that hold of me, and desire my frendship, be they here or where soeuer they be, that they with their counsell & dedes help me to auenge these our great trespasses, that we
and

of Reynard the Fox.

and ours may abide in honour & worship, & this false theefe in shame, that he no more trespasse against our sauegard, I will my selfe helpe therto al that I may. ¶ Isegrim the woulfe & Bruine the Beare hard well the kinges wordes, and hoped well to be auenged on Reynard the Fox, but they durst not speake one word. The kyng was so sore moued that none durst well speake. At the last the Queene spake and sayd: *Sir pour dieu ne croyes mye toutes choses que on vous dye, et ne iures pas legierement.* A man of worshippe shoulde not lightely beleue ne sweare greatly vnto the tyme he knowe the matter clerely, and also ought of right to heare that other partie speake. There be many that complaine on other, and bene in the defaute them selfe. Audi alteram partem. Heare that other partie. I haue truely holden the faith, yea for good and vpon that he ment no falshode, I helped him all that I might, but how so euer it commeth or goeth, is he euill or good, me thinketh for your worshippe that ye shoulde not procede against him ouer hastely, that were not good ne honest, for he may not escape fro you. Ye may prison him or slea him, he must needes obey your commaundement. Than said Fyrapell the Libbard: my Lord, me thinketh my Lady here hath sayd to you trueth, and hath giuen you good counsell, do ye wel and followe her, & take aduise of your wise counsell. And if he be founden giltie in the trespasses that now to you be shewed, let him be sore punished, according to his trespasses. And if he come not hither or this feast be ended & excuse him, as he ought of right to do, than do you as your counsayle shall aduise you. But and if he
A.iij. were

58 *Noble, enthroned, presides over his Whitsuntide court. Wynkyn de Worde woodcut, c.1495. This, and all the illustrations numbered 55 to 85, are reproduced by kind permission from books in the library of Mr Wilfried Grauwels.*

One may reasonably guess that this is the one picture most readers of *Roman de Renart* manuscripts would remember and associate with *Reynard's Trial*.

It is very doubtful if the small miniatures in MS *I* were widely known and represent an established or influential iconography chiefly because they occur in an unusual manuscript in that all the branches it presents have been abbreviated (in some cases quite markedly so), and the miniature between the two columns of text on the first folio which depicts a Madonna and Child suggests a special, religious-minded owner and relatively restricted readership. Indeed, some of the parts that have been omitted in the abbrieviating process are some of the ones more likely to offend a reader with 'proper' religious sensibilities such as the rape of Hersent. The first narrative picture in MS *I* , at the top of the first column of text, f.1, is larger than all the others (about 7 cm square) and depicts a procession entering Noble's castle from which the enthroned lion looks at Reynard walking on his hind legs and being brought forcibly by several animals into the royal presence. This and the next 34 narrative miniatures all illustrate moments in Branch I. Beginning on f.1v, three animals stand in a kind of queue before an enthroned lion; f.2, a fox (?) confronts a cat (?); f.3, three animals stand in a kind of queue before an enthroned lion; f.4, a funeral procession: a cock and a hen lead a two-wheeled bier (a hen lies on the bier) and are met by a crowned lion; a bull (?) and a cat (?) follow, and behind them stands an empty throne; also f.4, an altar with candles at the centre; a bull to the right, a cat (?) and a wolf (?) to the left hold an open book between them and sing; f.4v, a wolf and a fox (?) with a hare lying on a slab (a gravestone?) around which is written 'ci gist Couppée la suer Pintain que R occist' ('here lies Couppée, little Pinte's sister killed by R'); also 4v, three animals standing below an enthroned lion; f.5, a cat confronts a fox looking out of a round hole; f.5v, a bear confronts a fox looking out of a round hole; f.6, a fox pushes a bear into a tree trunk; also f.6, a bear is beaten by two peasants one of whom brandishes an axe; also f.6, a bleeding bear escapes from two peasants; f.6v, eight people surround a bear (?) which they strike (the bear is not visible); also f.6v, a woman (?) hits a bleeding bear; also f.6v, three peasants pursue a bleeding bear; f.7, three animals queue before an enthroned lion; also f.7, a cat rides on horseback towards the entrance to the fox's den; f.7v, a fox leads a cat (towards a barn?); f.8, a fox looks at a cat caught in a snare; also f.8, a cat is beaten by a woman wielding a distaff and a man with a stick; f.8v, two men and a woman are close to a cat caught in a trap; also f.8v, two men and a woman are near a cat which attacks one of the men by the testicles; also f.8v, a cat and another animal stand before an enthroned lion; f.9, either two animals and a cat sing from a book on a lectern, or they receive a sealed summons of some kind, all before an enthroned lion; f.10, two animals (a fox and a badger (?)) approach a large building, two foxes look over the battlements; 10v, a kneeling or prostrate animal, possibly a fox; also 10v, two erect animals (foxes?) approach a castle at the entrance of which stands a cock, while a human face peeps over the battlements; also f.10v, two foxes on horseback (or a fox and a badger?), leave a crenellated buiding; f.11, two erect foxes (or a fox and a badger?) approach a saddled horse; f.12, three animals, of which one is a sheep, approach an enthroned lion; also f.12, three animals, of which one is a hare, approach an enthroned lion; also f.12, a fox with a rope around his neck stands before a crowned lion, and there are gallows in the distance to the left; f.12v, a lion seems to be comforting a fox standing at the gallows while a lioness offers a ring to the fox; also f.12v, a fox pilgrim takes his leave of an enthroned and crowned lion. Two other animals stand behind the fox.

A few of these miniatures correspond in subject matter (but not in style) to pictures in the earliest cycle of English woodcut illustrations which may be reasonably thought to imitate not these miniatures, but the woodcut illustrations made by the Haarlem Master for a Dutch text published sometime between 1487 and 1490. The miniatures in question are the ones on ff 1 and 2 (the enthroned lion presiding over his assembled court); on f 4 (the murdered hen's funeral procession and service); ff 5v and 6 (the bear arriving at the fox's den, then caught in the split log, then being beaten by peasants and making his escape); ff 8 and 8v (the cat caught in a snare, being beaten, attacking a man's genitals); f 12 (the fox at the gallows); and f 12v (the fox begins his journey dressed as a pilgrim).

DUTCH MINATURES AND WOODCUTS

Where the (pre-Wynkyn de Worde) Dutch iconographic tradition is concerned, there is only the evidence of the Haarlem Master's work of c.1487 to consider. None of the manuscripts or fragments of manuscripts of *Van den vos Reynaerde* contains any illustrations. *Reinaerts Historie* survives intact in one manuscript at the Royal Library in Brussels, and in a fragment at the Royal Library in The Hague. The fragment contains no miniatures, but on several pages in the Brussels manuscript, space has been left for illustrations. In 1836, when Jan Frans Willems was preparing his edition of *Reinaerts Historie*, the Brussels manuscript contained five vignettes or miniatures which were pasted in, presumably where the gaps are now found. Willems' edition is illustrated with lithographs by F. Gyselinck, three of which are said to have been inspired by the pasted-in miniatures which have since disappeared.

The Haarlem Master's work is found in a seven-leaf fragment of an edition of a rhyming *Reinaerts Historie* published by Gheraert Leeu in Antwerp between 2nd August 1487 and 1st September 1490. These are known as the Culeman fragments and are kept in the University of Cambridge Library. Only two of his woodcut pictures and about three-quarters of a third one survive intact [78, 79, & 80] but they are sufficient to show that this, the first woodcut cycle of pictures to illustrate the Beast Epic, was the model for both the first English and the first German translations of *Reinaerts Historie* (London, Wynkyn de Worde, c.1495; Lübeck, publisher unknown, 1498). The Wynkyn de Worde cycle is not only earlier than the Lübeck cycle, but (going by the little evidence we have) closer to the Haarlem master's in format, style and subject matter. This may be deduced from a comparison of the cuts which shows Reynard stealing a capon from a priest's table [78 & 73]. The detail is especially striking, e.g. the shading on the roofs, the little oblong object on the table in front of one of the seated men, the gestures of every animal and human in the picture. Unfortunately, there is no Lübeck cut to compare with this, and no Wynkyn de Worde original corresponding to the two remaining examples of the Haarlem Master's work for which Lübeck parallels do exist (cf [75 & 77]). In the Lübeck copy of the Haarlem Master's scene depicting the fox and the badger passing a convent's poultry yard [75 & 79], one notes that it is substantially accurate, but the finer details are not copied as closely and carefully as is the case with the corresponding Wynkyn de

Worde cut. The wall enclosing the barn-like building is omitted from the Lübeck cut; the barn itself acquires three windows to the side, but loses the one by the door, the proportions of which have been altered. The details of the convent's architecture have been much changed: height of enclosing wall, size and style of porch, number and shape of windows, style of roof, etc. The grouping and the gestures of the poultry are subtly different; and the Lübeck artist seems unable to discern less subtle differences in the poultry as depicted by the Haarlem Master. His three big geese and one little one become four similar-sized birds, half geese, half ducks, in Lübeck; his strutting cock (in line with the convent porch) is just an ordinary hen in Lübeck. And so on. Unfortunately, not enough of the Haarlem Master's third extant cut suvives for such a detailed comparison to be made, but here, in the scene depicting the fox's and the badger's arrival at the lion's court, we note the Haarlem Master's greater ability to depict a cat-like cat (cf [80 & 77]). Even the English copy ([76]) of the presumed Wynkyn de Worde original is more convincing in these details. In short, the little evidence there is suggests that the Wynkyn de Worde series copies far more closely the Haarlem Master's work, and it may be possible to reconstruct his cycle more accurately by studying the Wynkyn de Worde pictures than by studying the Lübeck pictures. When, for example, in the Wynkyn de Worde picture of the hare's head being presented to the lion [211] we see a beaver with a very beaver-like tail sitting between the panther and the ram, we can be fairly sure that the Haarlem Master depicted a beaver here, perhaps with webbed feet, as in the Wynkyn de Worde cut, and not a shaggy dog with a stumpy, furry tail and clumsy paws. And we may guess that it was the German artist who gave the lion and lioness their robes, not the English artist who unrobed them, etc. It is also noteworthy that the English and German artists, in copying the Haarlem Master, reversed the subject matter due to the method of copying. We must therefore imagine that most of his cuts will have been the reverse of their reflection in the Wynkyn de Worde and the Lübeck cycles.

ENGLISH WOODCUTS

Caxton's immediate successors as printers of the *Historye of Reynart the Foxe*, Wynkyn de Worde and Richard Pynson, both published illustrated editions using the same woodcuts. Although neither a de Worde nor a Pynson edition survives intact, there are fragments, and there is circumstantial evidence to show that a Wynkyn de Worde edition of about 1495 (or earlier) was illustrated by a series of 43 woodcuts, 12.5 cm high by 9 cm wide, apparently newly made for that edition. One of these very same cuts appears in a Pynson fragment kept by the National Library of Scotland and dated c.1501-1505. Pynson is known to have printed an earlier edition of the *History of Reynard the Fox* (before 1500), and de Worde a later one (about 1515), and we may guess that both of these were illustrated with all or some of this series of 43 vertical oblong-shaped cuts. In fact a surviving fragment of de Worde's c.1515 edition, housed in Cambridge University Library, contains one of his vertical cuts. The earliest nearly complete fully illustrated *History of Reynard the Fox* to come down to us probably dates from the period 1560-1586. It survives in a unique copy in the private ownership of Mr W. Grauwels and is sometimes described as the 'Anonymous' edition because it lacks the first few and the last few pages where we would expect to find the name of the printer and the place of publication. It contains 39 of the 43 Wynkyn de Worde cuts. To judge by their worn state, in particular by their damaged thick black borders, they had been much used since they were first made. This Anonymous edition also contains a series of 19 smaller, artistically inferior pictures 7.5 cm high by 11 cm wide. They too are quite worn and may date from soon after the earliest illustrated editions. One guesses this horizontal series will have been used to supplement the original vertical series whose subject matter they repeat. It is partly by typographical but chiefly by textual detail that I have ascribed this Anonymous edition to the period 1560-1586. It is therefore just possible that it is either the lost William Powell edition of 1560-1561 or the lost Edward Allde edition of 1586, for both of these are mentioned in the Stationer's Register, but neither survives. It may, of course, be a little later, but it is unlikely that it is earlier.

Thirty-nine of the 43 cuts which one may reasonably guess were made for the original Wynkyn de Worde vertical picture cycle are reproduced here [58-66; 69-73; 81-82; 85-88; & 209-227]. Thirty-seven come from the Anonymous edition; one from Allde's 1620 edition and one from Bell's 1656 edition, for cuts belonging to this cycle went on being used till late in the seventeenth century. The subject matter of the four missing blocks may be deduced from two early and reliable sources. The first of these is the series of 19 horizontal cuts found in the Anonymous edition; the second is the series of nearly square-shaped cuts in the famous 1498 Lübeck edition of the Reynard story, *Reynke de Vos*, in the Low German translation of *Reinaerts Historie*. The subject matter of all four of the missing cuts is to be found in both these sources, and they are drawn on, at the appropriate points, to complete the following description of the first half of the first English picture cycle for the *History of Reynard the Fox*. To begin with, we confine our description and commentary to the first twenty-four pictures because they depict for the most part episodes to be found in both Branch I of the *Roman de Renart* and the first half of Caxton's *Historye of Reynart the Foxe*. They also depict most of the episodes we see carved on five misericords in Bristol Cathedral.

THE FIRST ENGLISH PICTURE CYCLE FOR THE *HISTORY OF REYNARD THE FOX*

(Part I; from the beginning to the fox-pilgrim's departure from court)
1. The lion holds his Whitsuntide open court to which all the animals come except the fox [58]. This picture actually occurs as the 26 cut in the Anonymous edition, but one may guess that in this position it is, like so many others, a repeat illustration, a space-filler, and would have appeared as the frontispiece picture in one of the missing first few pages. 2. From left to right we see [59] a wolf, a cat, a dog and a badger (?) before the crowned and sceptred lion. The first three animals will shortly make complaints about the fox. In the background we see the fox pouncing upon an upturned hare, an attempted murder to which the panther will refer as he joins in the chorus of complaints. The badger, always loyal to the fox, will find excuses for his uncle and his friend. 3. The wolf eats a fish which has been thrown out of a cart driven by a fisherman intent upon the road ahead [60]. The fox looks hard at the wolf. This illustrates one of the grossly unfair treatments meted out to the fox by the wolf, an unfairness which the badger recalls as he makes excuses for the fox. 4. The cock, beating his wings in distress, arrives before the lion at the head of a bier on which lies the decapitated corpse of a hen [61]. On either side of the bier walks a hen carrying a tall, lighted taper. 5. The cock tells

59 *Curteyse the Hound complains to Noble. Wynkyn de Worde woodcut, c.1495.*

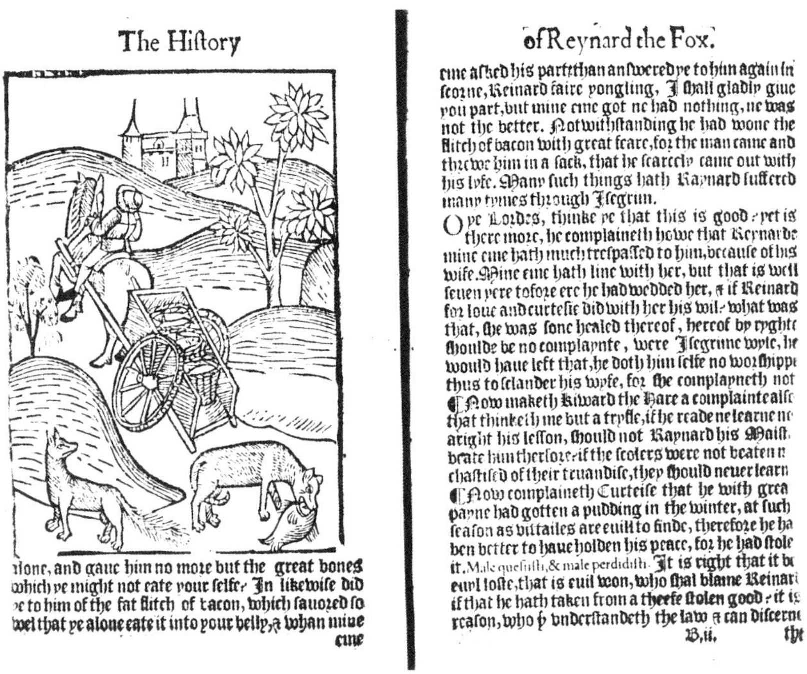

The History

alone, and gaue him no more but the great bones which ye might not eate your selfe. In likewise did ye to him of the fat flitch of bacon, which sauored so wel that ye alone eate it into your belly, & whan mine eme

of Reynard the Fox.

eme asked his part, than answered ye to him again in scorne, Reinard faire yongling, I shall gladly giue you part, but mine eme got ne had nothing, ne was not the better. Notwithstanding he had wone the flitch of bacon with great feare, for the man came and threwe him in a sack, that he scarcely came out with his lyfe. Many such things hath Raynard suffered many tymes through Isegrim.

O ye Lordes, thinke ye that this is good? yet is there more, he complaineth howe that Reynarde mine eme hath much trespassed to him, because of his wife. Mine eme hath line with her, but that is well seuen yere tofore ere he had wedded her, & if Reinard for loue and curtesie did with her his wil, what was that, she was sone healed thereof, hereof by ryghte shoulde be no complaynte, were Isegrime wyse, he would haue left that, he doth him selfe no worshippe thus to sclander his wyfe, for she complayneth not.

Now maketh Kiward the Hare a complainte also that thinketh me but a tryfle, if he reade ne learne not aright his lesson, should not Raynard his Maist. beate him therfore? if the scolers were not beaten nor chastised of their truandise, they should neuer learn.

Now complaineth Curteise that he with great payne had gotten a pudding in the winter, at such season as vittailes are euill to finde, therefore he had ben better to haue holden his peace, for he had stole it. Male quesisti, & male perdidisti. It is right that it be euyl loste, that is euil won, who shal blame Reinard if that he hath taken from a theefe stolen good? it is reason, who that understandeth the law & can discerne

B.ii. the

60 *Isegrim eats the fish thrown from a cart by Reynard. Wynkyn de Worde woodcut, c.1495.*

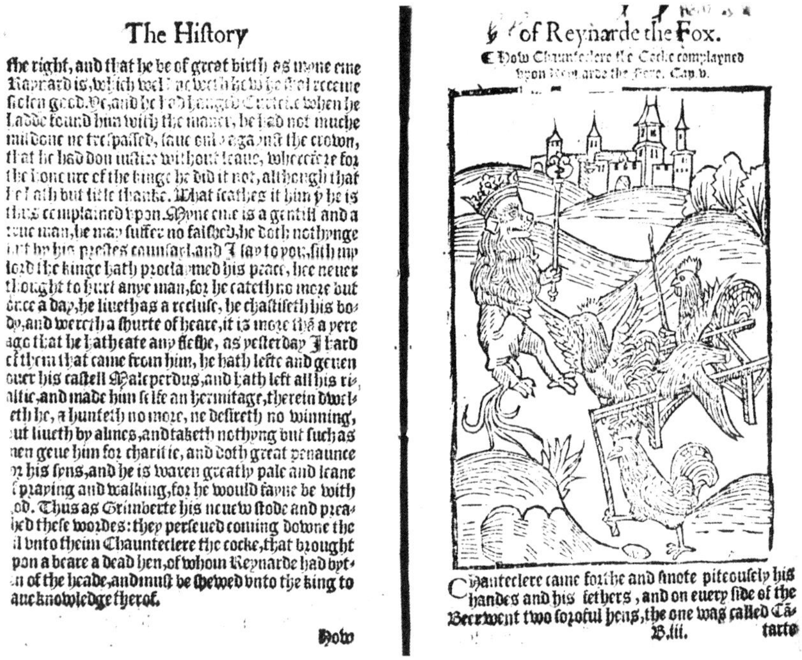

The History

the right, and that he be of great birth as myne eme Raynard is, which well knoweth how he shal receive stolen good. Ye, and he had hanged Curteise when he hadde found him with the maner, he had not muche mis done ne trespassed, save only agaynst the crown, that he had don iustice without leave, wherefore for the honoure of the kinge he did it not, although that he hath but litle thanke. What scathes it him y he is thus complained upon. Myne eme is a gentill and a true man, he may suffer no falshed, he doth nothynge but by his prestes counsayl, and I say to you, sith my lord the kinge hath proclaymed his peace, hee never thought to hurt anye man, for he eateth no more but once a day, he liveth as a recluse, he chastiseth his body, and wereth a shurte of heare, it is more thã a yere ago that he hath eate any fleshe, as yesterday I hard of them that came from him, he hath lefte and geven over his castell Maleperdus, and hath left all his rialtie, and made him selfe an hermitage, therein dwelleth he, a hunteth no more, ne desireth no winning, but liveth by almes, and taketh nothyng but such as men geve him for charitie, and doth great penaunce for his syns, and he is waxen greatly pale and leane [of] praying and walking, for he would fayne be with God. Thus as Grimberte his neuew stode and preached these wordes: they perseued coming downe the hil unto theim Chaunteclere the cocke, that brought upon a beare a dead hen, of whom Reynarde had byten of the heade, and must be shewed unto the king to haue knowledge therof.

How

of Reynarde the Fox.

¶ How Chaunteclere the Cocke complayned upon Reynarde the Foxe. Cap. v.

Chaunteclere came forthe and smote piteously his handes and his fethers, and on every side of the Beer went two sorowful hens, the one was called Cã[tarte]

B.iii. tarte

61 Chantecler complains to Noble. Wynkyn de Worde woodcut, c.1495.

62 Reynard shows Chantecler a copy of Noble's order for peace among his subjects. Wynkyn de Worde woodcut, c.1495.

63 *Coppe the Hen's funeral service. Wynkyn de Worde woodcut, c.1495.*

how the fox came to him in the guise of a hermit and carrying a letter [62] which he said was from the king, sealed with the king's seal, proclaiming peace among all his subjects. This woodcut also shows, in the background, how (when the cock and his hens had been put off their guard) the fox seized one of them by the throat. It is, then, the illustration of earlier events and, like the third picture in this cycle, of the flashback variety. 6. Returning to the present, we witness the decapitated hen's funeral service [63]. 7. Enraged by this crime in particular, the lion sends the bear as his emissary to bring the fox to court. Here we see the bear approaching the fox and displaying the royal, sealed message demanding that he should appear before him [64]. This woodcut, missing from the Anonymous edition, is drawn from Allde's 1620 edition. 8. Pretending that he will eventually accompany the bear back to the royal court after providing him with refreshment in the form of honey, the fox leads the bear towards a woodcutter's yard [65]. 9. In that yard he points (in the middle ground of the picture) to a half-split log held open by a wedge, telling the bear that there is honey inside the log [66]. In the foreground we see the bear trapped in the log from which the fox has pulled the wedge once the bear had inserted his forepaws and snout deep into it. The fox gloats over

64 *Bruin presents Noble's summons to Reynard to attend court. Wynkyn de Worde woodcut, c.1495.*

his victim's plight. 10. Missing from the Anonymous edition and all other surviving editions which use the Wynkyn de Worde vertical cuts is the scene depicting the bear being beaten by the woodcutter and other peasants. There can be little doubt that this scene was included in de Worde's picture cycle for it is among the smaller, cruder, early English horizontal cuts in the Anonymous edition [67], most of which copy the subject matter of the vertical cuts. And it is in the Lübeck cycle at this particular point [68], a cycle which parallels the one made to illustrate Wynkyn de Worde's 1495 edition. In both the Anonymous horizontal cut and in the Lübeck square cut, we see the beating inflicted upon the bear in the foreground, his escape into a nearby river in the middle ground, and the fox gloating over the bear's sufferings in the distant background. 11. It is then the cat's turn to be sent to bring the fox to court, and his turn to be duped by the fox with the promise of a meal (this time of mice) to be had in a country priest's barn. The artist shows us the moment when the cat has been caught in a snare set just inside a hole through a barn wall [69]. It looks as if the cat is on the outside of the

65 *Reynard leads Bruin to the woodcutter's yard. Wynkyn de Worde woodcut, c.1495.*

66 *Reynard tricks Bruin into getting caught in a trap. Wynkyn de Worde woodcut, c.1495.*

67 *The trapped Bruin is beaten by peasants. From the Anonymous c.1560 edition; an early 16th-C. woodcut based on a c.1495 Wynkyn de Worde cut.*

68 *Peasants beat the trapped Bruin. Lübeck woodcut, 1498.*

of Reynard the Fox.

ſet a grin tofore the hole to auenge him, for fayne he would haue taken the Fox. This knew we wel the falſe theefe the Fox, and ſaid: Syr Tibert coſin, crepe into this hole, and ye ſhall not long tary but that ye ſhall

E.ij. catch

69 *Reynard tricks Tibert into getting caught in a snare. Wynkyn de Worde woodcut, c.1495.*

barn, but this is simply the artist's way of showing us what happenened to the cat after he had got into it. In the foreground the fox taunts his victim. The Lübeck cycle has an interesting variant of this scene [234]. Here it looks as if the cat is being shown the way to the priest's barn in much the same way that the bear was shown the way to the woodcutter's yard; the cat has yet to be caught in the snare. 12. In order to escape, the cat attacks the naked priest's genitals [70], for this is supposed to take place at night, and the priest has just jumped out of bed. It is also supposed to take place inside the barn. The priest's concubine aims a blow at the fox with her distaff, while his two children (one also naked, the other wearing only a shirt) are armed with sticks with which they aim blows at the cat. The concubine, one notes, is clothed and wears both head-dress and shoes! 13. The badger is then sent to bring the fox to court, and we are shown [71], in the background, the moment of his arrival at the entrance to the fox's lair where he speaks to both the fox and his wife. The badger persuades the fox that, before returning to court, he should confess his sins and be shriven. The artist shows us the moment of the shriving of the fox in the foreground in this same cut. 14. Among the sins to which the fox confesses is the time when he got the wolf's forepaws tied to the bell ropes of a

The Hyſtory

catch Miſe by great heapes, harken how they pipe, whan ye be full, come againe, I will tary here after you before this hole, we will go to morowe together to the court. Tybert why tary ye ſo long? come of quickly, and than may we returne ſone to my wife, which wayteth after vs, and ſhall make good cheere. Tybert ſayd, Reinard coſin, is it than your counſaile that I go into this hole? theſe prieſtes be ſo wily and ſhrewiſh that I dread to take harme. O ho Tybert ſaid Reinard, I ſaw you neuer ſo ſore afrayde, what ayleth you. The Cat was aſhamed and ſprang into the hole, and anone he was caught in the gryn by the necke or he wiſt. Thus deceiued Reinard his gueſt ⁊ coſin. As ſone as Tibert was ware of the gryn: hee was afeard and ſprang forth, and the Grynne went together. Than began he to wrag, for he was al moſt ſtrangeled, he called, he cryed and made a ſhrewde noiſe. Reinard ſtode tofore the hole and hard all, and was well apaide, and ſaid: Tibert loue ye well Mice? be they fat and good? knew the prieſt hereof or Martinet, they be ſo gentle that they would bringe you ſauce. Tibert ye ſing and eate, is that the guiſe of the court? Lord God if Iſegrym were there by you in ſuch reſt as ye be now, than ſhould I be glad, for oft he hath done me ſcath and harme. Tibert could not go awaye, but he meawed and galped ſo loude, that Martinet ſprang vp and cried out. God be thanked, my grynne hath taken the theefe that hath ſtolen our hennes, ariſe vp we will reward him.

How

of Reynard the Fox.

How Tibert the Cat was maruelouſly ſmitten of Martinet and of Iullocke the prieſtes wife, and how the prieſt loſt his priuie member by Tybert the Cat. cap.xy

E.iij. With

70 Tibert attacks the naked priest's genitals. Wynkyn de Worde woodcut, c.1495.

The Hiſtory.

I trowe there is none here ſo much a foole. Grimberd ſpake, ſo helpe me God, I am ſo much a foole that I wil do this meſſage my ſelfe to Reinard if ye wil commaund me.

How Grimberd the Brocke was ſent for to bring the Fox to the court tofore the kyng. cap.xiij. Now

71 Grimberd the Badger persuades Reynard to attend court, and shrives him. Wynkyn de Worde woodcut, c.1495.

72 *Reynard recalls how he got Isegrim caught in a bell-rope and then beaten. Wynkyn de Worde woodcut, c.1495.*

73 *Reynard recalls how he stole a capon and led his pursuers to the trapped Isegrim who was then beaten by them. Wynkyn de Worde woodcut, c.1495.*

village church causing him to ring the bells till the villagers came and gave him a terrible beating, depicted here [72]. The fox may be seen making his escape in the top right-hand corner of the picture. 15. Another sin to which the fox confesses is that of leading the wolf into a rich priest's house through a narrow tunnel and there encouraging him to eat so heartily that he became too fat to return through the tunnel [73]. Then the fox made his way to the priest who was at table and there stole a capon from under his nose and ran off with it to the place where the wolf was, so drawing him and his followers to the wolf who got a terrible beating from them while the fox made his escape. In the left foreground of this cut we see the priest at table and the fox making off with the capon. In the middle ground and to the right we see the wolf being beaten while the fox makes his escape from an upstairs window. This and the previous cut are also of the flashback variety. The model for this cut is one of the three to survive from the Haarlem Master's cycle [78]. 16. Missing from the Anonymous edition at this point, and from all other surviving English editions using the Wynkyn de Worde vertical cuts, is a scene of the fox accompanied by the badger, on his way to the lion's court. It will have shown them as they pass a convent, and in particular the nuns' poultry yard which the fox feels tempted to raid. A good idea of the subject-matter is provided by one of the horizontal cuts from the Anonymous edition [74] and by the corresponding square-shaped cut from the Lübeck edition [75]. In both, it is to be noted that the fox has donned a religious's cowl. The model for these cuts also survives in the Haarlem Master's work [79]. 17. Also missing is a

The Hystory

The Fox promised that he would so do, and then they went both together towardes the kynges court. A little beside the way, as they went stode a Religion of blacke Nunnes, where many geese, hennes, & capons went without the walles, and as they went talking the Fox bethought Grinberd out of the right waye thither, and without the walles by the barne went the pullayne. The Fox espied them and sawe a fatte young capon, which went alone from his fellowes, he lept and caught him, so that the feathers flewe about his eares, but the capon escaped. Than Grynberd sayd: what Eme cursed man? what will ye do? wyll ye for one of these pullettes, fall againe into all your sinnes which ye haue shriuen you of, ye ought sore to repent you. Reinard answered: truely Cosin I had

of Reynard the Fox.

I had forgotten al, I pray god to forgiue it me, for I will neuer do so more. Than torned they ouer a little bridge, yet the Fox alway loked after the pullaine, he could not refrayne him selfe (that which cleaued by the bone might not out of the flesh) though hee should be hanged he could not leaue his loking after the pullaine, as farre as he might se them. Grinberd sawe his maner and sayd: Foule false deceiuer, how goe thine eyen so after the pullaine. The Fox sayd: cosin ye misdoe to saye to me any such wordes, yee bring me out of my deuocion and prayer, let me say a Pater noster for all the soules of the Pullaine & geese that I haue betraied, and oft with falshod stolen from the holy Nunnes. Grinberd was not well apaid, but the Fox had euer his eyen toward the pullayne tyll at the last they came into the way againe. And then went they toward the court, how sore quaked then Reinard, when they aproched nere to the court, for hee wist well that hee had for to answere to many a foule feate which he had done.

How the Fox came to the court, and how he excused him tofore the kyng. cap.xvij.

AT the first when it was knowne in the courte: that Reinard the Fox and Grinberd his cosin were come to the court: there was none so pore, ne so feble of kinne and frendes, but that he made him redy tofore to complaine upon Reynard the Fox. Than Reinard loked as he had bene afeard and held him better then he was, for he went forth proudly with his newew through the high streate, straight to the court

G.ii.

74 *The shriven Reynard passes a nuns' poultry yard and is tempted to sin again. From the Anonymous c.1560 edition; an early 16th-C. woodcut based on a c.1495 Wynkyn de Worde cut.*

75 *The shriven Reynard passes a nuns' poultry yard and is tempted to sin again. Lübeck woodcut, 1498.*

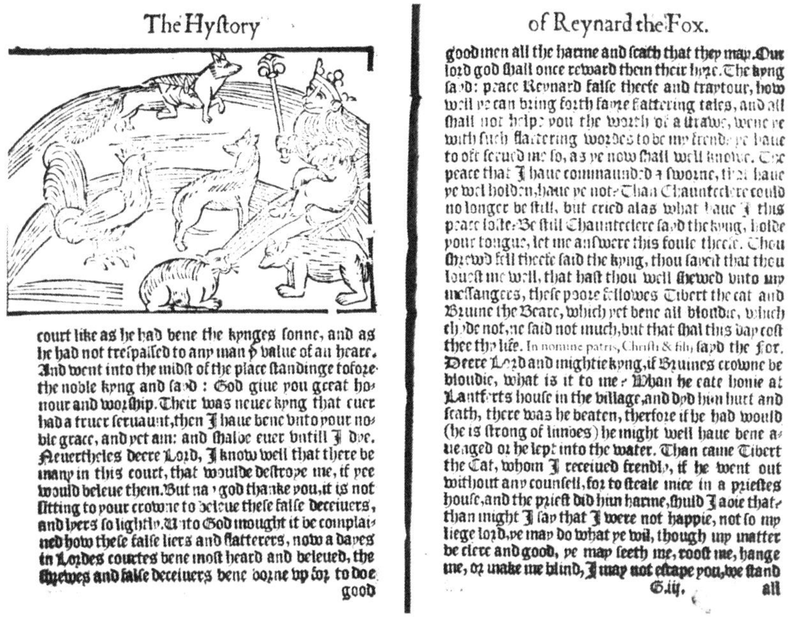

The Hystory of Reynard the Fox.

court like as he had bene the kynges sonne, and as he had not trespassed to any man y value of an heare. And went into the midst of the place standinge tofore the noble kyng and sayd: God giue you great honour and worship. Their was neuer kyng that euer had a truer seruaunt, then I haue bene vnto your noble grace, and yet am: and shal be euer vntill I dye. Neuertheles deere Lord, I know well that there be many in this court, that woulde destroye me, if yee would beleue them. But nay god thanke you, it is not fitting to your crowne to beleue these false deceiuers, and lyers so lightly. Unto God mought it be complained how these false liers and flatterers, now a dayes in Lordes courtes bene most heard and beleued, the shrewes and false deceiuers bene borne vp for to doe good

good men all the harme and scath that they may. Mutt lord god shall once reward them their hire. The kyng sayd: peace Reynard false theefe and traytour, how well ye can bring forth faire flattering tales, and all shall not helpe you the worth of a strawe, wene ye with such flattering wordes to be my frende: ye haue so oft serued me so, as ye now shall well knowe. The peace that I haue commaunded & sworne, that haue ye wel holden, haue ye not? Than Chaunteclere could no longer be still, but cried alas what haue I this peace loste? Be still Chaunteclere sayd the kyng, holde your tongue, let me answere this foule theefe. Thou shrewd fell theefe said the kyng, thou sayeist that thou louest me well, that hast thou well shewed vnto my messangers, these poore fellowes Tibert the cat and Bruine the Beare, which yet bene all bloudie, which chyde not, ne said not much, but that shal this day cost thee thy life. In nomine patris, Christi & filij sayd the Fox. Deere Lord and mightie kyng, if Bruines crowne be bloudie, what is it to me? When he eate honie at Lantferts house in the village, and dyd him hurt and scath, there was he beaten, therfore if he had would (he is strong of limmes) he might well haue bene auenged or he lept into the water. Than came Tibert the Cat, whom I receiued frendly, if he went out without any counsell, for to steale mice in a priestes house, and the priest did him harme, shuld I aoie that? than might I say that I were not happie, not so my liege lord, ye may do what ye wil, though my matter be clere and good, ye may seeth me, roost me, hange me, or make me blind, I may not escape you, we stand

G.iij. all

76 *Reynard, accompanied by Grimberd, arrives before Noble. From the Anonymous c.1560 edition; an early 16th-C. woodcut based on a c.1495 Wynkyn de Worde cut.*

77 *Reynard, accompanied by Grimberd, arrives before Noble. Lübeck woodcut, 1498.*

78 *Reynard recalls how he stole a capon and led his pursuers to the trapped Isegrim who was then beaten by them. The Haarlem Master, c.1487.*

79 *The shriven Reynard passes a nuns' poultry yard and is tempted to sin again. The Haarlem Master, c.1487.*

scene of the fox and the badger as they arrive at the lion's court. This, too, occurs in both the horizontal series of cuts in the Anonymous edition [76] and in the Lübeck edition [77]. Here we see the two travellers prostrate themselves before the crowned, sceptred, cloaked and seated lion who is encircled by four of the fox's chief enemies: the wolf, bear, cat and cock. The model for these cuts also survives in the Haarlem Master's work [80]. 18. The fox's plea of not guilty to the charge of murder fails, and he is sentenced to death. Urged on by the cat, the bear seizes the fox and the wolf binds him with a rope [81]. In the middle ground, to the right, the badger and other friends of the fox (mostly apes) slink away. 19. The fox mounts the gallows ladder, led by the cat who holds on to the rope and plays the role of hangman [82]. The wolf and the bear stand on either side of the foot of the ladder The crowned lion and lioness are in the front rank of the crowd gathered to witness the execution, and in the crowd one recognizes a ram, a stag, a dog and, strangely, a unicorn. Strangely, because the unicorn plays no part in the text. Here the artist makes room for one of the enduring medieval symbols of justice and truth. Another common symbol for these values, especially for justice, was the stag, so it is almost certainly no coincidence that the stag stands at the side of the unicorn, and that his antlers are as prominent as the unicorn's horn. One cannot but admire the excellence of the composition and the impact of this particular picture, one of the finest in the de Worde cycle. 20. Also missing from the vertical series of cuts is one which will have shown, in the foreground, the fox seated between the lion and the lioness immediately after he had been pardoned. (He gained his pardon by telling the lion from the gallows ladder [from the way he stands on the ladder and gestures, one would say he had already begun to speak to the lion in the last picture] about

80 *Reynard, accompanied by Grimberd, arrives before Noble. The Haarlem Master, woodcut fragment, c.1487.*

81 *Reynard is bound after being sentenced to the gallows. Wynkyn de Worde woodcut, c.1495.*

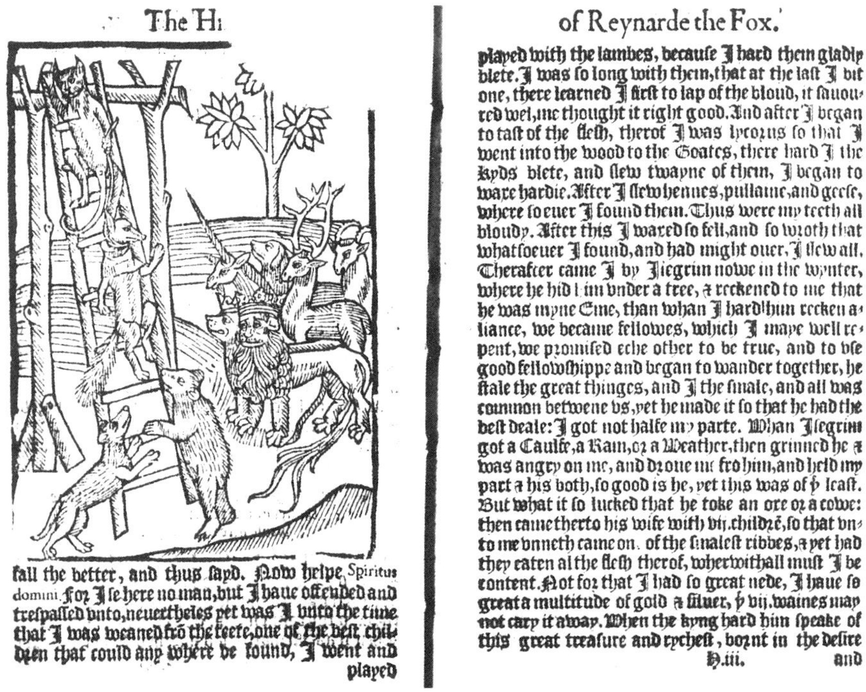

The Hi | of Reynarde the Fox.

fall the better, and thus sayd. Now helpe Spiritus domini. For I se here no man, but I haue offended and trespassed vnto, neuertheles yet was I vnto the time that I was weaned fro the teete, one of the best children that could any where be found, I went and played with the lambes, because I hard them gladly blete. I was so long with them, that at the last I bit one, there learned I first to lap of the bloud, it sauoured wel, me thought it right good. And after I began to tast of the flesh, therof I was lycorus so that I went into the wood to the Goates, there hard I the kyds blete, and slew twayne of them, I began to ware hardie. After I slew hennes, pullaine, and geese, where so euer I found them. Thus were my teeth all bloudy. After this I wared so fell, and so wroth that whatsoeuer I found, and had might ouer, I slew all. Therafter came I by Isegrim nowe in the wynter, where he hid him vnder a tree, & reckened to me that he was myne Eme, than whan I hard him recken aliance, we became fellowes, which I maye well repent, we promised eche other to be true, and to vse good fellowshippe and began to wander together, he stale the great thinges, and I the smale, and all was common betwene vs, yet he made it so that he had the best deale: I got not halfe my parte. Whan Isegrim got a Caulfe, a Ram, or a Weather, then grinned he & was angry on me, and droue me fro him, and held my part & his both, so good is he, yet this was of ye least. But what it so lucked that he toke an oxe or a cowe: then came therto his wife with vij. childrē, so that vnto me vnneth came one of the smalest ribbes, & yet had they eaten al the flesh therof, wherwithall must I be content. Not for that I had so great nede, I haue so great a multitude of gold & siluer, ye vij. waines may not cary it away. When the kyng hard him speake of this great treasure and rychest, bornt in the desire

H.iii. and

82 *Reynard confesses his sins from the gallows' ladder. Wynkyn de Worde woodcut, c.1495.*

83 *Reynard is released and placed between Noble and Fiere. From the Anoymous c.1560 edition; an early 16th-C. woodcut based on a c.1495 Wynkyn de Worde cut.*

84 *Reynard, placed between Noble and Fiere, is pardoned. Lübeck woodcut, 1498.*

buried treasure, the whereabouts of which he is willing to reveal if he is pardoned and allowed to go on a pilgrimage.) In the background will have been shown, looking on, a disconsolate group of animals: the bear, wolf and cat. The subject matter of this cut is guaranteed by one from the horizontal series in the Anonymous edition [83] and one from the Lübeck series [84]. 21 The fox is then shown on a raised platform seated between the crowned lion and lioness, dominating a group of animals who look up at them [85]. In this group, five of the fox's chief enemies and victims are clearly visible: bear, cat, wolf, dog and hare. This is when the lion announces to all his subjects that he has pardoned the fox who, together with his wife and children, is henceforth to be held by them in the greatest respect. 22. Still seated between the lion and the lioness on a slight eminence, the fox watches the bear and the wolf being arrested for speaking ill of him to the king [86]. One notes that the cat, anxious to be restored to favour with the fox, is the one who arrests the wolf though the text does not say that he did, nor does it say that a monkey arrests the bear! 23. In the background [87], seated next to the lion and the lioness, the fox observes the mutilation of the bear and the wolf as hide is cut from them to provide him with a scrip and a pair of boots for his journey to Rome. 24. In the foreground [88] the ram-priest bestows upon the fox a staff and a blessing. In the background the lion bids farewell to the fox-pilgrim equipped with his new staff (or bourdon), wolfskin boots and bearskin scrip.

The History

As sone as this speaking was done, ꝥ noble king went and stode vpon an high stage of stone, and commaunded silence to all beastes, and that they should sit downe in a round ring vppon the grasse, uerych one in his place after his estate and byrth.

Reinard

of Reynard the Fox.

Reinard the Fox stode by the Queen, whom he ought wel to loue. Than said the kyng here ye all that bee poore and rich, young & old that standeth here. Reynard one of the head officers of my house had done so euil, which this day should haue bene hanged, hath now in this court done so much, that I and my wyfe the Queen haue promised him our grace & frendship. The Queene hath much praied for him, in so much ꝥ I haue made peace with him, and giuen him life and member freely againe, and I commaund you vppon your life that ye do worship to Reinard, to his wyfe and to his children wheresoeuer ye meete them by day or by night, and also I wil here no more complaints of Reynard, if he hath heretofore misdone and trespassed, he wil no more misdoe nor trespasse, but anned him he will to morowe early go to the Pope for pardon and forgiuenes of al his sinnes, and so forth ouer the sea to the holy land, and he will not come againe till he bring pardon of all his sinnes. This talke hard Tiselin the Rauen, and lept to Isegrim, to Bruine, & to Tibert where as they were and sayd: ye caitiues how goeth it nowe, ye vnhappie folke what do ye here? Reinard the Fox is now a squyre and a courtier and right great and mightie in the court. The kyng hath quit him of all his felony, and forgiuen him all his trespasses and misdeeds, and ye be all betrayed & apeached. Isegrim sayd: how may this be? I trowe Tiselin that ye lye. Certaynly I do not sayd the Rauen. Than went the woulfe & the Beare to the king. Tibert the Cat was in great sorowe, he was sore afeard, that for to haue the Foxes frendship, he would

K.ij. well

85 *Reynard's pardon is publicly proclaimed, and the animal-barons are told to hold him henceforward in the greatest respect. Wynkyn de Worde woodcut, c.1495.*

The History

wel forgiue him the losse of his one eye that he had lost in the priestes house, he was so woe he wist not what to do, he would wel ꝥ he neuer had sene the fox.

How the Woulfe and the Beare were arested by the labour of Reinard the Fox. cap. xxiij.

Isegrim

of Reynarde the Fox.

Isegrim came proudly ouer the feild tofore the kyng, he thancked the Queene, and spake with a fell mode euill wordes on the Fox, in such wise that the king heard it, & was wroth, and made the woulfe & the beare anone to be arested, ye saw neuer wod dogs do more harme than was done vnto them, they were both fast bound so sore, that all the night they might not stere hand ne foote, they might not scarcely moue one ioynt. Now here how the Fox did forth to them that hated him, he laboured to ꝥ Queene that he gat leaue for to haue as much of the Beares skinne vpon his ridge, as a fote long, and a fote brode, for to make him thereof a scrippe. Than was the Fox ready if he had foure strong shone. Now here how he did for to get those shone. He said to the Queene. Madam I am your pilgrim, here is mine eme Syr Isegrim that hath foure strong shone, which were good for me, if ye would let me haue two of them, I would on the way besily thinke on your soule, for it is right that a pilgrim should alway thinke and pray for them that do him good. Thus may ye do your soule good, if ye will. And also if he might get of myne aunt Dame Erswind also two of her shone to giue me, she maye well do it, for she goeth but little out, but abideth alway at home. Than said the Queene Reinard you behoueth well such shoes ye may not be without them, they shal be good for you to kepe your feete hole, for to passe with them many sharpe mountaines and stony rockes, ye can find no better shoes for you, than such as Isegrym and his wife haue, and because they be good and strong, though it should touch their life,

K.iii. eche

86 *Isegrim and Bruin are arrested and bound for speaking ill of Reynard. Wynkyn de Worde woodcut, c.1495.*

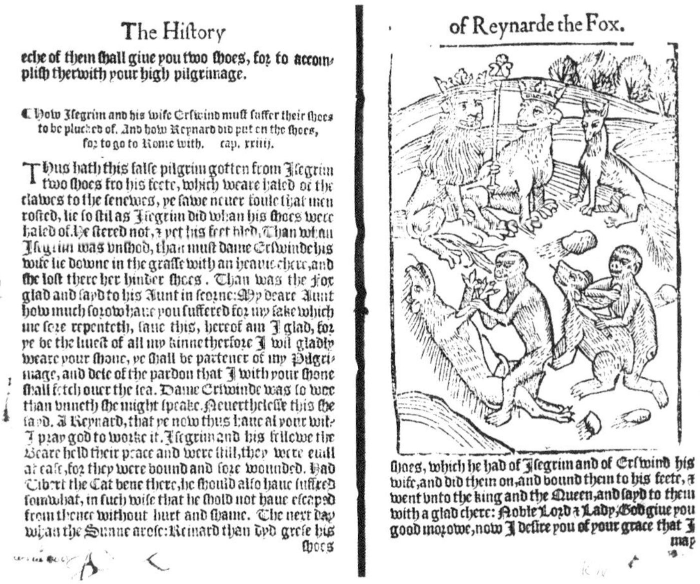

The History

eche of them shall giue you two shoes, for to accomplish therwith your high pilgrimage.

¶ How Isegrim and his wife Erswind must suffer their shoes to be plucked of. And how Reynard did put on the shoes, for to go to Rome with. cap. xxiiij.

Thus hath this false pilgrim gotten from Isegrim two shoes fro his feete, which weare haled of the clawes to the senewes, ye sawe neuer foule that men rosted, lie so stil as Isegrim did whan his shoes were haled of. He stered not, & yet his feet bled, Than whan Isegrim was unshod, than must dame Erswinde his wife lie downe in the grasse with an heauie chere, and she lost there her hinder shoes. Than was the Fox glad and sayd to his Aunt in scorne: My deare Aunt how much sorow haue you suffered for my sake which me sore repenteth, saue this, hereof am I glad, for ye be the liuest of all my kinne therfore I wil gladly weare your shone, ye shall be partener of my Pilgrimage, and dele of the pardon that I with your shone shall fetch ouer the sea. Dame Erswinde was so woe than unneth she might speake. Neuerthelesse this she sayd. A Reynard, that ye now thus haue al your wil: I pray god to worke it. Isegrim and his fellowe the Beare held their peace and were still, they were euill at ease, for they were bound and sore wounded. Had Tibert the Cat bene there, he should also haue suffred somwhat, in such wise that he shold not haue escaped from thence without hurt and shame. The next day whan the Sunne arose: Reinard than dyd grese his shoes

of Reynarde the Fox.

shoes, which he had of Isegrim and of Erswind his wife, and did them on, and bound them to his feete, & went unto the king and the Queen, and sayd to them with a glad chere: Noble Lord & Lady, God giue you good morowe, now I desire you of your grace that I may

87 *Isegrim and Bruin lose parts of their hide to provide Reynard with a scrip and boots. Wynkyn de Worde woodcut, c.1495.*

88 *Bellin the Ram hands to Reynard his pilgrim's staff, and Noble bids the pilgrim-fox farewell. Wynkyn de Worde woodcut, c.1495.*

It is at this point that the original twelfth-century French story and a three-centuries-later Dutch version of it, made English by Caxton, part company. The extraordinary fact is that, if one knew only the original French story, one might think most of these woodcuts were made to illustrate it, for successive generations of storytellers telling their story for different audiences and readers in different cultures have remained faithful to the chief dramatic moments around which it is structured. Its iconography is compelling proof of this.

THE BRISTOL CATHEDRAL MISERICORDS

Five misericord scenes in Bristol Cathedral, thought to have been carved around 1520, illustrate episodes from this story. The eminent English medievalist Kenneth Sisam thought that they were inspired by Caxton's text: 'At Bristol, the subjects and the late date indicate they derive from Caxton's version,' he wrote in the introduction to his edition of Chaucer's *Nun's Priest's Tale*. When I first commented on these carvings in 1967, I was inclined to disagree. Since then I have learned about the Haarlem Master's work and that of his disciples, the Wynkyn de Worde Master and the Lübeck Master and, though I still disagree in part with Sisam's overall view, I have to admit he was nearer the mark than perhaps even he could have known.

Following the order of the narrative, the first carving to consider depicts Bruin the Bear trapped in a half-split log [89]. He is shown with his head and forepaws fast in the cleft of what appears to be a nearly upright log. He is being beaten by three men while Reynard looks on from a safe distance. If the carver had worked from the text, he could have used either the French or the Anglo-Dutch versions. In both the essential details are the same. The bear gets trapped, head and forepaws in a cleft log; he is soundly beaten; and the fox watches and taunts from a safe distance. Inevitably, the carver would have to leave things out and concentrate on the essentials. In the French version a swarm of country folk runs towards the bear with clubs, axes, flails and hawthorn sticks. But, and this is perhaps important, we are told that, before they reach him, the bear escapes from the log, leaving behind much skin and some claws. They beat him only when they catch up with him as he flees through the woods where they are joined by others who land blows on him with a garden fork and a bull's horn. So, even if the carver were basing his work directly on the French text, he took greater liberties with it than he would have had to had he used the Anglo-Dutch text. There the bear's assailants beat him as he stands caught in the log, and they use hooks, staffs, rakes, brooms, flails, a crucifix and a distaff. At the climax of the assault, the text singles out Lantfert the woodcutter and his brother who 'sprang forth... with a staff and smote the bear on the head'. In simplifying the scene, the carver reduces the crowd to three men all using sticks, one of which is clearly aimed at the bear's head.

It has long been established that the Bristol carver used prints as models for many of his other misericord scenes, so did he use them for his Reynard the Fox sequence? The best comparison we can make for the scene depicting Bruin's plight is to be found in the Lübeck Master's corresponding woodcut [68], for it has not survived in either the Haarlem Master's or the Wynkyn de Worde Master's cycle. Particularly striking are the positions of the fox in the

89 *Bruin is trapped in a half-split log, and beaten. Bristol Cathedral, misericord; c.1520. D.R. Maxted.*

middle background, of the two peasants to the left and the third to the right of the log, but still more striking is the position of the log itself. In the Bristol carving it seems to be standing, unaccountably, on one end, while in the Lübeck woodcut it lies, as it should, on the ground. The angle of the log is, however, not so very different, and one realizes that the Bristol carver has merely given it a slightly more vertical angle while failing to show the receding horizontal lines of the ground's surface which the Lübeck artist has ably shown. There is in the Anonymous edition's series of horizontal cuts (which usually copied in reverse and fairly crudely the subject-matter of the original Wynkyn de Worde vertical cuts) a parallel scene [67], but it differs in one or two important details from the Lübeck cut and the Bristol misericord. In particular, there is only one figure on either side of the log. However, the log is at the same strange angle. Furthermore, this cut occurs in the place it ought to have in the narrative sequence of events, suggesting that it is replacing a lost original by the Wynkyn de Worde Master with which it would have been interesting to make a comparison.

In the second misericord of the Bristol sequence, we see Tibert the Cat in trouble [90], as well as the naked priest. His naked son holds the rope which ensnares Tibert, while his concubine wields her distaff. It is in the French, not the Anglo-Dutch account, that the priest's concubine beats the cat with her distaff, though she joined in the assault on Bruin with this weapon, and it could be that the Bristol carver was remembering the part she played in that battle, and getting her roles a bit muddled. Or that the arming of a belligerent woman with a

90 *Tibert, ensnared and beaten, attacks a naked priest's genitals. Bristol Cathedral, misericord; c.1520. D.R. Maxted.*

distaff was just a commonplace notion and of no particular significance. In both the French and the Anglo-Dutch accounts the priest loses only a bit of his masculinity when Tibert attacks him just before he can land a heavy blow with a stake. In this carving Reynard stands between the feet of son and concubine to watch the cat's discomfiture. Behind the woman one sees the priest's barn and the hole through which Tibert jumped into the snare. A woodcut of this scene has not survived from either the Haarlem Master's or the Lübeck Master's work, but there is one in that of the Wynkyn de Worde Master [70]. If the Bristol carver had it in mind, or even in front of him as he worked, he modified it by including the fox, by placing a distaff in the concubine's hands, by depicting only two men of whom one plays a completely passive role, and by having the priest turn his back on the cat who attacks him from the rear and keep all four paws firmly on the ground. One is tempted to argue that this Bristol carver was able to depart from pictorial models and draw on what he knew of the story (be it from a recollection of his own or somebody else's reading of it, or from a retelling he had heard) and to depict the event in his own way. However, without the evidence of the Haarlem Master's version of this event (if ever there was one), we must be cautious. No other illustration of it, other than Wynkyn de Worde's, has come down to us from before 1520 with which to compare the Bristol carver's work.

The artistic independence of the Bristol carver seems to be confirmed when we come to the third misericord in this sequence. Tibert's attack upon the priest so delighted him that he

91 *Tibert jumps up and scratches the naked priest's back. A woman tries to pull the cat away. Bristol Cathedral, misericord; c.1520. D.R. Maxted.*

made another version of it [91]. In this Tibert is shown jumping up the poor priest's back. His concubine tries to knock the cat down while Reynard watches from the safety of a tree fork. The barn and the priest's son are no longer shown, while the concubine has apparently found time to don an apron and put on her shoes! The priest, now lacking a part of his genitals, is depicted in almost exactly the same pose as in the previous scene. It looks as if he even continues to hold the stick in his right hand, but it has been lost through damage. Evidently the events in this scene are supposed to happen only seconds after those in the previous scene. Nothing like this exists in any woodcut cycle or book illustration before or after its creation in Bristol.

The fourth scene in this sequence depicts the moment when Reynard is brought to the gallows. In both the French and Anglo-Dutch texts, the fox is persuaded to answer for his crimes. In one of the early French versions (the one in manuscript *B*, Paris, Bibliothèque Nationale, f fr 371), he finds himself immediately face to face with five of his chief enemies and victims: the wolf, the cat, the bear, the cock and the dog, four of whom may be seen in the Bristol gallows scene. Although the Anglo-Dutch text does not mention an immediate confrontation with any of these animals, the cock is the first to cry out against him after the lion has spoken harsh words to his rebellious baron. Only later do first the ram and the ewe, then the bear, the cat, the wolf, the hare, panther, boar, camel, goose, kid, goat, ass, bull, ox and weasel rise up in a chorus of complaint. So, when the Haarlem Master depicts Reynard and his cousin,

92 *Reynard mounts the gallows ladder. Bristol Cathedral, misericord; c.1520. Elaine Block.*

the badger, arriving at court and being met by the cock, the wolf, the cat and the bear (visible only by his face [80]), his concentration on these animals seems to reflect not so much what the text says, but what he knows about the fox's chief escapades and victims. And this may be the case with the Bristol carver. Four of the five members of the hanging party at Bristol are easily identifiable: the bear, to the left and muzzled, assisting the fox up the gallows ladder; the cat on the gallows cross-bar, helping to pull the fox up by the rope (partly missing through damage); the cock who stands to the right of the gallows ladder (head missing through damage); and the wolf, just below and before the lion. I used to think the animal below the gallows cross-bar was a dog, Roenel, but I now note that this animal has cloven hoofs and a short horn (a second horn having been lost through damage?). Is it the ram who spoke first after the cock to accuse the fox, or the goat who also joined in the complaints? More likely the ram who, as priest in the animal kingdom, has a certain role to play on this kind of occasion, and who was so cruelly tricked by the fox at the beginning of his 'pilgrimage' in the Anglo-Dutch version of events. And is the rabbit face peeping out of a hole below the ram's (or goat's) rear hoofs at all significant? In the Anglo-Dutch story he suffers even more than the ram at the beginning of the 'pilgrimage', but is only mentioned in passing in the list of complainants. In the French version, he dares to throw a stone at the fox who then, just by wagging his head at him, threw him into such a panic that he disappeared from view: 'terrified by the gesture... he then hid in a hedge, thinking he would keep an eye on Reynard's punish-

93 *Isegrim and Bruin dance. Bristol Cathedral, misericord; c.1520. J.C.D. Smith.*

ment from there'. I would be surprised if the Bristol carver had this in mind, but it is a possibility.

The Haarlem Master's gallows scene has not survived, but it is present in both the Wynkyn de Worde and Lübeck cycles [82 & 235]. In fact, it is depicted twice in the Anonymous edition, once in the original vertical series, and one in the horizontal copies [82 & 230]. The Bristol artist's work seems slightly nearer to the Lübeck Master's than to the Wynkyn de Worde Master's, especially in the positioning of the cat on top of the gallows and in depicting the lion and the lioness seated. However, the Bristol artist here begins to assert his independence once more (that is, if he knew these woodcuts) and at the same time to reveal his knowledge of a literary version (written or spoken) of this episode. This is particularly evident in his decision to include Chanticler the Cock in his representation of it and to exclude from it that complete foreigner, the unicorn. One notes, in passing, that he gives Bruin a muzzle, and that he dispenses with a ladder in an admirably economic use of line and space.

This artist's apparent independence has already been noted in his rendering of the moment when the ensnared cat attacks the priest, and especially in his depiction of the cat scratching the priest's back. This quality is also evident in the fifth and final carving in this sequence where he depicts the wolf and the bear (muzzled again) dancing to the rhythm of the drum beaten by a monkey [93]. Presumably, they are rejoicing at the fox's imminent execution. Again, there is nothing like this in any early printed book nor, for that matter, in any of the later illustrated books in which the Haarlem Master's influence, however distant, may be traced. Even so, there are lines in both the French and the Anglo-Dutch versions of this story which could have inspired him if he knew them. 'Now Reynard is taken and bound. God! How happy are Isengrin, Pinte and Chantecler the Cock, for they think they are safe' writes one of the French poets. The Dutch poet, however, picks out the bear and the wolf at this point in the story: '...Along the way with mighty glee,/ And vied with one another playfully/ In jumping over many a fence,/ Did Bruin and Isegrim...' he says in Adriaan Barnouw's translation. Yet again one feels the Bristol carver, influenced to some extent by available woodcuts, was an independent artist whose independence stemmed in part from his knowledge and love of the story, most probably in one of its Dutch forms, drawing on its spirit as well as on some of its details.

REFLECTIONS ON THE BRISTOL MISERICORD REYNARDIAN SEQUENCE

There are a few lessons to be learned from this sequence of carvings in Bristol Cathedral. If all written versions of the story were lost, the one we would reconstruct from these five scenes would differ greatly from any of the masterpieces which have in fact come down to us. It would seem to tell us that a bear and a cat got trapped and badly hurt, as did a naked man when attacked by a cat. We would guess this was all probably due to the fox because he is shown witnessing these violent happenings and is brought to the gallows by (among other animals) a bear and a cat. We would deduce that the impending execution of the fox gave particular pleasure to a monkey, a bear and a wolf who are seen rejoicing nearby, and we might think they too had been harmed by the fox in one way or another. The real reasons for the fox's being brought to the gallows, for the bear's, the cat's and the naked man's sufferings; the roles played by other animals, in particular the badger and the cock; the fact that the fox was not executed, the reasons for his being pardoned; his setting off on a false pilgrimage and its immediate consequences: all these and much else besides could not be recovered from this evidence. We would assume the cat played a specially big part in this story given that he is centre-stage in two out of five scenes, and prominent in the gallows scene. And we might think the back-scratching episode was especially important. On the other hand, knowing the story well from quite a few different versions, we are made aware that visual retellings can be changed, especially in emphasis, by a number of factors such as the existence of a visual model which may be relatively easy or difficult for a carver to copy; by his knowledge of the story and preference for certain episodes in it; and, presumably, by the instructions he is given and the instructor's aim. Here, it looks as if the instructor wanted to turn a highly entertaining episode in a newly (?) popular story into a moral lesson, for the implication of the story as told in these five misericord carvings is that the perpetrator of such wrong-doing will come to a bad end and get his just deserts. (There are two other carvings nearby in the Cathedral choir stalls which first show the fox deceiving his trusting congregation of geese, then being well and truly hanged by them [41 & 105]). Clearly, recovering lost literature from visual evidence of this kind is a hazardous undertaking!

ANOTHER UNIQUE SEQUENCE OF ILLUSTRATIONS OF THIS STORY: BODLEY MS DOUCE 360

There is yet one more sequence, in this case of drawings, which illustrate several episodes in this story of Reynard's trial. They may or may not be of English origin; they may or may not be from the late Middle Ages. They are crude, almost child-like in style, done in fading brown ink and wash, eleven in number, and to be found in the lower margins of the first few folios in manuscript *D* of the *Roman de Renart*, kept in the Bodleian Library (Douce 360). The text above these drawings is that of Branch I, the story of Reynard's trial, and it starts on f.1 with a larger-than-usual miniature [57] showing Noble presiding over his Whitsuntide court, a miniature contemporary with the manuscript which is dated at the end by the scribe who copied it 1339 (the only *Roman de Renart* manuscript to be precisely dated). These later, added lower margin drawings are difficult to date. Librarians consulted at the Bodleian say that this kind of ink and wash drawing could be from the fifteenth or sixteenth century. They have obviously been added at a later date than the miniatures, and I would guess at a much later date. They begin (1) on f.3 with a drawing of a saddled horse pulling a cart which serves as a bier [94]. The body it contains is completely covered with a cloth.The fact that this is led by a large cock, together with its position in the text and in the sequence of drawings, all indicate that this is part of the funeral procession of the hen Coppée. They continue (2) on f.4 with an upright bear and hare carrying a bier on which the body is completely covered by a sheet [95]. The projecting shafts of the bier are carried on the animals' shoulders with the bear before and the hare after. Then, (3), f.5, a crouching fox looks at a bear trapped in a split log [96]. The log stands vertically, and the bear, standing on its hind legs, is caught by the left forepaw and snout in the cleft in the log. Separating the two animals is a large bee-hive, presumably meant

94 *Chantecler heads Coppée's funeral procession. (This sketch and the others numbered 92 to 101 are by Kenneth Varty, based on the originals in the Bodleian Library, MS Douce 360. These were added in the lower margins of ff. 1-10 and are of uncertain date.). This is on f. 1.*

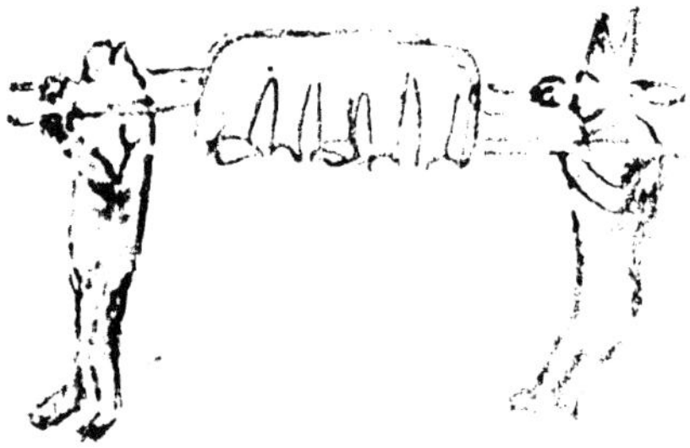

95 *Two animals (a bear and a hare?) carry Coppée's bier; f.3.*

96 *Reynard looks at Bruin trapped in a half-split upright log; f.5.*

97 *Tibert hesitates before the entrance to Reynard's castle-den; f.6.*

to indicate the 'real' presence of honey. (4), f.6, a cat stands before a large hole in a mound of earth which, above and almost encircling the hole, has been given the shape of crenellations [97]. This is no doubt meant to be Tibert hesitating at the entrance to Reynard's castle, Maupertuys. (5), f.6v, a cat, half-inside a hole into a building (presumably the priest's barn) is being beaten by a man and a woman wielding staves [98]. (6), f.7, a fox peeps out of its earth, shaped a little like the one on f.6 [99]. Presumably, this is Reynard contemplating (from the safety of his castle entrance) his success in dealing with the last of the royal envoys. (7), f.7v, a lion (?) on a low round-backed throne reaches out with a forepaw to touch the outstretched forepaw of an erect animal which might be a badly drawn badger [100]. Three other animals

98 *Tibert is caught and beaten in the priest's barn; f.6v.*

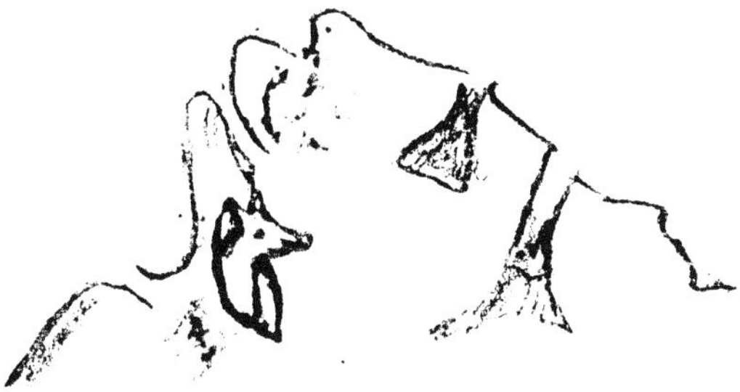

99 *Reynard looks out from his castle-den; f.7.*

100 *Noble, enthroned, commissions Grimbert to summon Reynard to court; f.7v.*

surround the badger (?), among them a bear and a cat. This is probably meant to depict the commissioning of Grimbert. (8), f.8, a fox follows a badger (?). Both animals are on all fours [101]. This is probably meant to depict Reynard and Grimbert making their way to the royal court. (9), f.8v, a fox sitting on its hind quarters, erect, both forepaws reaching out to an erect badger (?) which confronts the fox and extends both its forepaws towards the fox [102]. This

101 *Grimbert escorts Reynard; f.8.*

102 *Grimbert shrives Reynard; f.8v.*

103 *Noble receives Reynard before his assembled court; f.9.*

is probably meant to depict the time when Reynard confesses his sins to Grimbert and is shriven by him. (10), f.9, an enthroned lion receives a fox accompanied by a badger (?). Six other animals surround them, confronting the lion [103]. The three nearest the fox and badger look like a large wolf, a bear and a cat. Behind them is a large bird (crow, hen, or cock ?), a monkey and a hare (or rabbit, with too long a tail!). This is probable meant to show Reynard finally arriving at court to answer the charges against him. Lastly, (11), f.10, a fox-pilgrim mounted on horseback sets off on his journey, alone [104]. The horse is saddled, and the fox

104 Reynard rides away on horseback; f. 10.

holds the reins in his right hand, the pilgrim's staff in his left, and resting over his shoulder. His scrip dangles from a belt at his waist.

The omission of drawings of the hen's funeral service, the bear being beaten, the cat attacking the priest's genitals, the fox and the badger passing the nuns' poultry yard, and the fox at the gallows, as well as the inclusion of the commissioning of the badger, is surprising. The picture of the hen being carried on her bier [95] is reminiscent of the fox being carried on his bier in drawings of his funeral (e.g., [119]) and makes one wonder if the artist knew some of them. Depiction of animals on horseback only comes late in *Roman de Renart* and related manuscripts (e.g., in MS *I*, fourteenth century). It does not occur in the Wynkyn de Worde woodcuts nor in anything else English from the late Middle Ages. I guess these drawings were made by a young person, perhaps the son or daughter of a later owner of this manuscript, perhaps inspired by a series of simple miniatures such as one finds in MS I, but whether in France or England, it is impossible to say for the whereabouts and ownership of this manuscript are not known until recent times.

Notes

BASIC TEXTS:

For English translations of Branches II, Va, and I, see Owen 1994, pp. 53, 92 and 5, respectively. For the Old French texts and a translation into modern French, see Dufournet 1985 I, beginning, respectively, pp. 208, 346, and 42.
For Caxton's text, see (among others), Blake 1970; and (in modernized spelling), Sands 1960.

For the positioning of Branches II, Va, and I in the different *Renart* manuscripts, see Varty 1998, pp. 5-6.
On the illustrated *Renart* manuscripts, and on the illustrating of the Beast Epic to the eighteenth century, see Varty 1983, pp. 243-58. Also Varty 1991, pp. 415-44.
On the work of the Haarlem Master, the Wynkyn de Worde cycle of woodcuts, its later fortunes, and the work of other disciples of the Haarlem Master, see Varty 1980, pp. 160-95, plus illustrations pp. 365-444.
Sisam's comments on the Bristol Cathedral misericords are in his edition of the *Nun's Priest's Tale* 1927, p.xxiv, note 3. My earlier comments on the Bristol Cathedral misericords are to be found in the Leicester University Press book (1967), pp. 45-48; also in the New Alyth book (1991) mentioned above, pp. 434-435; and the *Mélanges Shimmura* 1998, pp. 93-99.
Dr Martin Kauffmann, Assistant Librarian at the Bodleian Library, says that our knowledge of the provenance of MS Douce 360 goes back only as far as the eighteenth century. The manuscript was lot 2717 in the sale of the Duc de la Vallière in 1783, and subsequently lot 1376 in the sale of the collection of Charles-Gilbert, Vicomte de Morel-Vindé, held in Paris on 17 March 1823. There it was bought by Francis Douce through the bookseller Payne. On his death in 1834, Douce bequeathed his collection to the Bodleian.

CHAPTER FOUR

The Fox's Death and Resurrection

In the many pre-fifteenth-century stories about him, Reynard is often threatened with execution, usually by hanging, but is never executed. The nearest he comes to death on the gallows is in that branch of the *Roman de Renart* usually called *Le Plaid* (The Trial). This is the story that came to England, considerably modified, via the Dutch Beast Epics, through Caxton's translation. In this story, it will be recalled, Reynard successfully appeals to the king for clemency as he stands on the rungs of the gallows' ladder [82]. In the plastic and graphic arts, however, the fox may be seen being hanged, dead, carried in funeral procession, and even buried. More often than not, geese are the executioners.

In Bristol Cathedral eight geese are present at the fox's hanging [105]. To expedite his demise, two pull on the ropes and one on his brush. It will be remembered that, in this same Cathedral, there is an interesting variant on the motif of the preacher-fox who gets his congregation of geese off their guard in order to grab one of them for his dinner [41]: interesting

105 *Geese hang a fox. Bristol Cathedral, misericord; c.1520. D.R. Maxted.*

106 A robed fox preaches to geese from a pulpit. Beverley Minster, misericord; c.1520. J.C.D. Smith.

because we do not see him actually grab one of them; instead he (or an accomplice) is shown descending from the pulpit and, holding a thick stick in a threatening way, making for one of the nearer geese. The gallows depicted on the left are no doubt the ones from which we now see him hanged by the survivors of his vicious attack [105]. Although the two misericords on which these scenes are carved are no longer side by side, they probably were originally next to each other and formed a kind of diptych.

This is also probably true of two misericords in Beverley Minster. First we see the fox in a pulpit [106], robed, a rosary in his right hand, addressing a group of seven geese, all but one of which seem to be paying close attention to his sermon. The one which is not, on the back row, seems to be asleep, and is probably the one which gets carried off by the fox over to the left, behind the ape-like accomplice which also has a dead goose dangling from a stake held over its shoulder. Only three seats removed from this scene is one of the geese hanging the fox [107]. The carving of the left supporter is perhaps a reminder of what happened to the sleeping goose, for here we see a fox stealthily approaching two geese having a nap. In the centre, five geese form a hanging party while, to the right of them, two more watch the execution. One carries a cross and the other a mace. It looks as if there is to be a funeral procession after the hanging (and following the removal of the noose, depicted in the right supporter) which will be led by these two. If this is so, if there is to be a procession taking the fox to his grave, it is highly probable that the artist had in mind a late variant of one of the most successful of the Reynardian stories (*Reynard's Death and Funeral Procession*), to which we will soon come. (Perhaps a clue that the two Bristol Cathedral misericords were also linked in the artist's mind with the Beast Epic and the animal kingdom ruled over by Noble is to be found in the lion

107 *Geese hang a fox. Beverley Minster, misericord; c.1520. D.R. Maxted.*

108 *A mitred fox preaches to birds. Brent Knoll, St Michael, bench end; 14th or 15th C. J.C.D. Smith.*

109 *Birds footcuff a fox, then he is put in the stocks. Brent Knoll, St Michael, bench end; 14th or 15th-C. J.C.D. Smith.*

peeping out of the foliage to the right in the scene depicting the murderous preacher [41]. Is he a witness to the crime, and the one who will sentence the fox to death?)

We may only guess that these misericords in Bristol Cathedral and Beverley Minster were meant to be sets, but in other places there is no need to guess. In St Michael's at Brent Knoll, for example, three bench ends tell the story of the fox's fall in four vivid scenes. On the first of these bench ends [108] is a fox dressed as a monk-bishop preaching to a congregation of birds. Among them one distinguishes (behind the fox's ear), a cock; (top left), an owl; some hens (they have claws); some geese (with webbed feet); and a stork (close to the top of the crozier). A dead bird dangling from the fox's right hand (though it may be attached to the crozier) speaks of his perfidiousness. (The scene carved at the top of this bench-end is also probably a comment on hypocrisy since the chained ape-like creature holding a urinal is almost certainly meant to be a doctor, the butt of much satire and ridicule in those times; while the scene at the bottom showing two ape-humans roasting a pig on a spit [the one to the left is using a pair of

110 *A fox is hanged by geese. Brent Knoll, St Michael, bench end; 14th or 15th-C. J.C.D. Smith.*

bellows to fan the flames] is probably a comment on gluttony.) At the top of the next bench end [109], the owl, symbol of spiritual blindness and prophet of doom and disaster, looms larger than before, and we soon see why. In the upper register, the fox, stripped of his religious habit and accoutrements, is footcuffed and then, in the lower register, transferred to the stocks. The upper register carving is framed to the left and above by what may be a choir of birds (rejoicing at the imprisonment of their enemy?) conducted by a crudely carved figure which could just be a lion. It could also be another ape-like human similar to the two roasting the pig at the foot of the first panel, but if one looks closely, it has a mane indicated by wavy lines around its neck and shoulders, and clearer still in the depiction, in the lower register of the jailor holding a giant axe. A mane like this usually indicated a lion. That the prisoner in the stocks is the false bishop is proved by the mitre suspended in the space between him and his jailor. In the third bench-end [110], justice is done, and the fox is hanged by four geese, three of them sitting on top of the gallows while a fourth flies upwards to join them, and a fifth stays on the ground to tug at the rope.

111-14 *A fox seizes a goose by the head (111); flings it over his back (112); is caught by a goose with a rope (113); and is hanged by the goose (114). Tower of London, Chapel of St Peter ad Vincula, tomb of John Holland (Duke of Exeter), formerly in St Katherine's Hospital, stone frieze. The Courtauld Institute of Art.*

115 *A fully armed goose rides a saddled fox; a fully armed fox rides a saddled goose. Westminster Abbey, Henry VII's Chapel, misericord supporters; 1509. The National Buildings Record.*

One of the best illustrations of this particular turning of Fortune's wheel is part of a stone frieze running round the tomb of John Holland, Duke of Exeter, now in the Tower of London but which used to be in St Katherine's Hospital. First a fox seizes a goose by the wing [111], then drags it off by the neck [112]. A demon-ape divides these two scenes from the next two which, as if to emphasize the turning of Fortune's wheel, face the other way. Now a goose drags a fox by a rope round his neck [113], then it hangs him [114]. Medieval imagery abounds in parallel reversals of fortune as when rats hang a cat, and rabbits hang a mastiff or roast a hunter. However, the fox is also involved in other less violent reversals of fortune. In Lincoln Cathedral he rides a goose and is then ridden by it. Similar but more interesting scenes are depicted in Westminster Abbey [115]; more interesting because of the armour worn by both the fox and the goose, suggesting familiarity with at least the spirit of some of the later branches of the *Roman de Renart* such as the one entitled *Renart Empereur* (Emperor Reynard, Branch XI). We find the fox riding or being ridden by other enemies in other places as, for example, in Manchester Cathedral [116] where he rides a wolf (or dog). Might there still be faint echoes of a Beast Epic tale here, for he holds over his shoulder a staff from which dangles a dead hare. Couard? And might the bird in the tree to which he seems to speak be another of his intended vitims, the crow Tiecelin?

Although Reynard is hanged in medieval art, he is never hanged in medieval literature until Henryson's *The Tod* at the end of the fifteenth century. However, in one of the most popular branches of the *Roman de Renart*, the one called *La Mort et Procession Renart* (Reynard's Death and

116 *A fox rides a hound through a wood. Manchester Cathedral, misericord; 1508. D.R. Maxted.*

Funeral Procession, Branch XVII), probably composed at the beginning of the thirteenth century, he is thought to be dead, mourned, given State and Church funeral rites, then taken in solemn procession to a place of burial where he is put into a grave.

The unknown author of this lively tale begins with a couple of episodes which bring together Reynard and Couart the Hare who decide to accompany each other as far as King Noble the Lion's court to settle a dispute between the hare and a peasant. When this has been settled, all the animals sit down to an excellent meal, drinking and eating abundantly. Games and betting follow. Reynard gets into a game of chess with his old enemy, Ysengrin the Wolf. They play for money. Reynard loses again and again till he has none left. Desperate, he bets his skin against everything the wolf has won. The wolf accepts, and the fox loses. Reynard weeps tears of rage as Ysengrin calls for a hammer and nails with which he nails the fox to the chessboard by his testicles. There he leaves him, howling in agony. Worried by the howling, the queen herself, Fière the Lioness, traces it to its source. Having a very soft spot for the fox, she has him released and taken to her bed where he makes something of a recovery and there confesses his sins to a priest. Then he falls into a deep faint, so deep that everybody is convinced he has died. Hearing cries of distress, the king comes to the queen's room. Deeply saddened to find Reynard apparently dead, he orders court mourning and sends messengers to Reynard's castle to break the news to the fox's 'widow'. His body is taken to the great hall of the palace where the animals conduct a service for the dead. Immediately afterwards, leaving Reynard's body lying in state, the animals continue their feasting and gaming right through the night. At daybreak, Bernard the Ass (who is archbishop) orders the bells to be tolled. Then Reynard's body is carried from the great hall to the church where they lay him before the altar. Here Bernard pronounces the funeral oration and says a special prayer recalling the fox's virtues. Brichemer the Stag reads the epistle and absolves Reynard of his sins. Ferrant the Horse reads the gospel and Bernard concludes the proceedings by saying mass. After this, Brun the Bear goes ahead to dig Reynard's grave while Noble draws up the funeral procession. He orders Chantecler the Cock to immediately precede the bier and to carry the censer. The stag and the ram are to carry the bier and Ysengrin to follow it, carrying the cross. The goat is to beat a drum and the horse to play a harp. Tibert the Cat, Couart the Hare and Hubert the Kite are to hold candles alongside the bier. The mice are to toll the bell and the ape to weep as the body is laid to rest. Reynard, head uncovered, is thus borne in procession to his grave. Just as the bear is about to shovel earth on him, Reynard recovers from his deep faint, opens his eyes and looks about him. He quickly weighs up the situation, jumps out of the grave, seizes the cock by the neck as he goes, and makes off as fast as he can. The story continues for quite a while, recounting several more of the fox's escapades. Briefly, a chase follows, the cock manages to escape, and Reynard gets home so far ahead of his pursuers that he has time to arrange for a grave to be dug and marked by a headstone with his name on it so that, when his pursuers reach his castle, they find his wife, now apparently a widow (yet again!) mourning his recent death. Once again Reynard's enemies are duped, once more he 'dies' to live again.

To judge by numerous representations in stone, mosaics, drawings and paintings which seem to reflect variants of this story all over Europe; by its numerous reappearances in *Roman de Renart* manuscripts (especially in the fourteenth century); by references to it in later branches of the *Roman de Renart*; and by the fact that it was mimed in the streets of Paris in the 1313 Pentecost Festivities (referred to in the penultimate paragraph of Chapter Two), this version of the story was widely known over a long period of time. And it has left some interesting traces in medieval English art, including a set of coloured drawings which are the most complete and faithful of all extant representations of that part of the text which describes the funeral procession.

The most authentic illustration of the literary version of Reynard's funeral procession must surely be the miniature in a fourteenth-century French manuscript of the *Roman de Renart*, MS. f.fr. 12583 at the Bibliothèque Nationale in Paris. This is the only frontispiece miniature in a *Roman de Renart* manuscript to depict an episode from this particular story [117]. Because it appears at the beginning of the manuscript, it is much worn, and it is not easy to see all the details. I have therefore made a sketch of it to help interpret it [118]. It depicts a bier of which the projecting shafts are supported on the shoulders of an upright boar (behind) and a ram (in front). Leading them is a donkey walking on its hind legs and carrying a cross with a long upright shaft. The fox is shown jumping off the bier and seizing the cock as he goes. In this way the artist produces an abbreviated visual account of what happens in the text.

The earliest (about 1300) and most faithful-to-the-text visual rendering of the funeral procession in medieval English art adorns the lower margins of (most appropriately) the Service for the Dead in a Book of Hours which, according to art historians, was probably made in the Peterborough or London area. It is now kept in the Walters Art Gallery, Baltimore, Maryland (MS. 102).

117 *Renart's bier and funeral procession led by Bernart the Ass. Paris, Bibliothèque Nationale, MS f. fr. 12583, f. 1.*

118 *Sketch of the same by Kenneth Varty.*

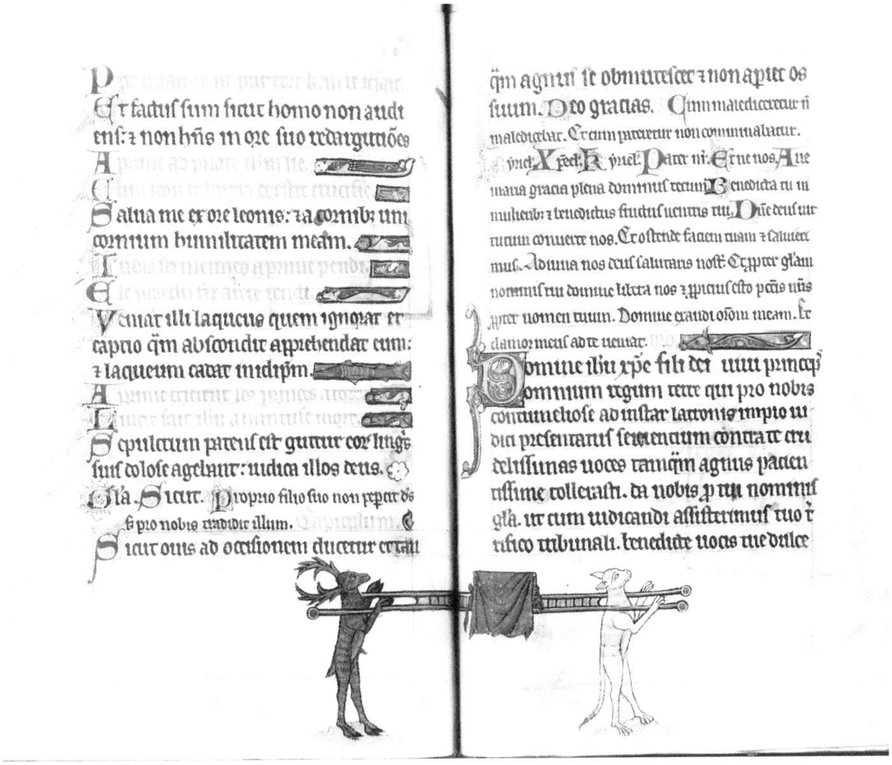

119 *A fox carried on a bier by a stag and a cat. This and all the illustrations which follow up to and including 131 are from MS 102 kept in the Walters Art Gallery, Baltimore, dated c.1300. They are reproduced here by the kind permission of the Director and Trustees of that Gallery. This is from the lower margins of ff.76v and 77.*

The procession wends its way across the lower margins of 17 sides of parchment (folios 73-81). At the centre, across two sides of parchment, is the fox on his bier [119], the shafts of which are supported on the shoulders of a stag (behind) and a cat (in front). The fox lies on his back under a cloth, head projecting from one end, brush from the other. An open eye shows that he is not dead. Immediately ahead of this group, on the next page, is a cock carrying, as he does in the story, a censer [120]. Before the cock is a wolf dressed as a bishop [121], then a cat beating a square-shaped tambourine [122], then a goat carrying a cross [123], then a tail-less quadruped blowing some kind of horn [124], then a ram carrying an aspergillum and holy water in a deep handled vessel [125]. Ahead of the procession a boar is shown in the process of making a grave [126], and a hare tugs at the bellropes in a church [127]. The rear of the procession is brought up by a camel ringing handbells [128]. In front of him, a pilgrim elephant [129], then a bull blowing a great horn [130], then a dappled horse beating a drum

[131], then an ass blowing a pipe with one hand and ringing a handbell with the other [132], and then a dog playing bagpipes [133]. He is presumably immediately behind the stag at the rear of the bier, although a group of apes (a female with three young) is depicted between the dog and the stag [134]. They seem to be standing on a little mound of earth and are probably meant to be bystanders, watching the procession, perhaps inspired by the lion's instruction to the ape to weep, to be the official mourner, at the interment of the fox.

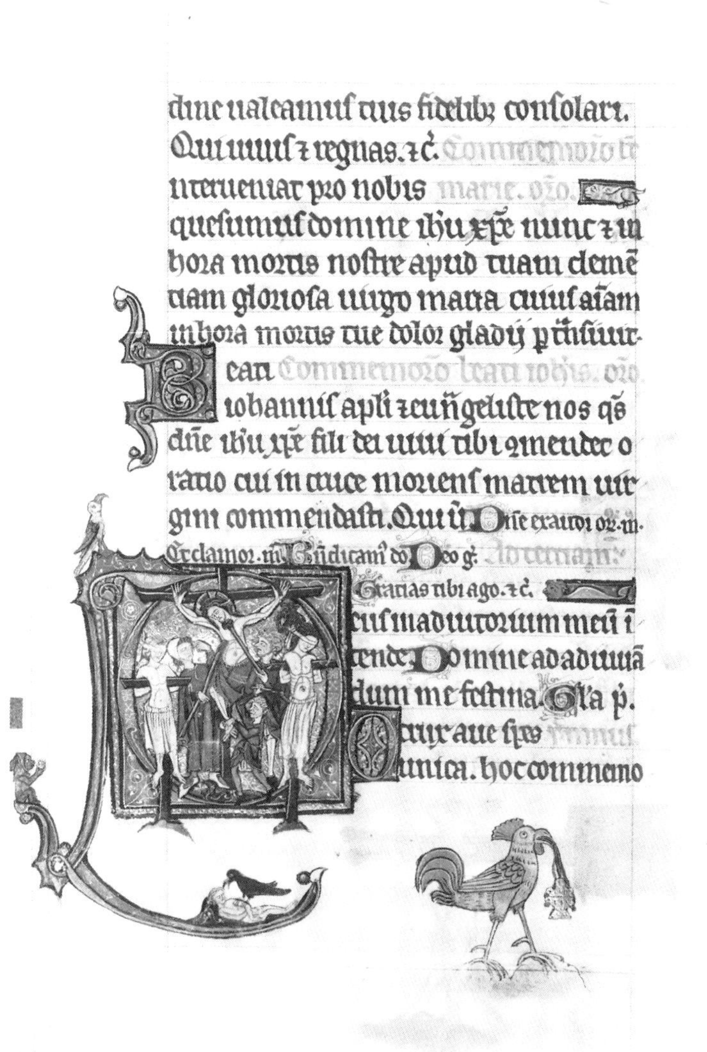

120 *A cock carries a censer immediately before the bearers of the fox's bier; f.77v.*

121 *A wolf-bishop precedes the cock; f.78.*

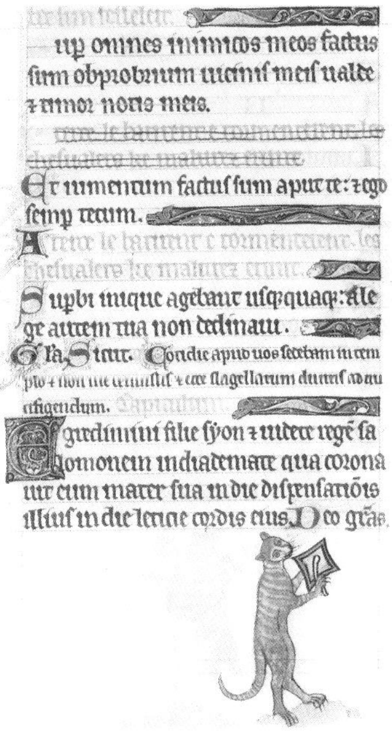

122 *A striped cat (or tiger) beats a tambourine and precedes the wolf-bishop; f.78v.*

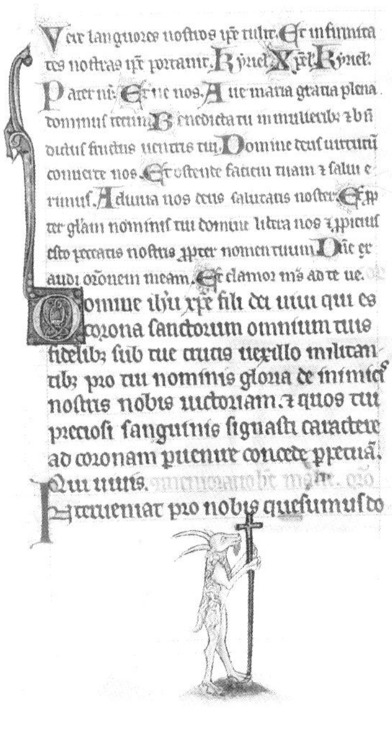

123 *A goat carrying a cross precedes the cat; f.79.*

124 *A quadruped horn-blower precedes the goat; f.79v.*

125 *A ram carrying an aspergillum precedes the cat and leads the procession; f.80.*

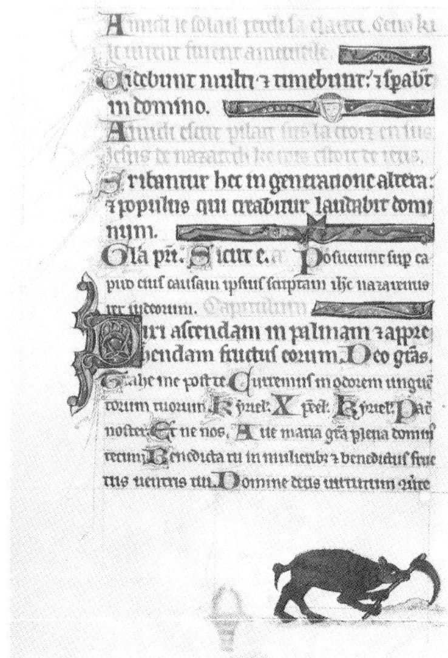

126 *Ahead of the procession, a boar digs a grave; f.80v.*

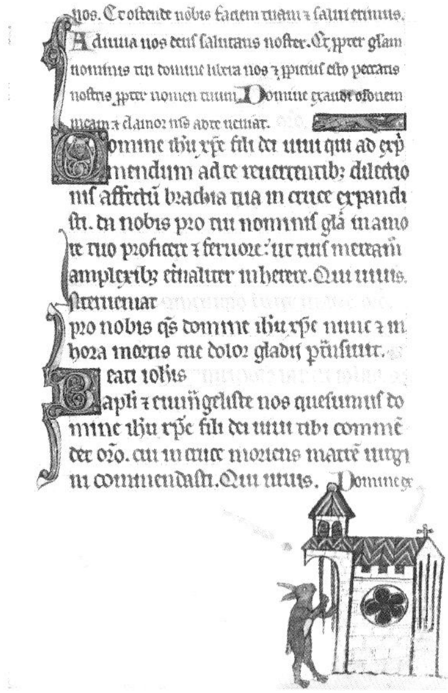

127 *A hare tolls church bells; f.81.*

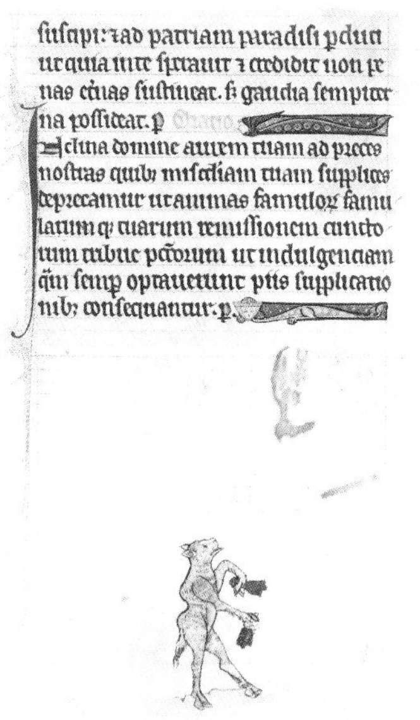

128 *A camel ringing handbells brings up the rear of the procession; f.73.*

129 *An elephant-pilgrim precedes the camel; f.73v.*

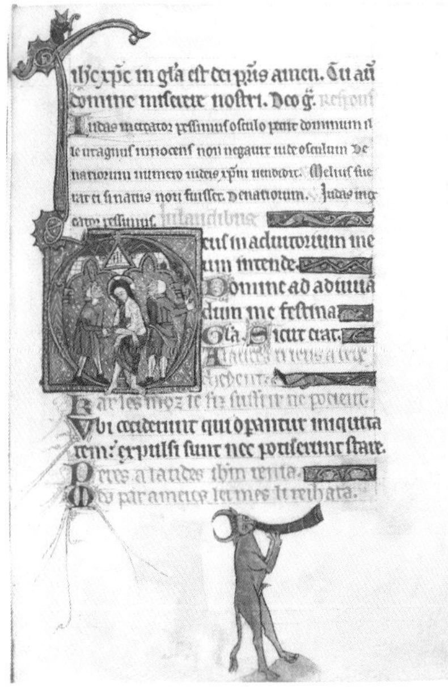

130 *A horn-blowing bull precedes the elephant; f.74.*

131 *A dappled horse precedes the bull; f.74v.*

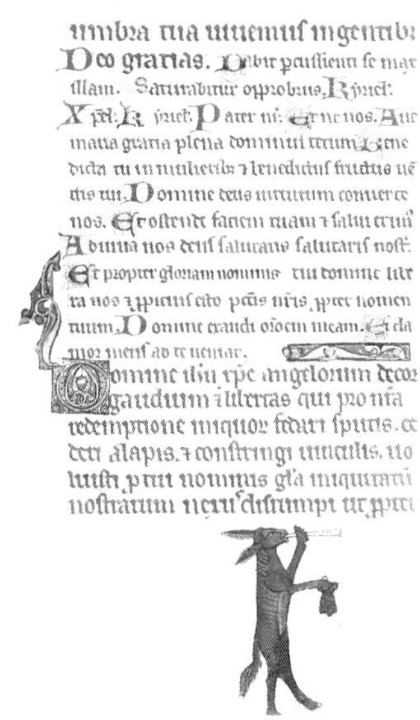

132 *An ass blowing a pipe and ringing a bell precedes the horse; f.75.*

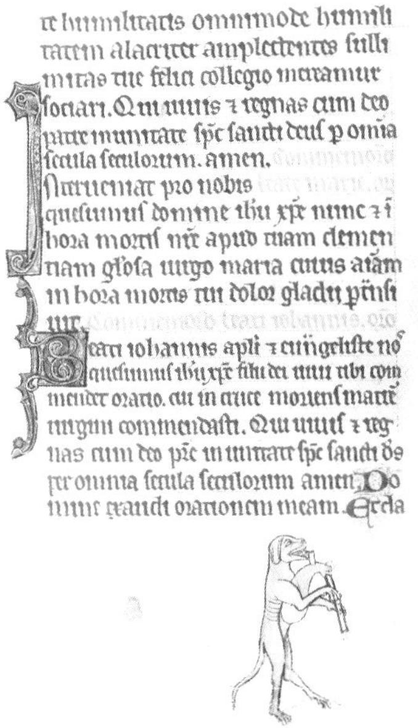

133 *A dog playing bagpipes precedes the ass and comes immediately behind the stag which bears the rear shafts of the fox's bier; f.75v.*

134 *A group of apes watches from the roadside, between the dog and the stag; f.76.*

Most of the animals instructed to take part in the literary account of the procession do so in the visual one: horse, stag, cock, wolf, cat, goat, ram, bear, ape. Several of the roles that are to be played are also depicted here: the carrying of the bier by two animals, of a censer immediately before the bier, of a cross, as well as the playing of some instruments, the digging of the grave, the tolling of the bells, and the shedding of official tears. A few of the parts played are identical in both the literary and the visual accounts: the stag is one of the pall-bearers, the cock carries the censer immediately before the bier, the horse is one of the performers on an instrument, and the ape is a mourner. If other animals are included, and roles are exchanged between some of them, this is also true of at least one other literary account. The one followed above is the one usually printed in editions of the *Roman de Renart*, but there is another one (in MS. cod. varia 151 kept at the Biblioteca Reale in Turin) in which the stag (still) and the horse (instead of the ram) carry the bier. The cock still immediately precedes the bier and carries the censer, but is accompanied by a rat, while the dog carries the cross. On the dog's back sits a squirrel carrying the aspergillum and holy water. The two musicians in the 'standard' literary account are replaced by quite a few more: the wolf plays a flageolet (like the Walters ass), the bull a tabor (like the Walters cat), the ram rings two handbells (like the Walters camel), and a monkey plays the harp on which sit two singing thrushes. A singing sparrow sits atop a hare which also plays an instument, followed by a music-making ass. In short, this variant literary account is a great deal more festive and musical than the 'standard' account, and the Walters Art Gallery procession is closer to it in spirit as well as in the odd detail.

A mere ten years may separate the Walters Art Gallery Book of Hours procession from a panel of stained and painted glass in York Minster which depicts what is usually called 'the monkey's funeral', and which may be related to our story [135]. Monkeys play most of the roles in this scene which depicts a service for a dead animal which lies on a bier and is covered by a green cloth and locally is said to be a monkey. However, the French text says that the cloth which covers Reynard on his bier is green, and the fox does play a part in this funeral service. Here he faces a cock across a lectern on which is an open book from which they read or chant as they take part in this service for the dead. The fact that these two old enemies face each other and are the only non-simians in the scene suggests some link with stories about their confrontations, one of which lies at the heart of the literary accounts of the fox's funeral. And right next to this panel is the scene of the fox seizing a goose and being chased by a distaff-wielding woman [7]. Were these two scenes connected, one wonders, in the mind of the artist who designed the whole window?

Next in time comes a funeral procession in the c.1335 Smithfield Decretals [136]. This is headed by a pompous, strutting cock which wears a smooth, bulbous crown and sports a broad wattle-beard. In the claws of its raised left leg it holds a mace. Behind him come six geese in pairs, harnessed by a rope which goes round the base of their necks and is tied to the hind legs of a supine fox, just above the paws. He is supported not by a bier, but by the arms of two

135 *A monkey's funeral. York Minster, lower panel of the St Peter window, stained glass; c.1310-20. The Royal Commission on Historical Monuments (England).*

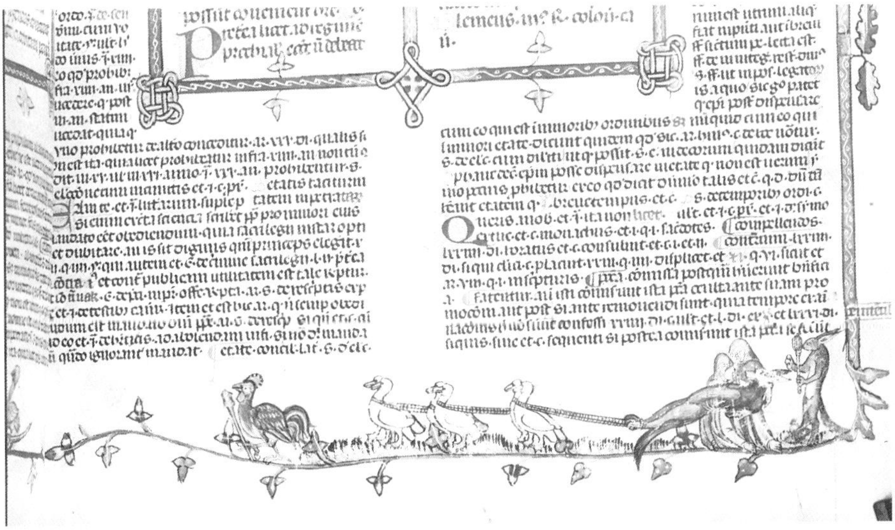

136 *A fox's funeral procession. The British Library, MS Royal 10. E. IV; c.1335.*

weeping nuns who stand on the far side of the fox and face the observer. One of the nuns supports his head, held in a way which suggests that he is still alive, as does the faintest trace of a cunning smile. He wears a thrown-back cowl, a reminder of some religious role he has been playing. Bringing up the rear is a very big hare, erect and carrying an aspergillum. The hare is easily mistaken for a fox because it sports a brush, but if one looks carefully one can see the short stumpy tail which it was first given. A later artist has added the brush. The head and ears are clearly those of a hare. The drawing in the lower margin immediately preceding this procession depicts a fox being hanged from a tree-branch by several birds [137]. A cock and a hen pull at the fox's hind legs with their beaks, while a goose with a long sword and carrying a buckler tugs at the end of the rope with its bill. Another goose, airborne, tugs at the rope at the point where it has been looped over the branch. To the right stands a goose preparing to shoot an arrow from an enormous bow. To the left two ducks watch the execution, and a goose holds an aspergillum in readiness for the ceremony to follow. The fox wears a thrown-back cowl just like the one he wears in the funeral procession. Clearly, these two drawings form a pair much like the carvings in Bristol Cathedral and Beverley Minster [41 & 105; 106 & 107]. On the page following the funeral procession, there are the coupled drawings which we have already examined in another context: the preaching fox-bishop and the chase [24]. The close proximity of these scenes (fox preaching, making off with a victim, being hanged, funeral procession) make one feel that they form a moralizing, narrative whole; and some of the details such as the mace, the aspergillum, the prominence of the cock, and the open-eyed fox suggest that the artist knew something, a variant, of a Beast Epic tale about the fox's 'death' and resurrection.

137 *A fox is executed at the gallows. The British Library, MS Royal 10. E. IV; c.1335.*

In 1974 the eminent restorer of mural paintings, Clive Rouse, discovered in the Dean's Vestry of Gloucester Cathedral a remarkable series of paintings on wood which depict yet another truly fascinating version of the fox's death and funeral, and the events which led up to and followed it. He found them beneath the peeling paint of some rather crude ornamental paintings of brocade patterns with trees, foliage, a vase of flowers and other motifs probably done in the sixteenth century. They are on the outside back of the wooden panels which form the north range of the choir stalls. On the choir side are the stalls themselves, on the other side, the Dean's Vestry. Records show that these panels were put in place sometime between 1350 and 1377, and Mr Rouse was sure that the Reynardian paintings were the first to be painted on them, most probably very soon after the choir-stalls had been completed. It is therefore reasonable to ascribe them to the late 1370s or early 1380s. The paintings are on the outside back of two stall seats on two panels, each of which measures 56.5 by 59.7 cm. Each panel is divided into an upper and a lower register, and each register contains at least two scenes. There are thus at least eight distinctly different pictures which, it seems, are to be read from left to right. The upper row begins with a fox making off with a goose and ends with his execution; the lower row starts with two animals singing from an open book and ends with the lion and lioness feasting at table.

Because the condition of these paintings is so poor, and some of the detail is lost in the photographs, I have made sketches to help appreciate their content. Beginning with the left side of the upper register of the left-hand panel [138 & 139] we see, out in the open and below some trees, a fox who has just thrown a goose over his back. Towards the middle of this register the fox, now upright, is taken prisoner and accompanied by several animals of which the most easily recognizable is a very tall hare and a boar. The hare stands in front of the fox and looks back at him, holding in its forepaws a rope which appears to go round the fox at shoulder height. Immediately behind the fox, holding a tall, thin stake, is a goat, identifiable partly because of its hoofs but chiefly because of the pale yellow colouring reserved for it when it makes its easily identifiable reappearance later on. The stake is probably all that is left of an elongated wooden cross which has lost its cross-piece due to the flaking of the paint. Behind the goat is a clearly delineated boar with its hairy spine, snout and hoofs. It seems to hold a staff. At the right end of this register we see a seated, fierce-looking wolf, wearing a skull-cap and flowing red robes edged with pearls. The wolf's fangs and pearls are very clearly painted. The bound fox is being led into the presence of this judge-like character, facing whom is a magnificent cock and a hen, eager spectators, one would say, of the impending trial and condemnation of their great enemy. Surely, we see here Baucent the Boar, Couard the Hare, Chantecler the Cock, Pinte the Hen, and Ysengrin the Wolf (or the English equivalents thereof), all at one time or another victims and enemies of Reynard the Fox? If so, this scene is unique. Nothing like it survives anywhere else either in word or image. In literary accounts of the fox's trial it is the lion, Noble, who usually judges the fox. But, as we have often seen in the visual arts, it is usually the fox's goose-victims which do the judging and the hanging. Here, however, it is his Beast Epic victims who do the judging, while the role of his folklore goose-victims is limited to their dragging him off to execution. This is shown in the next scene, depicted to the left of the upper register of the neighbouring panel [141 & 142]. Six yoked geese pull him by a rope which seems to encircle his neck (a reminder of their execution-er role?), though it may be that what looks like a rope collar is all that is left of a cowl. He lies on his back without any visible means of support, his forepaws sticking upwards and perhaps bound. His rear paws are certainly bound. On the right side of this register we come to his execution where two Beast Epic characters are especially prominent: the Goat (never named in any of the Beast Epics), and the Hare, Couard. The Goat holds what could be a stake with which he seems to be helping to dispatch the fox. A comparison with the procession in the Walters Art Gallery Book of Hours suggests that this is really a processional cross turned upside down. It is almost certainly the same object which the goat holds in the centre of the top register of the left-hand panel. And a tall processional cross is prominent in several of these fox funeral processions, including the one in the fourteenth-century French manuscript miniature referred to above [117& 118]. Apart from the Goat and Couard, a solitary goose (just beyond the hare's legs) assists at the fox's execution. Here then, in the Gloucester gallows scene, literary Beast Epic and popular fox-goose imagery are nicely blended. Returning to the left-hand panel [138 & 140], but to the lower register, we first see what could be an ass singing alongside a stag. Musical notation is clearly visible on the open pages of the book which is mounted on a lectern standing between them. Here perhaps are Bernard the Ass and Brichemer the Stag singing part of the Service for the Dead: in the *Roman de Renart* we are told that, in this service, Bernard the Ass read the ninth lesson and that the versicle linked with this was sung by Brichemer the Stag. (In passing we recall the cock and the fox at the lectern in the York Minster panel of glass depicting the 'monkey's funeral' [135].) The least well preserved and most difficult scene to interpret is the one which follows to the right of this register. It almost certainly has something to do with a game the mourners played immediately after the Service

138 *Scenes from a version of the fox's trial, execution and burial. Gloucester Cathedral, Dean's Vestry, painted wooden panels; c.1350-75. The National Monuments Record (England).*

for the Dead as recounted in the *Roman de Renart*. Leaving Reynard's supposed corpse on a bier in front of the chapel altar, the animals go off together for a meal. This develops into a riotous feast, and rough games follow. The principle game they play may be described as 'foot-banging'. Each animal in turn stretches out its foot and its partner strikes the outstretched limb as hard as it can in an approved manner (not easy to say exactly what this is) with the aim of unbalancing its owner. Trouble develops when one animal strikes another before it has had time to stick its leg out to receive a blow according to the rules. Perhaps this is what we see here. One round in the game is played between the wolf and the cat, and it is just possible they are depicted in the middle of this rather chaotic scene which does seem to represent feasting and carousing.

139 *A sketch of the upper register of illustration 138. Kenneth Varty.*

140 *A sketch of the lower register of illustration 138. Kenneth Varty.*

There is at least one outstretched paw, and the dog-like creature on the left seems to hold out a round vessel, perhaps for wine. There is a big lectern or desk to the right on the edge of which sits a little ape-like figure. Going on to the lower register of the right-hand panel we witness the moment when the fox is either lifted on to his bier at the beginning of the funeral procession or, more likely, when he is lifted off it to be lowered into the grave [141 & 143]. Reynard is scarcely visible, but his head and upturned snout are clear to see. We also see a mitred, doggy creature, probably Ysengin the Wolf, who plays a similar role in the Walters Art Gallery funeral procession [121]. Whoever he is, he is conducting a religious service. It is Couard the Hare who pulls Reynard off the bier, while Baucent the Boar rings a bell. A spotted, patchy hound (no doubt Courtois) stands behind the boar. Lastly, we see the King and Queen of the animals, Noble and Fière, rejoicing at the fox's demise. Though this departs from the literary account in which there is no such feasting at this point, it is a pure Beast Epic scene. This has to be

141 *More scenes from a version of the fox's trial, execution and burial. Gloucester Cathedral, Dean's Vestry, painted wooden panel; c.1350-75. The National Monuments Record (England).*

Noble and Fière (or whatever an observer in late fourteenth-century Gloucester would have called them), wearing their crowns and sitting at a table laden with food. In front of them one can just make out Brun the Bear and Belin the Ram (or is it the goat again?) bringing food from the left, while an ape is also just discernible in the bottom right corner.

This is all very intriguing. We have no medieval written account of the fox's trial and execution in England, and in the only story we have in French, written over two hundred years earlier (but 'reprinted' many times, especially in the fourteenth century), the fox is not hanged and there is no final party. Also very interesting is the fact that these paintings would have been at head height and very visible to the pilgrims who came here to visit Edward II's tomb, being on the path they would have taken within the Abbey (as it then was) to get to that tomb. During his lifetime, Edward had anything but a saintly reputation, but not long after his death,

142 *A sketch of the upper register of illustration 141. Kenneth Varty.*

143 *A sketch of the lower register of illustration 141. Kenneth Varty.*

miracles of healing are said to have taken place at his tomb, and very many came to it over a long period of time. If these pilgrims did not know a version of the tale we know in French before they came to Gloucester, they would almost certainly know one by the time they left; that is, if they asked questions about these paintings as they passed by, and if somebody was on hand to explain them. And what, one wonders, might that explanation have been? Were they, in the mind of those who commissioned these paintings, some wry, ironic comment on the fact that here lay Edward who, in his lifetime might have been compared in some ways to Reynard, performing miracles after his death? There is, after all, in parts of the Beast Epic, some ridicule of the miracles of healing that were alleged to take place at the tombs of unlikely saints. And how significant is the fact that these paintings occupy what one may call a 'lower margin' position? As art historians have often pointed out, lower margin drawings and paintings in manuscripts sometimes make an antithetical comment on the main point made in the text above. Clearly, the funeral procession which extends over the lower margins of the Service for the Dead in the Walters Art Gallery Book of Hours forms a kind of comic antithesis to the solemnity of that Service. It may even go further, for it is well known that funeral orations sometimes celebrated the 'virtues' of the unvirtuous, and this is certainly what happens during the course of the ceremonies described in that branch of the *Roman de Renart* in which the fox is thought to be dead. And the panel of glass in York Minster depicting the devil-fox making off with a goose (the soul of an unwary person?) is in a lower margin position of a window at the centre of which sits St Peter holding the keys to the gate of Heaven [7]. Above the panels depicting the fox's execution behind the stalls in Gloucester Cathedral were paintings of saints. There may have been six, but only two survive. These are St Margaret of Antioch emerging from a dragon, and St Anthony with his attributes of pig, bell, and rosary, and carrying his tau-headed cross or staff. These are painted on tall panels so that they may be compared with the

144 *Geese hang a fox. Ludgvan, St Lugdvan; late medieval wall painting, now lost. Drawing by Dr Borlase, c.1750, copied by E.Clive Rouse.*

145 *A Fox attacks geese, then is hanged by them. Wellington, Cothay Manor, Great Hall; late medieval wall painting. E. Clive Rouse.*

stained glass windows to which the fox paintings form the lower margins, and make a devilish contrast to the saintly scenes above. The lives of some saints (whose reward will have been life eternal) contrasted with the life, and death, of the devil incarnate in Reynard the Fox?

To the best of my knowledge, there is no further iconographical evidence in England about this story until the second half of the fifteenth century. Dating from this period we have two wall paintings: the one that was in St Ludgvan's in Ludgvan, Cornwall [144]; and the other that is in the Great Hall of Cothay Manor near Wellington in Somerset [145]. The Ludgvan mural has long since been destroyed, but a drawing of it was made in about 1750, and it shows that, on the west side of the north door, balancing a picture of St Christopher on the east side, was a picture of geese hanging a fox, but there is no evidence of a funeral procession. The Cothay Manor mural not only shows the fox being set upon by geese, then hanged by them, but also a funeral procession. It is not at all easy to see, especially in the photograph, but if one looks carefully one can discern between the dark patches in the foreground the partial outlines of yoked geese. This brings us back to the Smithfield Decretals situation [136 & 137] in which fox-geese world-upside-down imagery predominates, but in which there seem to be reminiscences of the Beast Epic funeral procession. It may be that further restoration of the Cothay Manor mural will show Reynard lying on his bier, but the details so far revealed only hint that this will prove to be the case. Here, however, the fox's funeral is not in a marginal position. It is high up on the wall of the Great Hall of a secular building. Lastly, where the iconographic evidence about this story in medieval England is concerned, and it is only just medieval, we return to those traces of a funeral procession to follow execution carved on a c.1520 misericord in Beverley Minster [107]. In England, popular fox-goose world-upside-down imagery seems finally to have crowded out the Beast Epic proper. However, in Scotland, in Henryson's *The Tod*, from the late fifteenth century (and later than Caxton's 1481 translation), this

146 *An owl rings a bell either announcing a fox's funeral, or at the moment of committal. Yarnton, St Bartholomew, stained glass quarry; 16th C. (?). P.S. Spokes.*

popular imagery is set aside, Noble's animal-barons resume their normal roles, and in it the fox is indeed hanged; this for the very first time in any version of the Beast Epic. Finally, there is that intriguing bit of evidence of the stained glass diamond-shaped quarrel in St Bartholomew's, Yarnton, Oxfordshire [146] in which an owl rings a bell (just like the one rung by the boar in the Dean's Vestry in Gloucester Cathedral [141 & 143]), and says 'Ye schal praye for ye foxe.'

In effect, the fox's victims finally win in both traditions, the literary and the iconographic.

By way of conclusion to this chapter, I offer a few comparisons with some of the continental representations of the fox's execution and funeral procession.

As noted in the preceding chapter and at the beginning of this one, and splendidly demonstrated by Kerstin Rodin, the iconography of the preaching fox who attacks one of his flock which then turns on him and hangs him is widespread in Europe. One of the finest examples of this is to be found in three scenes in the church at Kungs-Husby, Norway. Each scene is painted at the top of a capital, and dated c.1500. In the first [147], the fox leans forward over a pulpit as he preaches to geese on either side and below him. In the second [148], he is attacked by the geese and taken prisoner. This compares with the Cothay Manor mural [145] and is relatively rare. In the third scene [148], they hang him, all of them pulling at the gallows' rope.

The most important continental drawing of the Beast Epic funeral procession is, of course, the miniature in the fourteenth-century manuscript of the *Roman de Renart* [117 & 118], discussed above. Earlier than this are some scenes which were sculpted towards the end of the thirteenth century on the capital of a massive polygonal pillar which supports the south wall of the nave opposite the pulpit in Strasburg Cathedral, but which were deliberately destroyed in 1685 by a zealous Catholic who felt strongly about the anti-Catholic propaganda put out by Protestants using these scenes as criticism of Roman Catholic rites. Fortunately for us, woodcut drawings were made of these stone carvings and published in 1576 in an anti-Catholic broadsheet with verses by the Protestant satirist Johann Fischart [150].

Translated from the German, some of these verses describe the carvings thus: 'Here they bear a sleeping fox as if he were a holy shrine. This indicates hypocrisy. Hypocrites pretend to be like sheep, whereas they are in fact lurking like a sleeping fox. This is the hellish fox of Rome, ancestor of all foxes and a burden to all mankind...Two handsome fellows are bearing the hypocritical fox of Rome: a dissolute sow and a foul-smelling he-goat heap lasting shame on clerical habit. The sow represents epicureans, fat hogs, devourers of benefices, slaves of the gut, fornicators, for this is the nature of the band of clerics profiting from that holy shrine...The he-goat stands for the high clergy and its foul-reeking carnal cravings. Beneath their two-horned hats they ravage the herd like licentious he-goats.' This is especially interesting because, to the best of my knowledge (and apart from the rare survival of a few words incorporated into a picture), this is the earliest extant explanation of the representation of a fox-centred scene in a church. If only something like this existed to explain a fifteenth- or sixteenth-century view of the creatures depicted in the Dean's vestry in Gloucester Cathedral! What these woodcuts really show us are, firstly, part of the religious service for the 'dead' fox, then the funeral

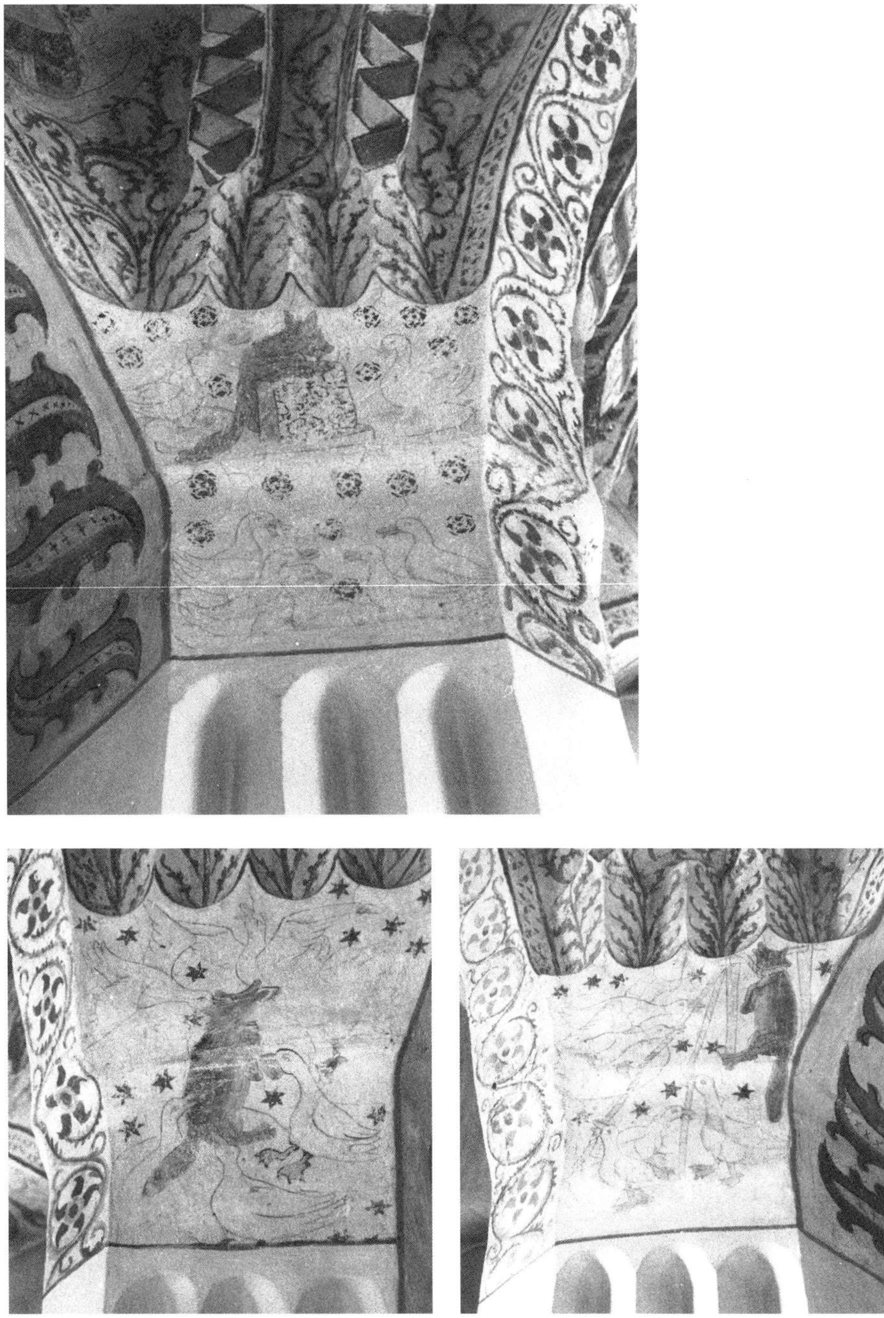

147-9 *A fox preaches to geese from a pulpit (147); the geese then attack the fox and take it prisoner (148); then they hang it (149). Kungs-Husby Church (Norway), frescoes on capitals; c.1500. K. Rodin.*

150 *A fox's funeral service and procession. Strasbourg Cathedral. Etchings made in 1576 based on late 12th C. sculptures made around a capital. The sculptures were destroyed in the 17th C.*

procession. In the former, one sees a stag at a small altar on which stands a chalice and an open book on the edge of which the stag rests a hoof. Just behind the stag-priest are a cat and an ass. They sit upright, the cat supporting an open book from which the ass seems to be reading music and singing. The scene of the stag at the altar is framed by what appear to be two columns on the capitals of which we see depicted the two carved scenes being described. Evidently, this is the one column being shown from both sides so that we may see where the carvings were and how they appeared. The funeral procession carving shows the fox on his bier, curled up as if he were sleeping, and being carried by a ram or goat (probably a goat) to the rear and by a boar to the front. The boar turns its head back to look suspiciously at the fox. A little monkey-like creature sits beneath the bier. In front of the boar marches a hare carrying a tall, lighted candle; and in front of the hare walks a wolf carrying a crucifix bigger than himself, and he is preceded by a collared bear who leads the procession carrying in one hand a holy water vessel and in the other an aspergillum. On the ground, just in front of the bear's feet, is planted a little cross to mark the fox's grave. Chronologically, this is one of the earliest and most detailed representations of the central episodes in the story of the fox's death and resurrection as recounted in the seventeenth branch of the *Roman de Renart*, but it is not that much earlier than the one depicted in the Walters Art Gallery Book of Hours, nor is it as close to the text.

Notes

BASIC TEXTS

For the text of the Old French *Mort et Procession Renart* and for a translation into modern French, see Combarieu du Grès & Subrenat 1985. For Henryson's *The Tod*, see MacQueen 1972, pp. 55-85.

CRITICAL STUDIES

On the Walters Art Gallery Book of Hours, see McCulloch 1962-63, pp. 9-26. For the iconography of the fox's funeral in Europe, including examples in Bourges, c.1095; Murano, 1111; Modena, c.1130; Verona, c.1160; Vercelli, c.1170; Ravenna, c.1210; Tarragona, c.1210; Strasbourg, c.1280; Marienhafe, c.1300; Venice, c.1300; Oviedo, c.1320; the Smithfield Decretals, c.1335; a Flemish drawing, c.1340; see Varty 1966, pp. 70-93. On this topic, see also Rouse & Varty 1976, pp. 104-117; also Varty 1991, pp. 361-90; also Schouwink 1993, pp. 169-79.

SUPPORTING INFORMATION

A photograph of a misericord depicting rats hanging a cat appears in Varty 1967 as illustration 135; of rabbits roasting a hunter, ibid. illustration 140; of the armed goose riding a fox, and vice versa, ibid. illustrations 137 and 138.

CHAPTER FIVE

The Fox and the Wolf in the Well

Vox and Wolf is another death-and-resurrection story, and the only other piece of medieval English fox literature to survive from pre-Caxton times. In this tale, the fox, accidentally trapped at the bottom of a well, is discovered there by the wolf. The quick-witted fox immediately pretends that he has died, that he is a spirit who has been transported to paradise where there is delicious food aplenty (especially of the kind preferred by wolves). Gradually, he persuades the wolf that this is really so, and that he can join him if he repents all his sins and jumps into the bucket which he can see in front of him. The wolf's weight takes him down and brings up the other bucket with the fox sitting in it, thereby 'resurrecting' him.

Written accounts

The motif of the fox and the wolf in the well has often been treated in fable, short story, sermon-exemplum, and folklore. In his *Types of the Folktale*, Aarne lists it as Type 32 under the descriptive heading 'The wolf descends into a well in one bucket and rescues the fox in the other'. The all-important mechanism on which this motif and much of the ensuing comedy depends is a pulley suspended above the well, a pulley around which runs a rope with a bucket attached to either end so that, as one bucket descends to the bottom of the well to gather water, the other, filled with water, is hauled to the surface. Versions of Aarne's Type 32 abound in different regions and cultures, from ancient to modern times. Quite a few scholars have studied its likely evolution on its way to the *Roman de Renart* (in which there are two different versions, the best one being known as Branch IV), and thence to its English *Vox and Wolf* version. Particularly interesting is Haim Schwarzbaum's re-examination of this subject as he studied the Rabbi Berechia Ha-Nakdan's 117th fable of the *Mishlé Shu'Alim* (Fox Fables), dated by him mid-thirteenth century. He, like most others who have gone into this, agrees that the immediate forerunners and most likely sources of the two *Roman de Renart* versions were, firstly, Rabbi Rashi (c.1070); secondly, Petrus Alphonsus, a converted Spanish Jew (between 1109 and 1114). According to Schwarzbaum, these two Hebrew sources may in their turn, have been influenced by both Rabbi Meir who flourished c.135-170 A.D. and Rabbi Hai Gam, who died in 1038. In short, there seems to have been a strong Jewish link in the evolutionary chain of this motif before it appears first in the *Roman de Renart* and then, eventually, in *Vox and Wolf*. Rabbi Rashi's version is a two-part fable exemplum which serves as a commentary on three Talmudic passages. It is in the second part that the fox, at night, under a full moon, leads the wolf to a well, then quite deliberately gets into the upper bucket causing it to descend and to raise the lower one. The wolf asks the fox why he has done this. Now at the bottom of the well, the fox calls up 'Look here', and points to the reflection of the moon. 'Here's a big cheese'. The wolf then asks how he can join the fox to get at the cheese. The fox points to the other bucket and invites the wolf to get in, which he does... Petrus Alphonsus's version is embedded in an exemplum fable, the amoral moral of which is 'take what is on offer at any given moment, and do not refuse it in the hope of better in the future'. This is also a two-part fable, and it is also in the second part that the wolf is duped. Here the fox takes the wolf on a moonlit night to a well and there points to the reflection of the moon, telling the wolf that it is a cheese. The wolf refuses to go down and get it for himself. He tells the fox to go and get it for him, but agrees that if it should prove too heavy for the fox, he will go down and help bring it up. The fox descends in the upper bucket then pretends the 'cheese' is indeed too heavy for him, so the wolf goes down in the other bucket...

It is in the *Roman de Renart* that this motif undergoes some radical and highly entertaining modifications. There are, as already stated, two versions: a little-known one preserved in only one manuscript, and a very well-known one which occurs in full (sometimes with substantial variants) in no less than 13 manuscripts, one of which also contains the unique, variant version. The comic qualities of both depend chiefly on the way that the fox, Renart, dupes the wolf, Ysengrin, into believing that he is dead, is a spirit, and in paradise, with all the food and drink he could wish for. The image of the fox in paradise is, of course, at the heart not only of both the standard and the variant *Renart* versions, but also of the Middle English poem. It is the chief innovation in this motif's long history, and it first occurs, it seems, in the *Roman de Renart*. The comic effect of the standard form of Branch IV is made even greater by the way the notorious affairs between the fox and the she-wolf, first told in the *Ysengrimus*, then in Branch II, are drawn into the narrative, and especially by the wolf's mistaking his own reflection in the well-water for his wife who, he presumes, is enjoying yet another round of sex with the fox. This comic element (not in the variant *Renart* version) is enriched when the fox tells the wolf that his suspicions about being cuckolded are groundless, and that he must accept that he was mistaken, especially if he wants to join him in paradise. The wolf then admits having thought the worst, and says he was indeed wrong, providing us with the comic spectacle of the cuckold grovelling before the cuckolder. The dénouement, which tells how the wolf got out of the well and what happened to him then, also incorporates another part of the tale of the fox's adultery with the she-wolf (not present in the variant version). The distressed and badly wounded wolf is found not far from the well by one of the wolf-cubs who had witnessed his mother commit adultery and had been called a bastard by her elated lover who, adding injury to insult, had then urinated all over him.

From the variant *Renart* version, the Middle English poem seems to draw on the way the wolf discovers the fox in the well (by overhearing the invisible fox, whose voice he recognizes) talking to himself. Their subsequent conversation is developed in a masterfully comic way. All three Renardian versions include lively and entertaining direct speech, but the best is in the English. It is easily the funniest with the psychologically best battle of wits, beginning with the wolf pretending not to recognize the fox's voice, and clearly relishing the knowledge that his old enemy is down a well. This heightens the comic effect when, finally, the wolf is duped. The way the fox's adultery with the she-wolf is drawn into the narrative is admirably ironic. From totally rejecting the fox's claim to be dead, to be a spirit and in paradise, the wolf is, it seems, gradually convinced that this is so; or, rather, lets his greed convince him that it is so. Before he too may enter paradise, he must confess his sins. But there is nobody to confess to, except the fox. And the fox makes him go on and on with his catalogue of sins till he gets him to admit that he had believed a tale about an affair between the fox and his wife, the she-wolf. He had actually, and stupidly, believed what he had seen with his own eyes! In the variant *Renart* version, the fox tells the wolf he has to forgive everyone everything before he can enter paradise. Forgiving the fox is of course implied, and in particular forgiving his adultery with the she-wolf; but it is only implied. In the standard *Renart* version, the fox tells the wolf he must confess as well as forgive. The wolf says he has already confessed, to an old hare and to a she-goat. No details are reported. It is only in the English poem that the wolf confesses to the fox and brings in the notorious affair between the 'confessor' and the she-wolf. In this way it is all the more comically outrageous, comically dramatic, in particular the wolf's repudiating the evidence of his own eyes.

Illustrations

The unique manuscript of *Vox and Wolf* (Bodleian, Digby 86, c.1300?) is not illustrated nor is there, it seems, any pictorial representation of medieval English origin depicting any incident of any version of this story until Caxton's *Aesop*, 1484. This reappears in Pynson's 1497 edition, and again in the same printer's c.1500 edition, referred to by Hodnett at 202 and 1816. Apart from these, I have found nothing else of medieval English origin. English libraries do, however, house three of the best illustrations to have come down to us, all of French origin. Two of these are in *Roman de Renart* manuscripts, one in Oxford, the other in London. The third is in a non-Reynardian manuscript kept in Cambridge. In all three, the mechanism for lowering and raising the buckets is particularly prominent, as is the rounded, raised wall of the well. Indeed, in the earlier of the two *Renart* miniatures (the Bodleian, Douce 360, f.46, dated 1339), the well wall resembles the shape of a baptismal font. In this picture [151] the artist has chosen to illustrate the moment when Renart reaches the top of the well, and he shows him hanging on to the rope rather than sitting in a bucket. Realistically, Ysengrin should, at this moment, be out of sight and at the bottom of the well. The artist, however, prefers to show the wolf, forepaws raised, about to disappear into the depths of the well. In this way he probably wanted to bring to mind the words exchanged as these old enemies passed each other travelling in opposite directions. (Ysengrin: 'Good friend, why are you coming up?' Renart: 'When one comes down, the other comes up: that's the normal procedure. I'm going up to Paradise, and you're going down into Hell'.) And he wanted to underline the fox's successful duping of the wolf.

After Renart's escape, Ysengrin is left for the rest of the night to lament his lot at the bottom of the well. In the morning, led by their cook, three monks and their ass come to the well to draw water. After strenuous but vain efforts by the ass to draw up the bucket, one of the monks leans over the well wall and espies the wolf. They all return to the monastery for

151 *While Ysengrin descends into a well, Renart ascends. The Bodleian Library, MS Douce 360, f.46v; 1338.*

weapons and dogs. Thus armed, they haul Ysengrin to the surface, beat him up, and set the dogs on him. Eventually, they leave him for dead. The artist who made the miniatures for the British Library's manuscript (Add. 15229, f.42, dated late fourteenth or early fifteenth century) shows something of what happened to Ysengrin when he was pulled out of the well. A white-robed monk (the author of Branch IV says that these events took place in the grounds of an abbey of white monks) is shown [152] about to bring an enormous cudgel down upon the wolf as he emerges from the well, seated in a bucket.

The third French artist's illustration is a very simple lower-margin outline drawing in the Metz Pontifical (Fitzwilliam Museum, MS 298, f.138v.) made for Raynaud de Bar, Bishop of Metz 1302-1316, the earliest of the three pictures. It also shows [153] the moment when

152 *Ysengrin is hauled to the top of a well and attacked by a monk. The British Library, MS Add. 15229, f.42; late 14th or early 15th C.*

Ysengrin, seated in a bucket, is brought to the surface, apparently by one man, possibly a monk. There is no hint of the man's or the wolf's reactions to their confrontation, nor of the fate awaiting the wolf. The artist has telescoped the sequence of events and chosen to depict the fox running away from the well as if this happened just as the wolf was drawn up. He also has the fox look back at the unfolding drama. Nothing like this happens in any extant version of the tale. It is probably the artist's way of underlining the fox's success over his old enemy.

Although this motif was so widely known, very few illustrations of it were made, it seems. If they were, few have survived. Perhaps the single most interesting one is that embroidered (with several other fox fables) on what was almost certainly an altar cloth made between 1300 and 1330, perhaps for the Cathedral of St Catherine's in Lübeck, and presently kept in the

153 *Ysengrin is hauled to the top of a well as Renart makes his escape. Cambridge, Fitzwilliam Museum, MS 298, f.138v; c.1302-16.*

154 *While a wolf descends into a well, a fox ascends. Lübeck, the St Annan Museum; sketch based on a woollen design embroidered on cloth; c.1300-30.*

155 *Reinaert escaping from a well as Isegrim descends. On the front of a drawer (third from top, left-hand scene) in private ownership in Wales. Pewter on wood; mid 17th C.*

St Annan Museum close by the cathedral. The scene of the fox and the wolf at the well is depicted fairly near the centre of the cloth [154]. Each of them sits in a bucket suspended from the pulley and above the well wall. Prusumably, the fox is the one to the right, a little higher than the wolf who is about to descend. Other scenes depict the fable of the fox and the stork who invite each other to a meal; the fox and the crow with the cheese; the fox and the cock; the fox (cowled) preaching to birds, then hanged under the gaze of birds; the fox with a goose held by the neck and in the process of being flung over his back; the wolf (or she-wolf) fishing with his (her) tail, then having the tail chopped off by a peasant wielding an axe; and a fox making off with a sausage (?) in his jaws. A veritable anthology of fox fables, several of which were drawn into the Beast Epic.

In passing, and to conclude, mention may be made here of yet another pictorial anthology which contains a scene of the fox and the wolf at the well; an anthology which draws entirely on a long-established Beast Epic iconographic tradition and is housed privately in Wales. These images are in pewter and set into the fronts of the drawers and a cupboard door of a splendid chest of drawers [155] which dates from the last quarter of the seventeenth century. The central cupboard door is decorated with a large-scale scene of the lion presiding over his court. Each of the surrounding ten drawers is decorated with two scenes, one on either side of a raised and ornate boss for the keyhole. To read the story which these pictures illustrate, the spectator starts with the central panel, goes to the top-left drawer and proceeds anticlockwise around the central panel, and reads each drawer from right to left. The well episode is on the left of the central cupboard door, third drawer down, and to the left of the keyhole. Here one sees the fox jumping out of his bucket as the wolf disappears in his, head down, with only his tail protruding above the well wall's rim. These pictures were mostly copied from a series of woodcuts made by Erasmus Quellijn de Jongere (1607-1678) and Jan Christoffel Jegher (1617-1667) both of Antwerp, and who almost certainly drew on a Flemish tradition which goes back to the 1500s. Although six other similar cabinets are known, this is the only one housed in Britain, and of great interest to Reynardians.

Notes

BASIC TEXTS

Editions of *Vox and Wolf* are many. The one by Bennett & Smithers (1968, pp. 65-79) is found in most libraries. The text is here preceded by a useful literary-historical and critical section. For the text of Branch IV of the *Roman de Renart*, see Dufournet & Méline 1985, pp. 308-337 where the Old French text faces a modern French translation. For a translation into English, see Owen 1994, pp. 81-87. The text of the variant version of Branch IV has been most recently edited by Strubel, 1998, pp. 1029-1037.

OTHER RELEVANT TEXTS

Aarne 1964; Dicke & Grubmüller 1987, pp. 264-65; Schwarzbaum 1979.

CRITICAL STUDIES AND SUPPORTING INFORMATION

Vox and Wolf has been the subject of several studies in recent times: see Honegger 1996, pp. 59-74 both for its comprehensive argument and the rich bibliographical information in the footnotes.

A detailed comparison between *Vox and Wolf*, both the *Roman de Renart* versions and their fable predecesors (in particular Rabbi Rashi and Petrus Alfonsus) is made by Varty 1997, pp. 17-30. On the Lübeck altar cloth and the Flemish cabinet, see Varty 1991 B, pp. 415-444. See also Wackers & Van Daele 1988, pp. 377-92; and Van Daele & Wackers 1988, pp. 128-34.

CHAPTER SIX

The Fox-Devil

When Fischart called the fox in the Strasbourg Cathedral carvings 'the hellish fox', he will have had in mind a very old belief about the nature of the fox.

Before the fox was given a proper name and achieved fame, first as Reinardus, then as Renart, then Reineke, and so on, he played a role in the *Physiologus* (The Naturalist) which was to become well known and to lead to great things, a role that the named fox and his descendants were to reinterpret again and again. According to some, the *Physiologus* was composed in the second century B.C. as a kind of introduction to zoology, a compendium of knowledge about animals and birds, some real, some imaginary (though then some of the imaginary ones may have been thought to be real). After the spread of Christianity, exhortations and moralizations were added to the description of each creature, and although the book was denounced as heretical in a papal decree of about the year 500, its popularity seems to have continued unhindered into the Middle Ages. By the early twelfth century, it had developed into a compendium of up to 200 creatures, became known as the Bestiary, and was divided into separate sections: one for animals, one for birds, and one for reptiles and fishes. In a few versions there were sections for plants and stones. The Bestiary seems to have been most popular in the twelfth, thirteenth and fourteenth centuries, especially in England and in France. It was also known in many other countries, and as far afield as the Middle East. The sudden growth in its popularity in the twelfth century may have been due not so much to the text as to a series of pictures which were then created to illustrate it. There can be no doubt that these illustrations greatly influenced the decoration of many buildings and manuscripts, and were used as models by sculptors, carvers and artists. On the whole the descriptions of the creatures in the Bestiary are remarkable for their fantasy. Rarely do they reveal careful observation even where common creatures are concerned. Often the imagination ran riot, and one encounters the siren, dragon, manticore (a man-headed lion) and the caladrius (a kind of bird which could predict the recovery or death of an invalid: if it turned its head towards him he would recover, if it looked away, he would die). The main object of the Bestiary was not of course to entertain with its poetic flights of fancy, but to teach, and in particular to remind the reader of basic Christian truths. It is not therefore surprising if one of the most frequently depicted subjects in the Middle Ages was the 'pelican in her piety'. According to the Bestiary, the male pelican often killed its young and the female restored them to life by pecking into her breast and letting her blood flow over them. She therefore came to symbolize Man's redemption through the blood of Christ after his fall through sin, and was often depicted standing above her young and opening her breast.

This is how, in one typical Bestiary, the description of the fox reads: ' "The foxes have holes and the birds of the air have nests", thus says the Scripture concerning the Lord; and in the *Song of Solomon*, Salome says: "Bring us the little foxes, for they destroy the grapes," and David says in a psalm: "They will become the portion of foxes". Physiologus relates of the fox that he is a very crafty animal. When he is hungry and can find no prey, he entices it thus: he seats himself in a warm place where there is chaff, or else casts himself on his back and holds his breath and swells up his body completely, so that he appears dead. The birds believe that he is really dead, and they fly down in order to eat him up; but he springs up and catches them and eats them up. So also is the Devil very crafty in his ways. He who would partake of flesh dies. To this flesh belong adultery, covetousness, lust, murder. Thence also Herod is likened to this animal: "Go", says the Lord, "and speak to that fox". '

Versions of this Bestiary account of the fox-devil lying in wait to trick and capture the unwary must have been told again and again in churches and by the clergy, and it is frequently incorporated into fox fable and the Beast Epic in all its forms. It will have been at the back of the mind of the author of that branch of the *Roman de Renart* which tells of the fox's funeral procession and in particular of his 'resurrection' when he seizes and makes off with the cock who was standing by the graveside. Later in that same story, Reynard and Chantecler fight a duel. The cock does so well that, in order not to be killed by him, Reynard feigns death and is left for dead close by the site of the duel. Along come Rohart the Crow and his wife Brune. The crow, convinced the fox is dead, lands on him and is about to take a peck when the 'dead' fox comes to life, bites off one of Rohart's thighs and makes off with it. Another version of this appears in the Dutch Beast Epics and comes through into Caxton's translation and all its derivatives and, as we will see, was illustrated by Wynkyn de Worde's artist [214].

Just as the Bestiary fox crept into the *Roman de Renart* and all the Beast Epics, so did Reynard make his way into the Bestiary. In Philippe de Thaun's Bestiary, written during the twelfth century, the fox is referred to only by his generic name (*goupil*). 'The fox signifies the Devil in this life. To people living carnally he shows pretence of death, till they are entered into evil, caught in his mouth. Then he takes them by a jump and slays and devours them, as the fox does the bird when he has allured it.' In Richard de Fournival's thirteenth-century Bestiary, the fox is first referred to by his generic name, then by the proper name 'Renart'. 'The fox's nature is such that, when he is hungry and cannot find anything to eat, he rolls over in red mud and lies down with his mouth wide open and tongue hanging out as if he had bled to death. Then magpies, who think he is dead, come hoping to eat his tongue. Then he snaps his jaws together, seizes them by the head and devours them... Oh, Reynard, how deceitfully you let your tongue hang out!' A later, anonymous thirteenth-century Bestiary uses only the proper name (*Renart*): 'Reynard is so full of trickery that there is no bird he cannot draw to him...' Clearly, as the reputation of Pierre de Saint Cloud's fox grew, the Bestiary fox became identified with him.

Having stressed above how fantastic some of the Bestiary descriptions are, it emerges that what Physiologus says about the fox simulating death to capture unwary birds is true and based on observation. This was proved in 1961 by the Russian naturalist F. Rossif who, with the help of the Moscow Pavlov Insitute, filmed a fox in the Caucasus as it feigned death and managed to catch a carrion crow. Four stills from his film show the fox settling down into a 'dead' position [156]; then, a little later, with a crow perched on its hind quarters [157]; then 'coming to life', the startled crow leaping into the air [158]; then caught in the fox's jaws [159]. Most Bestiary pictures show only the fox feigning death and a number of birds settled on or around him, sometimes pecking him. The picture in the twelfth-century Latin Bestiary kept in the University of Cambridge Library (MS Ii.4.26) is a fine early example of this [160].

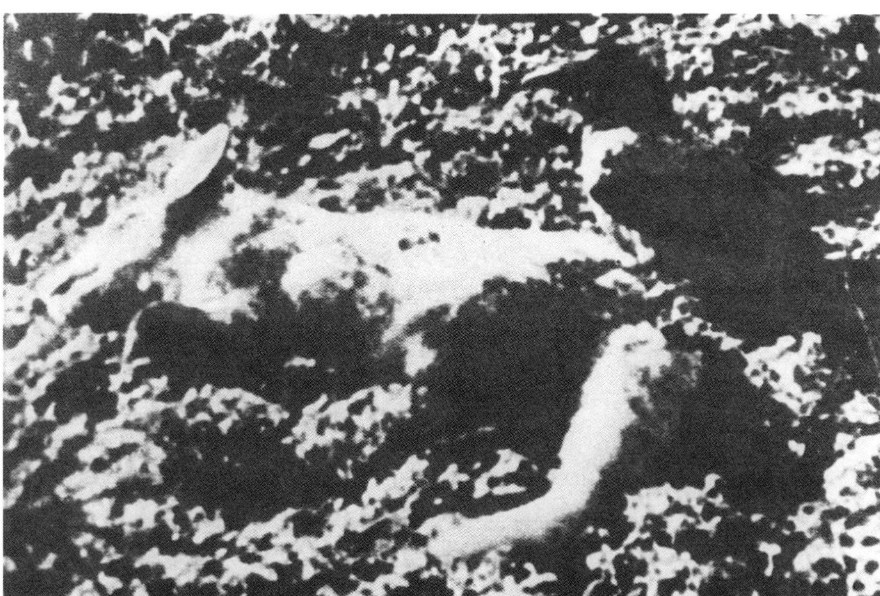

156-9 *These four pictures are stills from a Russian film made in 1961 by F. Rossif and published in Paris Match on 23rd November 1963. A fox prepares to feign death (156); a crow settles on the fox (157); the fox springs to life (158); and seizes the crow (159).*

160 A fox feigns death and crows come to feed on him. Cambridge, University Library, MS Ii. 4. 26; 12th C.

As if it were illustrating Richard de Fournival's text, one of the birds is indeed pecking at the fox's outstretched tongue. Sometimes two scenes are drawn, especially in the margins of non-bestiary manuscripts, as in the Queen Mary Psalter. The first depicts the fox feigning death and being pecked [161], the second his 'resurrection' and the capture of one of the birds which tried to feed on him [162]. What is especially interesting here is an echo of one of the oldest and most enduring Beast Epic tales, the one of the fox and the cock. In the first drawing, none of the four birds which peck at the fox is a cock, but in the second, one of them has in effect turned into a cock. In short, the artist began by depicting the Bestiary fox and ended by portraying Reynard making off with Chantecler. This is exactly parallel with Richard de Fournival's Bestiary which first refers to the fox by its generic name, then switches to his proper, Beast Epic name. The 'Reynardization' of the Bestiary fox was completed in a marginal painting in a French Froissart manuscript just as it was in the thirteenth-century anonymous Bestiary referred to above [163]. Here a fox looks up at a cock which seems to have been startled. Further down, the fox lies on his back, paws in the air, apparently feigning death. The cock peers at him and is about to peck at his belly. One guesses, returning to the upper part of

161-2 A fox feigns death and birds come to feed on him (161); he then leaps up and seizes a cock (162). The British Library, MS Roy. B VII, ff.99v and 100; early 14th C.

this drawing, that the cock is startled because the fox has sprung to life and is about to try and grab him. Chantecler the Cock is one of Reynard's most ancient and respected enemies, perhaps second in importance only to Ysengrin the Wolf, but nowhere in the *Roman de Renart* or in any other Beast Epic does the fox feign death in order to capture the cock. It seems that, in this Froissart manuscript, the artist has superimposed the image of Pierre de Saint Cloud's fox on to the traditional image of the Bestiary fox.

In medieval English art, I know of only two other examples of the Bestiary fox coupled with other images which may reveal a knowledge of some parts or variants of the Beast Epic. They are both from the late fourteenth century, both misericords, both in Cheshire. They are, however, dissimilar in detail, and the reasons for seeing in them links with the Beast Epic are

163 *A fox creeps up on a cock (top); then feigns death as the cock approaches. The British Library, MS Harley 4380, f.174v.*

also different. In St Mary's, Nantwich, we find a fox feigning death beneath some trees on which are perched two birds, now mutilated [164]. To the right, there are traces of a bird which had flown down and was pecking at the fox's tongue. It is on the supporters that we find details which suggest that the carver had in mind Reynard or one of his devilish cousins. On the left stands a fox in a Franciscan friar's habit with a dead hare (a relation of Couard's?) dangling from a stake held over his left shoulder, and a dead goose dangling by the neck from his left hand. We have seen how the fox-religious, and especially the fox-preacher, got hold of

164 *A fox feigns death beneath crows perched on tree branches; on either supporter is an upright, robed and armed fox. Nantwich, St Mary, misericord; c.1390. Kenneth Varty.*

unwary geese, but the hare is never captured by the fox in this guise. The most notorious occasion on which he takes a hare is at the beginning of his pilgrimage in the Dutch and English Beast Epic tradition, and the stake over his shoulder might just be a pilgrim's staff. On the right supporter the fox is again dressed as a Franciscan, but armed with a bow, a clear indication of his hypocrisy and intentions should he manage to gather together a congregation. In his left hand he clutches what looks like a money bag. This may contain the alms given to him after a sermon, for in St Mary's, Beverley, a goose is shown with a coin in its beak which it offers to the preacher [44]. And this money may well be the bribe he has ready for the lion, his sovereign-judge in the Beast Epic, before whom he may be brought to answer for his crimes. The readiness of the lion to be bribed by the fox is one of the basic characteristics of the Beast Epic, and it is depicted elsewhere in medieval English art, and nowhere more clearly than in the Smithfield Decretals [165]. Here a pilgrim-fox leaves a trail of dead geese and hares behind him. To the left, he is shriven by a pilgrim-lion to whom he offers a money-bag and, perhaps, one of his goose victims. Drawn about the same time that the Nantwich misericord was carved, these two representations of the fox who murders hares as well as geese, suggest a common oral or literary moralizing source. The other misericord is in Chester Cathedral [166]. Here we see a fox lying on his back, jaws gaping wide, tongue lolling out. Above, in the foliage of some trees, are three birds, two of them badly damaged. Three others have dared to descend and are pecking at the fox, two at his belly and one at his tongue. On the right supporter we see the

165 *A pilgrim-fox with booty approaches a pilgrim-lion, apparently to be shriven by him. The British Library, MS Roy. 10. E. IV, f.55; c.1335.*

fox, presumably moments later, killing one of the unwary birds beneath a tree. All these details speak of a typical Bestiary fox, but there are others which recall the Beast Epic. In the centre of the misericord, below the fox's back, is another scene on a smaller scale, as if it were in the distance. There are three or four holes leading into the fox's den, and at the furthest left we see a fox disappearing into it with a web-footed victim held by the neck. From the next hole to the right peep three more foxes: two little ones on either side of a big one. In several episodes in the *Roman de Renart* and other Beast Epics, Reynard takes prey home to his wife (Hermeline) and his sons (Percehaie, Malebranche and Renardel). This is the case in the seventeenth branch of the French epic, *Reynard's Death and Funeral Procession,* where he takes home Rohart the Rook's thigh. Then, another important detail, there is the lion on the left supporter (big shaggy mane, big clawed feet), crouching beneath some trees, and with his head and eyes turned towards the central scenes. This may be the Bestiary lion which symbolized vigilance, but he may also be the king of the animals before whom the fox will have to answer for his misdeeds, and in particular for this one which the lion has apparently witnessed.

In time, the Bestiary devil-fox gets 'Reynardized' in both texts and pictures, and representations of the fox, especially in churches and manuscripts of a religious nature, however Reynardian they may be, recall the hypocritical devil-fox of the Bestiary.

166 *A fox feigns death beneath trees whence birds fly down to feed on him. Chester Cathedral, misericord; c.1390. D.R. Maxted.*

Notes

BASIC TEXTS

For a translation of the *Physiologus* into English, see Carlill 1926, also Curley 1979. For an English translation of Cambridge University Library's twelfth-century Latin Bestiary, see White 1984. This also reproduces the illustrations. For an English translation of Richard de Fournival's Bestiary, see Beer 1984. Philippe de Thaun's Bestiary has not been translated into English; but for a critical edition, see Walberg 1930. The anonymous thirteenth-century Bestiary referred to is *Le Bestiaire d'Amour Rimé* edited by A. Thordstein, 1941. The translation is my own; the original is on pp. 105-106 of Thordstein's edition.

CRITICAL STUDIES AND SUPPLEMENTARY INFORMATION

Bestiaries flourished in medieval England in both Latin and English. A recent study and survey of them, paying particular attention to their illustration, is Hassig 1995. They also flourished in France, and the best general survey of Latin and French Bestiaries is the one by McCulloch 1960. Also useful and interesting for their influence on ecclesiastical and decorative art is Druce 1919. On the Bestiary fox's trick in the *Roman de Renart*, see Varty 1991, pp.344-60; also Combarieu du Grès 1991, pp. 159-69. For more information on the Russian film, see Bonheur 1963, pp. 94-97.

CHAPTER SEVEN

The Fox-Physician and the Lion-Patient

The part played by the fox in healing the sick lion is one of his most important. Some scholars think it is at the origin of the Beast Epic.

The earliest and best-known enactment of this role occurs in one of the fables attributed to Aesop, but the form in which we know it derives from Phaedrus (first century A.D.). He tells us that when the lion fell ill, all the animals came to see him except the fox. The wolf took it upon himself to point out the fox's absence, and argued that it showed disrespect for the king. The fox arrives, however, just as the wolf is concluding his speech, and the lion greets him with growls of anger. The fox is quick to excuse himself by arguing that he has been travelling far and wide in search of a remedy to cure the lion. Now he knows what the cure is: a freshly skinned, warm wolf's hide in which to wrap him. The wolf is promptly killed and skinned.

The fox physician next appears in the work of Paulus Diaconus during the eighth century. Here the bear plays the part given to the wolf in Phaedrus's fable. Again the fox appears late at the sick lion's court, and he uses the same argument to excuse himself, but this time it is, of course, a freshly flayed and warm bear's skin that will cure the lion. The bear is not killed, however, and is spared the fur on his head and feet. As the mutilated animal leaves the scene, the fox cruelly mocks him, asking him where he got his fine hat and boots from.

In the tenth century the fox physician reappears in the *Ecbasis Cuiusdam Captivi* (the Escape of a Certain Captive), apparently modelled on Paulus Diaconus's work. This time it is the wolf who is sick and asks all the animals to help him find a cure. The fox fails to answer the wolf's request, and all the other animals, prompted by the bear, decide he must be severely punished for what they consider to be criminal negligence. If they catch him, they will hang him. Because he feels sorry for the fox, the panther seeks him out and warns him of his impending fate. Forewarned, the fox turns up with what he claims is a marvellous ointment which will almost certainly cure the wolf, but to be quite sure of a complete recovery, the patient must be wrapped up in a bear's skin.

The fox physician enters the Beast Epic proper in the third book of the *Ysengrimus* (1149). In her summary of that book, Jill Mann writes: 'The lion, king of beasts, falls sick and summons the chief representatives of the animals to his court to give him counsel. Only Reynard stays away. Ysengrimus, pretending to be informed in medical matters, advises the king that he will be cured if he eats the flesh of a sheep and a goat. In response, the sheep and goat advise the king to send for Reynard again, and this time the fox obeys the summons. On arrival he pretends to have been away on a journey to Salerno' [then famous for its university's Faculty of Medicne] 'to seek medicine for the king, and produces six pairs of worn-out shoes (counting them out three times so that they appear more numerous) as evidence of his long journey. He recommends that the king, besides taking a potion of the medicinal herbs he has acquired, should undergo a sweating cure inside the skin of a three-and-a-half-year-old wolf. Ysengrimus' age then becomes the subject of some debate, but he is finally flayed by the bear, and his skin is used to cure the lion.' Perhaps one should add that the bear spares the wolf the fur of his head and feet. And, as the mutilated wolf leaves, the fox mocks him saying he can have his coat back if he cares to wait until the lion has sweated enough.

The longest and perhaps most entertaining story about the fox physician occurs in the tenth branch of the *Roman de Renart*, probably composed around 1185, and often retold through successive 'editions' in the fourteenth and fifteenth centuries. When Noble organizes a sumptuous feast, he expects all his chief barons to attend. Reynard, however, stubbornly stays away and even badly mistreats the king's envoys sent specially to bring him to court. Then Noble falls ill, and his doctors fail to cure him. Grimbert the Badger, who never misses a chance of helping his wayward cousin, suggests to Noble that he should ask Reynard if he could cure him (hoping, if he can, that he may be pardoned for his latest offences). Reynard likes the idea of playing physician to the king, realizing that, in addition to the pardon he may win, he may also manage to inflict some new injuries on his old enemies at court. He sets off. On the way he looks out for medicinal herbs and finds some, rather unexpectedly, in the pouch of a pilgrim fast asleep in a forest. One of these herbs is called *aliboron*, said to be an especially effective remedy for fevers. And the king, it is reported, is suffering from a fever. When Reynard reaches the court he says that he had failed to appear earlier only because he was busy travelling the world in search of a cure for the king. He claims to have been to Salerno, Rome and beyond. Noble allows Reynard to examine him. Then the fox declares that, to heal his king, he must first have a living wolf's skin, the chief nerve of a stag (thought to be in the antlers), a strip of stag's hide, and some cat's fur. The skin is to be used as a blanket, the stag's nerve as the chief ingredient in some medicine, the strip of hide to make into a belt to keep the wolf's skin tightly wrapped around the patient, the cat's fur to make some warm slippers for the lion. In spite of their protests, Ysengrin is skinned and Brichemer is polled. Tibert the Cat, however, makes a dash for freedom and escapes before anybody can lay a hand on him. Quite pleased by the harm done to Ysengrin and to Brichemer, Reynard says he will manage without the cat's fur. He administers his herbs to Noble, placing some *aliboron* in the lion's nose. Needless to say, he is cured and, in gratitude, makes the fox his chief adviser. Reynard returns in triumph to his wife and children, escorted by a hundred of Noble's troops.

The most interesting drawings depicting the fox physician in medieval English art are to be seen in the lower margins of a few pages in the Smithfield Decretals (c.1335). They are not easy to interpret chiefly because they do not illustrate any one extant literary version of the fox-physician story. The first of these drawings [167] depicts the fox being summoned, we suppose, to court by a hare, and this brings to mind the *Ysengrimus*. The hare proffers what we guess is the lion's summons, heavy with what looks like the royal seal, in his right hand; and, in his left, he carries a wand of office. A messenger's box or letter-pouch is fastened behind the hare's back to the belt around his waist. The fox carries a staff and also wears a belt from

167 *A fox is summoned by a hare. This and the next seven illustrations (up to and including 170) are from the British Library, MS Roy. 10. E. IV; c.1335. This is on f.53v.*

which dangle three pouches. The artist thus anticipates future events and already has the fox equipped for a journey to seek medicinal herbs, even before he has read or heard the message. The next stage in this graphic fox-physican story is when the fox approaches his patient who lies propped against a shrub, head swathed in bandages and slobbering over something between his jaws [168]. He looks more like a wolf than a lion, especially about the ears, paws and tail. The mane, characteristic of the lion (and much in evidence in other nearby drawings: see illustrations 170, 171 and 173), is also wanting, though it may be obscured by the bandages. It is possible that the artist was familiar with both the *Ysengrimus* and the *Ecbasis Cuiusdem Captivi* and that he now thinks of the sick wolf story rather than the sick lion story. There may even be a recollection of the *Roman de Renart* version of events because there we are told that Reynard came proudly before his patient and felt his pulse, which is just what the fox does here.

Attempts to pin these pictures down to one of the extant literary versions become even more difficult with the next picture [169] which vaguely recalls the *Ysengrimus*, for it shows the fox equipped in exactly the same way as when the hare came to fetch him, staff in hand and three pouches dangling from his belt [167]. He turns to bid either what we may guess to be a sarcastic farewell to the prostrate wolf (for in all the different literary versions of this tale, the fox taunts the flayed victim as it makes its exit), or he is is telling the wolf he will be back with

168 *A fox feels the pulse of a reclining wolf (?); f.54.*

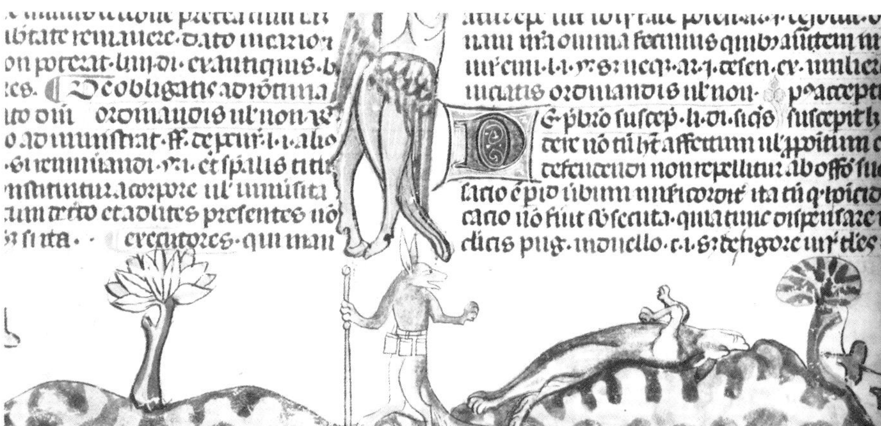

169 *A fox bids farewell to a prostrate wolf (?); f.54v.*

170 A bound fox is pulled by a wolf (?) before a seated lion; f.55v.

an effective treatment. In short, we seem to have three pictures which illustrate chiefly the sick wolf story, but with elements which could derive from the sick lion story as told in two different literary versions.

These three drawings of the fox being summoned to his patient, attending him, then leaving him, are separated from another fox-physican series by a couple of drawings on the next page (one in the upper margin, one in the lower) featuring the fox as a pilgrim.The second fox-physician sequence begins with a drawing [170] of the fox bound by a rope round his middle and being pulled by a wolf (?) before a seated lion. This fox looks very much like the one in the earlier series with the belt round his middle from which hang three pouches. He lacks only the staff. Is this the wolf bringing the fox by force before the lion? And is this the sick lion? He does not look particularly sick. And what is one to make of his outstretched paw? Today this would probably mean 'go away!', but in the Middle Ages, this was used to say 'welcome!', especially if the palm of the hand was exposed and the fingers stretched up (witness the welcome gesture made to the viewer in Botticelli's famous Primavera painting). We may guess that the wolf is treating the fox in a way of which the lion disapproves. The next drawing [171] depicts the fox-physician just as we saw him in the first sequence, but now he is alone with a very unhappy-looking lion, almost lying on the earth, cupping his chin in his hand,

171 *A fox offers the contents of a pouch to a sick lion; f.56.*

propping his elbow on the ground. Dr Fox seems to be offering the lion something from one of his half-open pouches, perhaps a herb, perhaps *aliboron*. The next drawing [172] shows two foxes skinning a wolf. Neither Phaedrus nor Paulus Diaconus says who skinned the scheming doctor's victim. In the *Ysengrimus* it is the bear. In the *Roman de Renart* several unnamed animals carry out this operation. But the fact that the whole of the wolf's skin is removed (only a part is removed in the *Ysengrimus*) may suggest the artist had in mind a version near to the *Roman de Renart*. Next, two foxes are shown wrapping the wolf's skin around the lion [173]. (In the *Roman de Renart*, Reynard does this alone.) One may guess that the depiction of two foxes in these last two drawings is meant to emphasize the fact that the fox is responsible for the flaying of the wolf. In short, this sequence of four pictures forms a version of the sick lion story with details which recall the way it is told in the French epic.

One more fox-physician picture in the Smithfield Decretals remains to be mentioned. It shows a fox holding a urinal in his right hand and a staff in his left [174]. This has to be a fox-physician. He stands before a seated, sick-looking wolf who holds his left paw out in an almost supplicating gesture. He needs the doctor's help. This is clearly inspired by the sick wolf story, but it is more than a hundred folios distant from the other pictures which illustrate it!

172 *Two foxes skin a prostrate wolf; f. 56v.*

173 *Two foxes wrap a wolfskin around a lion; f. 57.*

174 *A fox holds a urinal before a wolf (?); f.158v.*

There are, then, three groups of fox-physician pictures in the Smithfield Decretals. They begin with what turns out to be a sick wolf sequence beginning on the reverse side of folio 53, with the fox being summoned by the hare [167]; then, on folio 54, the fox feels his patient's pulse [168]; then, f.54 v., the fox takes leave of a prostrate wolf [169]. Dividing this sequence from one about the sick lion are two pictures on one page featuring the fox pilgrim. These are on f.55, where, in the upper margin, there is a fox pilgrim, staff in hand, scrip at hip, marked with a cross; then, in the lower margin, a fox pilgrim with loot, bowing before a lion pilgrim [165]. The sick lion sequence begins on f.55 v. where the fox is bound and pulled by a wolf (?) before the lion [170]; then, f.56 r, where the fox offers the contents of a pouch to the lion [171]; then, f.56 v. where two foxes skin a wolf [172]; then, finally, f.57, two foxes wrap a wolf-skin round a lion [173]. The third 'group' consists of the one, isolated fox physician before a sick wolf on f.158 v [174].

The only drawing I have found of the fox-physician apart from those in the Smithfield Decretals is in the Amesbury Psalter [175]. Here, in lower margin drawings added to the manuscript during the fourteenth century, Reynard, wearing a doctor's cap, is shown examining a urinal by Noble's bedside. The king is covered by a sheet and wears his crown, even as he lies in bed,

175 *A fox attends a lion in bed. Nearby a fox with a goose is pursued by a woman wielding a distaff. Oxford, All Souls College, MS 6, f.13; 13th C. with added 14th C. marginal drawings.*

176 *A fox attends a reclining lion. Gloucester Cathedral, misericord; c.1345. Kenneth Varty.*

awaiting Reynard's verdict. (In the *Roman de Renart* the first thing the fox does when he comes to treat Noble is to ask for a specimen of his urine. 'Fetch me a urinal,' says Reynard, 'and I will see the nature of his illness.' The urinal is brought to him, Noble sits up and fills it more than half full. Reynard says: 'Well done!' Then he takes it and goes towards the sun. He lifts the urinal up high and looks at it very carefully. He turns it round and round...') It might be thought that the Amesbury Psalter artist draws an ape and not a fox tending the lion, but a comparison with the fox to the left (pursued by a woman wielding a distaff) and the ape to the right (wrestling with a lion), confirms that this is the fox-physician in spite of his ears and the absence of a brush. The presence of two central scenes from Beast Epic tales, side by side, suggests the artist may have been familiar with the epic.

In addition to these drawings, I have found two carvings depicting the fox-physician examining a sick lion. One of these is on a misericord in Gloucester Cathedral [176] dated about 1345. Lying on the ground below stylized foliage is a lion, his head raised towards an erect fox who holds a urinal up to the light, away from the lion. This is in the fox's left hand. With his right, he reaches out to the lion's forehead. The other carving is in the Chapter House of Salisbury Cathedral [177]. Although it was made in the mid-nineteenth century, it is a copy of a thirteenth-century carving which it then replaced. There is in fact a series of fox scenes running round the base of the central column of the Chapter House which, worn and weakened, had to be replaced. The base of the old, medieval column is still to be seen in the southwest corner of the cloisters. A century of exposure to the open air has caused the almost complete erosion of the scenes with which it was decorated, though here and there bits of foxes may be recognized.

177 *A fox attends a lion in bed. Salisbury Cathedral Chapter House, central pillar, frieze at the base; a 19th C. (?) replica of an early medieval original. Kenneth Varty.*

As we enter the Chapter house, we find facing us (west) a sitting fox on either side of a stylized vine. It is to the east that one sees the fox, presumably in the role of physician, at the foot of the lion's bed. The crowned lion's head rests on a pillow and he looks mournfully at us, his right forepaw hanging down below his chin. His body is entirely covered by a sheet. The fox stands at the foot of the bed with his left arm raised. He probably held a urinal up to the light, but sadly whatever was shown above the elbow is now missing, as is the fox's snout.

Although there are not all that many drawings and sculptures of the fox-physician in medieval England, there are even fewer on the Continent. The chief examples are to be found in a late twelfth-century stone frieze in the crypt of Basel Cathedral [178] and in a few woodcuts in a late fifteenth-century German blockbook. The former is by far the most intriguing, and the scene of the fox tending the lion lying in bed makes an interesting comparison with the Salisbury Cathedral carving chiefly because it is the first of three related scenes. After the bedroom scene there is one which shows the fox bathing the lion [179], then one of the lion skinning the wolf himself. One wonders if, in the now lost Salisbury Cathedral series of fox-centred scenes, there were more episodes of the sick lion story, and if they too would have shown the lion being bathed and then skinning the wolf. None of this is evident in the modern

178-9 A fox attends a lion in bed (178); then helps the lion to take a bath (179). Basel Cathedral, crypt, stone frieze; c.1190. Kenneth Varty.

replacements. As the bathing of the lion as part of his cure takes place only in the Alsacian German Beast Epic by Heinrich der Glichezaere in the late twelfth century, it is highly unlikely that this scene would have been represented in Salisbury.

Christened Reynardine, a son of Reynard's, the fox-physician reappears in English literature in 1684, in the *Shifts of Reynardine*, a continuation of the Anglo-Flemish epic. In this story, Reynardine becomes a doctor after his meeting with Zani the Ape. Iconographically, much hangs on their meeting and on Zani's advice: 'Cosin, if you think you can please Fools, I would advise you to turn Doctor.' 'Well, Cosin,' said the Fox, 'jest not, as unlikely things have come to pass. I have read over Gallen's *Method of Physick* more than once; and am not a litttle Skilled in the use of Simples by him prescribed. Also I know how to prepare and administer Emeticks, Cathartícks, Diaphoreticks, and Diareticks.' 'What hard Names are these, Cosin?' said the Ape. 'These,' quoth the Fox, 'are only Terms of Art, used by Physicians, that their Patients may admire what they cannot understand. A few Cramp words spoken by a Doctor always creates Admiration in the Vulgar. For words or things commonly known are not regarded.' 'You say well, Cosin,' said the Ape. 'I see nothing to the contrary, but that you may very laudably practise Physick: but without some notable Disguise that cannot be done with Safety: Besides (I understand the temper of our Country Folk) it will be also necessary that you present yourself as a great Traveller and Stranger, come from Forrain Parts; otherwise (Doctor Simpleton having got so great repute) you will hardly ever come to be Famous or Eminent. And a Doctor without Fame (how Skilful soever) shall never get anything to purpose.' 'All this is true,' said the Fox. 'I can easily play the Counterfeit any way that shall be needful; but I have no Disguise to wear, nor know I how to procure any.' 'Leave that to me,' quoth the Ape, 'for I have all things necessary for the purpose. It is not long since I, with my Companions, going out upon a Frolick, found a Pedlar asleep, with his Pack lying by him. This Pack we took away, and as equally as we could, divided all the Wares amongst us. By this means I am stored with Razors, Lancets, Scissors, Combs, etc., by the help of which I doubt not but to make you a complete Disguise...'

There can be little doubt that some scenes in the Smithfield Decretals illustrate the time when a distant ancestor of Zani's was 'out upon a Frolick' with his companions and found a pedlar asleep 'with his Pack lying by him'. These scenes begin in the lower margin of f.149 [180] where a pedlar is shown falling asleep at the foot of a tree and two apes, a little apprehensive,

180 *A pedlar falls asleep, and monkeys steal his pack. This and the next four illustrations (up to 184) are from the British Library, MS Roy. 10. E. IV; c.1335. This is on f.149.*

181 Monkeys begin to steal from the contents of the sleeping pedlar's pack; f. 149v.

are in the process of seizing his pack. Over the page [181] the pedlar has slumped forward as he falls more deeply asleep, and the two apes are now emptying the pack. On the next page [182] we see four apes wearing or displaying some of the wares stolen from the pack, and so it goes on across the lower margins of the next two sides [183 & 184] where the apes play with, display or wear gloves, a hat, a towel, a belt, a dish, bandages, a cowl and a jug. Carvings of apes stealing from a sleeping pedlar are to be found in widely separated parts of the country, all dating from the fifteenth or sixteenth centuries. For example, they may be seen on misericords in St George's Chapel, Windsor, Manchester Cathedral, Bristol Cathedral, and Beverley Minster, as well as on a bench-end poppyhead in St Nicholas's, Halton Holegate. Although they differ in minor details, they are all very similar to each other. Some show the pedlar asleep, others awake; some show him treated with circumspection, others with brute force. The position of the pack is different every time, and so is the number of apes involved. Similar drawings and carvings are to be found on the Continent, and a detailed study of them shows that they all tell much the same story: a pedlar has fallen asleep at the foot of a tree, his pack by his side. A number of apes disport themselves in the tree and on the ground. They open the pack, examine and try on some of its contents. Usually a few of the simians are busy 'unpacking' the pedlar too; they pull off his boots, unbutton his trousers, examine his hair for vermin. Even taking into account all the Continental versions of this episode, the earliest iconographic

182 Four monkeys with items stolen from the pedlar's pack; f.150.

accounts remain those in the Smithfield Decretals. The leading expert on apes and ape lore, H.W.Janson, does not think that they are illustrations of an episode in a lost story; nor does he think the *Shifts* existed in an earlier oral or written form now lost. On the contrary, he thinks the author of the *Shifts* knew this iconographic theme and merely incorporated it in his story. Other scholars, Francis Bond and Mary Anderson, for example, both think there was an earlier, medieval version of the *Shifts*. What they all seem to have missed is that there was a literary model for at least the incident of the robbing of the pedlar, and that this model is in the tenth branch of the *Roman de Renart*, the story of the fox-physician.

Here, in translation, is what happens when Reynard unexpectedly comes across a sleeping pilgrim as he made his way to court, looking for medicinal herbs. 'Reynard...left the heath for the forest, which he preferred. In the forest, beneath a pine tree, he found a sleeping pilgrim. This pilgrim who lay there had an expensive pouch (*aumonière*) which was laced to his belt. Reynard quickly gets down from his mount and takes the pouch without him [the pilgrim] ever noticing anything. Reynard...opens it and finds in it a herb which is good for teeth, and he finds plenty of other herbs which will cure the king. He finds *aliboron* in it, which many people have tried out and which is good for raising the temperature and casting fevers out of the body.

183 *Three monkeys with stolen property; f. 150v.*

184 *Four monkeys with stolen property; f. 151.*

Reynard is most pleased by the pilgrim's hood (*esclavine*) which the man had under his head. He takes it...and promptly puts it on. Then he mounts his horse and rides quickly through the forest...'

If we return to the Smithfield Decretals, folio 149 recto and verso [180 & 181], we see that the pilgrim or pedlar, whichever he is, wears an *esclavine*, that is, a hood which covers both head and shoulders. Although he is not shown wearing an *aumonière*, that is, a pouch, the ape on the extreme right of f.149 v. [181] has one in his possession, laced to a belt. Also, the ape on the extreme right of f.151 r. [184] wears an *esclavine*. Obviously, these tiny details do not prove any link between these Smithfield Decretals scenes and the *Roman de Renart*, but added to the basic situation, the possibility if not the probability of a link, however distant, cannot be dismissed. In the *Roman de Renart* Reynard steals from a man sleeping beneath a tree material which will prove vital to him in his role as physician. In the *Shifts* and in the drawings and carvings which predate them, the ape provides the fox with equipment vital to him in his role as physician by stealing it from a man sleeping beneath a tree. Somewhere along the line, the age-old alliance between the fox and the ape (an alliance to be treated in the next chapter) produced a variant account of the way the fox-physician came by his dress and equipment, a variant in which the ape plays part of the fox-doctor's role.

Notes

BASIC TEXTS

For Phaedrus's fable in English translation, see Handford 1954, p. 28. For the text of Paulus Diaconus, see Neff 1908, pp. 191-197. For both the text and an English translation of *Ecbasis Cuiusdam Captivi*, see Zeydel 1966 where the fox-physician's role is played between lines 392 and 1097. For both the text and an English translation of the *Ysengrimus*, see Mann 1987 where the sick lion story is on pp. 300-363. For an English translation of *Renart Médecin* (Branch IV of the *Roman de Renart*), see Owen 1994, pp.178-201. For the relevant part of Heinrich der Glichezaere's text in a modern French translation, see Buschinger & Pastré 1984, pp. 61-64, lines 1965-2052.

CRITICAL STUDIES

On the foxes in the Smithfield Decretals, see Varty 1963, pp. 348-54. On the sick lion in the Basel Cathedral frieze and in the German Blockbook, see Field 1974. On apes and ape lore, see Janson 1952.

SUPPORTING INFORMATION

Other pictures of carvings showing apes stealing from a sleeping pedlar are to be seen in Varty 1967, illustrations 104-110. Details of their exact whereabouts are given in the relevant index of that book.

CHAPTER EIGHT

The Fox and the Ape

If, in the *Shifts of Reynardine*, the alliance between the fox and the ape eventually ends in recrimination and discord, their collaboration in mischievous adventures goes a long way back in Beast Epic time. In one of the earliest branches of the French epic, the one called *Le Serment de Renart* (Reynard's Solemn Oath), probably composed in the 1170s, the animal barons debate whether to put Reynard on trial. During the debate one of the two who speak up for the fox is the ape, Cointereau. 'The Devil take those who don't stick to the facts,' he says. To this Brun the Bear retorts: 'Aren't you out of your senses to take Reynard's side? Between the two of you there's a close understanding; you've thought up many a trick together...' However, no story about their collaboration has come down to us till much later. There is of course the possibility that there were earlier stories about them and that they have been lost. In this connection there is the evidence of Philippe de Novare's writings. Philippe composed a history of the wars fought from 1228 to 1243 in the eastern Mediterranean between the Emperor Frederick II and Jean d'Ibelin, lord of Cyprus and Beyrouth. As mentioned in the Introduction, Philippe took part in these wars on the side of Jean d'Ibelin, and he composed some satirical songs between 1229 and 1233 in which he gave to his enemies the names and characteristics of the fox, the badger and the ape, from the *Roman de Renart*. When the wars were over, he wrote his *Mémoires* (1258) which contain a long, satirical tale modelled on the branches of the *Roman de Renart*. In it he casts his lord, Jean d'Ibelin, in the role of Isengrin the Wolf, and himself as Chantecler the Cock. Other leaders on the Ibelin side were cast as Brun the Bear and Tibert the Cat, all of whom were, at some point or other in the French epic, victims of the fox. His chief enemies, Frederick's lieutenants in Cyprus, were cast as Reynard, Grimbert the Badger and Cointereau the Ape. He explains this grouping of the enemy leaders by saying that the badger and the ape are allied with the fox in the *Roman de Renart* itself ('celes bestes sont de la partie de Renart au roumans meisme'). This argument makes one think that Cointereau may have played a more prominent role in the French epic than he does in the branches that have come down to us.

An important relationship between the fox and the ape develops in that continuation of the French epic called *Renart le Nouvel* (1289), a largely allegorical story about the struggle between virtue (Noble) and vice (Reynard). To begin with, Cointereau is on Noble's side, but during the siege of Reynard's castle, numerous animals desert from Noble's army, among them Cointereau. He and his son Martin are banished to Norway as a punishment for desertion, so they rally behind Reynard's banner when he comes to that country. Cointereau proves himself to be a particularly valuable ally because he succeeds in convincing Reynard's high-ranking prisoners that they should join forces with the fox.

In an anonymous Latin tale of Italian origin from the late thirteenth or early fourteenth century, the ape is portrayed as Reynard's chamberlain, serving his guests with hens, cocks, pigeons and geese. Then, in Jean de Condé's *Renart, Mestres de l'Ostel le Roy* (Reynard, Master of the King's Household) from the late fourteenth century, the fox enjoys the lion's complete confidence and appoints whom he will to important posts. Monnequin, the elder son of Martin the Ape, is made Noble's secretary and treasurer, and Martinet, the ape's younger son, is appointed court minstrel. Martin himself is depicted as Reynard's close friend, and nothing is done at this court without their common consent.

Tales like these could well have made their mark in courtly, administrative and learned quarters in England where French was still understood well into the fourteenth century, and Latin throughout the entire Middle Ages. It is in the Dutch versions of the Beast Epic (*Reinaert de Vos* in the thirteenth century and *Reinaerts Historie* in the fourteenth century) that the ape plays an active and at times important role on Reynard's side, and this was to become well known in England after Caxton's 1481 translation from a Dutch text. Though Dutch was not at all well known in England at this time, Flemish craftsmen played a role in the carving of some church choir-stalls and in the making of some stained-glass windows, especially in East Anglia and other regions bordering on the Channel and the North Sea. Their collective influence and conversation, especially about the subjects they carved in wood, including Reynardian motifs, may have left its mark. In Caxton's *Historye of Reynart the Foxe*, it is Reynard's aunt, Rukenaw the Ape, who twice plays an important part on Reynard's side. Just as Cointereau did in the French epic when the tide was running against Reynard as his peers debated his fate, so Rukenaw does in Caxton's text: 'Tho was Reynard so sore afraid that he wist not what to say. He was at his wit's end and looked about him piteously and saw many of his kin and allies that heard all this, but nought they said...no man proffered him hand nor foot to help him. The king said, "Thou subtle fellow and false shrew, why speak you not? Now dumb? " The fox stood in great dread and sighed sore that all heard him. But the wolf and the bear were glad thereof. Dame Rukenaw the she-ape, Reynard's aunt, was not well pleased. She was great with the queen and well beloved. It happed well for the fox that she was there...She said, "My lord the king, you ought not to be angry when you sit in judgment for that becomes not your noblesse. A man that sits in judgment ought to put from him all wroth and anger...every man that stands here would well bethink him what he has done and bedriven in his days. He should the better have patience and pity on Reynard. Let every man know himself. That is my counsel..."

Later in Caxton's *Historye* we are told how Reynard has to fight Isengrin in single combat to determine the right and wrong of their quarrel. If the fox wins, it is largely thanks to the advice given him by his aunt the ape: 'The she-ape said to the fox, "Reynard, nephew, see that you take heed in your battle..." Dame Rukenaw...thought always on his profit and fordeal. And she did all his hair from the head to the tail be shorn off smooth and she annointed all his body with oil of olive. And then was his body also glat and slipper that the wolf should not have no hold on him and he was round and fat also on his body. And she said to him, "Dear cousin, you must now drink much that tomorrow you may the better make your urine, but you shall hold it in till you come to the field. And when need is and time, so shall you piss full your row tail and smite the wolf therewith in his beard. And if you might hit him therewith in his eyes, then shall you beneme him his sight. That should much hinder him...let him spring and run after you and run tofore whereas most dust is and stir it with your feet that it may flee in his eyes and that shall much hinder his sight. And while he rubs his eyes, take your advantage and smite and bite him there as you may most hurt him. And always to hit him with your tail full of piss in his visage...".'

Rukenaw appears prominently in some of the woodcuts made to illustrate Wynkyn de Worde's picture cycle. She is shown taking Reynard's side before the king and his court in illustration 217; she stands by Reynard's side when the king declares him free of all the charges that had been brought against him, just before the wolf challenges him [223]; and she watches from the sidelines as he fights his duel with the wolf [225]. An ape is prominent in illustration 218 when Reynard tells how well he was once supported by an ape uncle; and they share in Reynard's victory celebrations and in his triumphal return home at the end of the story [227]. Much earlier in the cycle, his ape friends are shown creeping away when they think the day is lost [81], but they return to the forefront when things are going well for him, and they help bind the bear [86], then flay him and the wolf [87].

Two late fifteenth-century carvings in St George's Chapel, Windsor, could depict Rukenaw preparing Reynard for his duel with the wolf. On the left supporter of a misericord, we see a seated fox holding a bowl between his hands [185]. A cloth is draped around his shoulders.

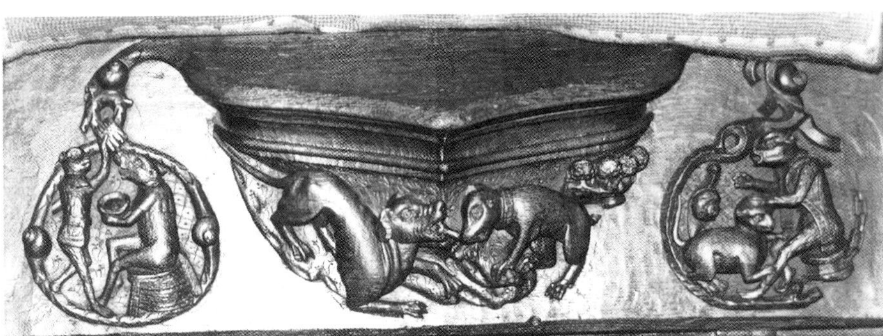

185 *An ape shaves a fox. Windsor Castle, St George's Chapel, misericord supporter; c.1480. Kenneth Varty.*

An ape stands before him and appears to be shaving or combing him. (A similar scene is carved on a bench end in All Saints, Branston.) The right supporter of another misericord in St George's Chapel shows an ape pouring liquid down the throat of a fox lying on his back. As Rukenaw stresses to Reynard, the smoothness of his body and the fullness of his bladder will be important factors in his battle strategy! There are other fox and ape carvings here which seem to illustrate a story, in particular the one decorating a spandrel of a desk front. Here, to the left, is an erect fox with a heart-shaped pouch hanging round his neck. He stands in front of a seated ape which holds a bowl into which both animals put their hands. To the right a fox holding a staff and carrying a pack on his back stands in front of a seated ape. Both scenes seem to be set in a forest.

The theme of the fox appearing before the lion to answer for his crimes has been touched on in the penultimate paragraph of Chapter Six and illustration 165. In St Peter's, Tilton-on-the-Hill, carved round a fourteenth-century capital, we find a procession of animals comprising a badger, an ape, a fox with a goose, and a crowned lion [186-188]. The fact that the lion wears a crown suggests a Beast Epic influence. This could well be a representation of the fox appearing before his lord and judge to answer for the crime he has just committed, accompanied and supported by his two principal allies, the fox and the badger. The ape wears a collar, chain and ball probably because this is how apes were often seen, kept in tow by travelling entertainers. Other carvings bear witness to this. For example, the carving on the mid-fourteenth-century capital in All Saints, Oakham, which depicts the fox making off with a goose and being chased by a woman wielding her distaff [5] also contains an ape wearing a collar, chain and ball [189].

186-8 A badger follows an ape wearing a chain and ball (186).

The chained ape follows a fox with a goose flung over his back (187); a crowned lion awaits the fox's arrival before him (188). Tilton-on-the-Hill, St Peter, capital; 14th-century. Kenneth Varty.

189 *An ape with a collar, chain and ball back-to-back with a woman. Oakham, All Saints, capital; 14th C. Kenneth Varty.*

This makes for an interesting comparison with the decoration of an early fourteenth-century capital in St Helen's, West Keal. First we see a fox making off with a goose followed by an ape wearing a collar, chain and ball [190]. In front of the fox is an owl, while further round the capital, diametrically opposite the fox, is a lion biting a serpent with a devilish-looking head [191]. Used as symbols, the goose seems to have stood for the unwary soul; both the fox and the ape stood for the Devil; the owl for stupidity, moral blindness and even death; the lion for Christian virtue; and the serpent for Satanic vice. The symbolic, moralizing purpose of these West Keal carvings is all too apparent, and it is difficult to imagine that they could tell a story (though informed clergy might draw on the relevant Bestiary texts). On the other hand, the Tilton-on-the-Hill and Oakham carvings do tell a story which, of course, like most fables, had its moral.

The medical profession was burlesqued not only in vulpine but also in simian terms. There are numerous examples, beginning with the mid-fourteenth century, of ape physicians inspecting urinals or applying ointments. In the parish church at Knowle, the ape is even depicted as a Professor of Medicine lecturing to four students [192]. Occasionally, the ape is shown in consultation with or attending to the fox. For example, in St Botolph's, Boston, a seated ape,

190-1 *An ape and a fox with a goose approach an owl (190); a lion bites a serpent (191). West Keal, St Helen, capital; early 14th C. Kenneth Varty.*

192 *An ape-physician seems to be giving a lecture on the contents of a flask. Knowle Parish Church, misericord; probably early 16th C. J.C.D. Smith.*

doctor's hood thrown back, inspects a urinal which, presumably, the worried-looking fox facing him has given to him [193]. The fox holds a bucket which may well contain a specimen of his droppings. Behind the ape is either another fox who, as he leaves the surgery, looks back quite happily at him; or it is the same fox a few minutes later, after receiving treatment and advice. In St Mary's, Beverley, we see a fox pierced through the middle by an arrow while the bowman runs up behind him [194]. In front of the wounded fox sits an ape who inspects (rather irrelevantly, in these circumstances, one would have thought) a urinal. The fox holds a bag which probably serves the same purpose as the basket in St Botolph's, Boston, but it may be a money-bag containing the physician's fee. In Beverley Minster the central scene of a misericord shows a fox hiding in a cavity as a bowman and his hounds descend upon him [195]. To the right, an ape tends a fox lying in bed. Perhaps we are meant to understand that the fox of the central scene escaped from his pursuers but was wounded and, once home, called on his ape physician. Quite a lot of Reynard's adventures as told by narrative poets end with him being badly wounded in his last-minute escape from trouble, and in need of medical attention and nursing. But this is usually provided by his wife and immediate family, never by apes.

193 *An ape-physician seems to be giving a lecture to two foxes. Boston, St Botolph, misericord; c.1390. D.R. Maxted.*

194 *A wounded fox consults an ape-physician. Beverley, St Mary, misericord; c.1445. D.R. Maxted.*

195 *An ape tends a fox in bed. Beverley Minster, misericord right supporter; c.1520. J.C.D. Smith.*

One is struck by the frequency with which, in churches, carvings of foxes have as neighbours carvings of apes. This happens, for example, at Beverley, Bloxham, Bristol, Fawsley, Halton Holegate, Manchester, Winchester, and Windsor. No doubt they called to mind related proverbs, fables, anecdotes or symbols.

Notes

BASIC TEXTS

For a translation into English of Branch Va of the *Roman de Renart* (*Le Serment*, 'Reynard's Solemn Oath'), see Owen 1994, pp. 92-106 (here called 'The Lawsuits of Isengrin and Bruin the Bear'). However, the translated quotation from this branch is my own and based on Roques 1954, lines 6606-6612, p. 33. There are no translations into English of any of the other basic texts mentioned in this chapter. For Philippe de Novare's *Mémoires*, see Köhler 1913; for *Renart le Nouvel*, see Roussel 1961; for *Renart Mestres de l'Ostel le Roy*, see Chabaille 1835, pp. 19-30; for the text of the thirteenth-century anonymous Latin tale, see Flinn 1963, pp. 693-95.

SUPPLEMENTARY INFORMATION

On Flemish craftsmen and the influence of Flanders, see Stone 1955, pp. 209-29; Rickert 1954, pp. 203-23; and Tracy 1990, p. 47.

CHAPTER NINE

The Fabulists' Fox

If there is one literary genre that was known at every level of medieval society, it was surely the fable; along with the shortest of literary genres, the proverb. Fables were studied in schools (such as they were), mostly in Latin, more as a language than as a literary exercise, by the few who were fortunate enough to receive an education. They were often recited as entertainent with a worldly-wise lesson for both the literate and the illiterate who would remember them and repeat them more or less well in one form or another. It is therefore not at all surprising if the authors of Beast Epics and animal tales often drew into their compositions some of the best-loved fables and proverbs. At the heart of the *Ysengrimus* is the fable of the sick lion, a fable that recurs in subsequent Beast Epics. In the earliest part of the first *Roman de Renart* is the fable of the fox, the crow and its cheese, brilliantly turned into a mini-mock-epic. Pictures of fables featuring the fox are to be found in almost every medium and in every culture throughout the Middle Ages. Are they all independent fable-pictures, or have they been 'Reynardized'? Did they conjure up in the mind of the beholder episodes in the Beast Epic, or simply an Aesopian fable with a worldly-wise moral? Or perhaps both? Does the use of proper names for some of the animals in both medieval French and English fable collections provide us with a few clues?

The history of the fable is especially complex. The following very short summary glosses over that complexity and many a thorny problem, and serves only as an introduction to this short essay on fable illustrations in medieval England and their links, if any, with Reynardian matter.

Most fables told in the Middle Ages go back to Phaedrus, who spent most of his life at Rome in the reign of the Emperor Augustus. Another important source of the medieval fable is the Roman Avianus who is generally thought to have flourished c.400 A.D. Paraphrases of the fables of Phaedrus and Avianus began to be made from the fifth century, and it was chiefly from them that medieval versions and anthologies derived. Medieval English collections were largely based on French fable collections which were called *Isopets*, a corruption of the name Aesop, thought to be the inventor of this literary form.

After the creation of the *Roman de Renart,* the proper names of some of its protagonists began to appear in fables, but the process was a slow one, as Flinn (1963, 125-131) has shown. For example, in the thirteenth-century collection of fables known as the *Isopet de Chartres,* there is a fable about the fox and the eagle in which the fox is always referred to by his generic name, *goupil* (Bastin 1929, I, 140-4). The same fable re-occurs in the fourteenth-century *Isopet II*, derived from exactly the same Latin source as the *Isopet de Chartres*, that is, from the *Novus*

Aesopus by Alexander Neckam, and in it the fox is referred to by his generic name, *goupil*, both in the title and in his first two appearances in the text; but in his third appearance he is *Renart li goupil*, Reynard the Fox (ibid. 74-5). The *Isopet II* also contains the well-known fable of the fox and the crow with the cheese, and in this fable, every time he is named (three times), the fox is called *Renart* (ibid. 83-4).

Turning to the thirteenth-century *Isopet de Lyon* and the fourteenth-century *Isopet I*, both derived, ultimately, from a common source (namely, the verse *Romulus* attributed to Walter the Englishman), we find a yet more marked influence of the *Roman de Renart*. In the earlier collection there are four fables about the fox: the fox and the eagle, the fox and the crow, the fox and the stork, and the fox and the monkey (Bastin, II, 108, 110-11, 136-8, & 181-2, respectively). In every case the name *vulpil* (= *goupil*) is used in the title, but *Renart* is used in the text. In the later collection there are six fables about the fox, and in all six, both in the title and in the text, he is called *Renart* (ibid. 222-7, 256-7, 265-7, 280-3, & 303-4). What is more, we also meet here a wolf called Ysangrin, a dog called Rouneaus (= Roonel, Roenel), a crow called Tiecelin, and a stag called Brichemer, all proper names made famous by the *Roman de Renart*.

The presence of some of these proper names in the works of some fabulists writing in England in the thirteenth and fourteenth centuries suggests, as already mentioned in the Introduction, that some parts of the French epic were known in England, and that the 'Reynardization' of fables was also taking place here. Mossé (1951, 70-84) is convincing on this topic. The two main fabulists referred to are (also mentioned in the Introduction), Odo of Cheriton who wrote in Latin and Nicholas Bozon who wrote in Anglo-Norman, so they were writing for the educated minority which would include the aristocracy of both State and Church. Even so, Odo (himself an aristocrat) may well have retold some of his fables in English because, in his *exempla*, English phrases and proverbs occasionally interrupt the Latin. It is he who, in three of his fables (Mossé 1951, 30-31) writes of a fox which he calls Reinardus here and Renaldus there who encounters a cock called Chantecler, a cat called Tebergus and a wolf called Ysingrinus, names most probably inspired by Pierre de Saint Cloud's Branch II of the *Roman de Renart*. Nicholas Bozon, a Franciscan monk, re-tells, much modified, many of the fables formerly told by Odo and occasionally uses the Anglo-Norman forms of the animals' proper names (Toulmin-Smith 1889, 184).

The Lion cured by the Fox

Perhaps the most important fable where the Beast Epic is concerned is the one about the sick lion who is cured by the fox at the expense of his chief enemy, whose skin, to be wrapped round the lion, is prescribed as part of the cure. Although this was well known over a wide area for a very long time, very few carvings or drawings of its central scenes have come down to us. And most of the ones that have are English. These are treated in Chapter Seven, 'The Fox-Physician and the Lion-Patient' [167-177]. Of these, only the drawings in the Smithfield Decretals seem to be inspired by the Beast Epic rather than by an independent non-Reynardized fable.

It has to be admitted at the outset that there are surprisingly few representations of fables in medieval English art (other than in illustrated books of fables) and that (apart from the fable of the sick lion) there are no drawings or carvings of fables which were drawn into the Beast Epic which depict, unambiguously, scenes from it. This generalisation is perhaps best illustrated with representations of the fable of the fox and the crow.

The Fox and the Crow

The story of Reynard's encounter with Tiecelin the Crow forms the fourth major episode in Pierre de Saint Cloud's poem, Branch II. After brushes with the cock, titmouse and cat, Reynard confronts the crow with his cheese, and the well-known fable is expanded into nearly two hundred lines of octosyllabic verse. Its roots may be traced to the account attributed to Aesop, but Pierre de Saint Cloud's immediate source may have been the fable by Marie de France (Foulet 1914, 158), writing in England. It must have been very popular in its mock epic form, at least in France, for it was soon Reynardized. In the *Isopet de Chartres* there is no obvious influence of the *Roman de Renart*, but in the *Isopet II* the fox is Renart, though the crow is referred to only by the generic term *corbel* (Bastin 1929, 83-4). In the *Isopet de Lyon* the fox is even Don Reynard (*Dam Renar*), while the crow remains the impersonal *corbel* (ibid. II, 110-11). In the *Isopet I* both animals have their proper name: the crow is even Sire Tiercelin (ibid. 225-7).

I know of just two possible medieval representations of this fable in England from the period of the Beast Epic. There is a drawing in the twelfth-century Dover Bible (Appendix 1, 7); and there is a rare piece of fifteenth-century stained glass in Clipsham Parish Church which shows a large bird on a token branch being approached by what could well be a fox [267]. Sadly the rear quarters of this animal are missing, so the characteristic, defining brush is not to be seen. Nor is there any sign of a cheese. There are, of course, the pre-*Roman-de-Renart* embroidered scenes in the margins of the Bayeux Tapestry which may, perhaps, be called 'English'. The only other English representations of some interest are, firstly, the nineteenth-century misericord in Chester Cathedral which, at first sight, looks medieval. Here we see two foxes below a tree in which is perched a crow holding a little bit of cheese in its beak [196]. This may copy a medieval model in which a sequence of two scenes are depicted in one and the same frame. The fox to the left, resting below the tree, may be Reynard at the beginning of the Pierre de Saint Cloud poem; and the fox to the right, sitting up, may be him a few minutes later when he has become aware of Tiecelin's presence. We know that a few misericords in Chester Cathedral were replaced during nineteenth-century restoration because they were then considered indecent and unfit to be in a holy place. As two other Chester Cathedral misericord fox-scenes are also replacements, it does seem possible that the carver had an illustrated fox-story to hand, possibly even an early one. (It is interesting to note that the miniature which illustrates this fable-based episode in the *Roman de Renart* is itself very fable-like [197]; that is to say, includes no detail which makes it distinctively of the Beast Epic.) The other, also modern, interesting representation of this fable is to be found in the spandrels of a choir-stall bench end in Somerton Parish Church [268]. It is beautifully designed and executed, with the crow in tree branches to the left, and the fox at ground level to the right.

196 *The fable of the fox and the crow with some cheese. Chester Cathedral, misericord; 19th C. D.R. Maxted.*

197 *Renart and Tiécelin with some cheese. The Bodleian Library, MS Douce 360, f.29v; 1338.*

The Fox and the Grapes

The Aesopian fable of the fox and the sour grapes also finds its way into Branch XI of the *Roman de Renart*, usually dated c.1200. This is one of the briefest of the Aesopian fables: a hungry fox tries to reach some clusters of grapes, but they are too high for him to reach, so he goes away comforting himself by saying 'they weren't ripe anyway'. This is expanded into some seventy lines of octosyllabic verse in the French epic, and the grapes are turned into blackberries. It ends with Reynard saying to himself: 'Blackberries? Why, I never eat them. I once used to like them, but I vowed I would never eat them again. I must keep my vow.'

The only (late) medieval English representation of this to come to light is a misericord carving in St Mary of Charity's, Faversham, Kent. This is probably fable-inspired for it shows the fox in a vineyard eating from a bunch of grapes. Two other nineteenth-century mock-medieval carvings of this fable have also come to light. One is in stone, at the base of the central column in the Chapter House of Salisbury Cathedral, and shows two foxes contemplating a colossal bunch of grapes. There is good reason to believe that this modern sculpture replaces a similar one of medieval origin. That nineteenth-century guardian of public decency in Chester Cathedral has left us a delightful scene of the fox first contemplating and then struggling to reach a luscious bunch of berries [198]. Once more, it seems as if he employs the medieval technique of two consecutive scenes in one. But it is of course possible that these illustrate neither the fable nor the Beast Epic, that they are the little foxes of the Bible (Song of Solomon, Chapter 2, Verse 15) who spoil the tender vines. Another modern (1880) representation of this fable carved in wood is to be found on a choirstall front in Tideswell's parish church.

198 *The fable of the fox and the sour grapes. Chester Cathedral, misericord; 19th C. D.R. Maxted.*

The Fox and the Stork

The fable of the fox and the stork who invite each other to a meal but serve it in such a way that the guest is unable to partake of the food on offer was widely illustrated over time and space. It is particularly frequent in Church art and religious books where, doubtless, it was intended as an illustration of Christ's teaching 'whatsoever ye would that men should do to you, do ye even so to them'. Although this fable was never drawn into the *Roman de Renart* (or, for that matter, into any of the Beast Epics), in its later medieval forms it was occasionally Reynardized as the following summary-translation of a fourteenth-century French version shows: 'Reynard (*Renart*), who never did any good, invited his friend the stork to dine with him. She did not refuse. She thought she would be well received, fed and feasted. She did not expect any trickery. But Reynard poured a pot of honey over the table, and offered this to his guest... She wondered how to pay Reynard back... She invited Reynard, and prepared a pot full of the very best meat. This pot had a very long and narrow neck so that Reynard was unable to taste the meat. But the stork took her fill...'

There is no similar proof of this fable's Reynardization in English literature where its only appearance is in Caxton's *Aesop*. Nor is there much to say about its English iconography.

There are just three pre-Beast-Epic carvings. There is an early (twelfth-century?) and much-worn stone carving of this fable on a capital at the north doorway of St Martin's at Holt in Worcestershire [199]. The fox is shown, as in all the English examples, with the tables turned against him. There is no contextual evidence here to suggest any Reynardian overtones. Another

199 *The fable of the fox and the stork who invite each other to a meal. Holt, St Martin, capital of north doorway; early 12th C. The National Buildings Record.*

200 *The fable of the fox and the stork who invite each other to a meal. Bridlington, Priory Church, stone coffin lid; 11th C. (?). The Courtauld Institute of Art.*

early (eleventh century?) much-worn carving is to be seen on a coffin lid in the Priory Church of Bridlington in Yorkshire [200]. This may not, however, be of English but rather of Flemish origin, from Tournai. Here, as at Holt, the fox is trying to get his snout into the mouth of the vessel at the same time as the stork. Immediately below the fox and the stork is a lion-like figure (none of the creatures depicted on this stone is particularly realistic). This lion (?) is carved upside down in relation to the fox and stork so that he witnesses the fox's discomfiture. If this lion had been crowned, one might have been more easily persuaded that there was some link with the animal kingdom and some form of the Beast Epic. The third of these early carvings is the only one which contains a few details which may justify a link with Reynardian matter. This is a very worn, twelfth-century carving on a capital which is part of the wide chancel arch in St Michael's, Melbourne, Derbyshire [201]. Only the stork, to the extreme right, is fairly clear, and the tall vessel from which it feeds. To the right of this vessel are the vague outlines of a fox standing on its hind legs. On the capital next to it, further to the right (south), it is just possible to make out a fox pursuing a bird through some stylized leaves and branches. Only the bird is reasonably easily recognized. The pointed ears and snout are all that can be distinguished of the fox. On an adjoining capital to the left (east) of the fox-and-stork scene is a clearly visible fox scene. A long-nosed, thick-lipped, big-eyed peasant leans backward

201 *The fable of the fox and the stork who invite each other. Melbourne, St Michael, chancel arch capital; 12th C. Kenneth Varty.*

with the effort he makes as he tugs at a fleeing fox's brush. The fox has something in his open jaws, possibly the head of a bird. On a capital on the opposite side of the chancel, facing this peasant and fox, is a lion-like creature. Even though he wears no crown, it seems reasonable to suggest, given all the elements in these carvings, that this is the king of the animals before whom the fox is going to have to account for his misdeeds, and gives a moral point to these prominently positioned carvings. Given the fact that this fable of the fox and the stork is so common outside medieval England, it is distinctly odd that there is no other church carving of it till the nineteenth century and then, it seems, only two. There is a beautiful poppyhead carving on the priest's prayer desk in the parish church at Swavesey near Cambridge where we see the fox licking at the liquid which overflows from a long-necked vessel into which a stork dips its bill [202]. And there is a particularly fine misericord carving in Chester Cathedral, another replacement for an earlier, indecent scene [203]. The leading expert on scenes depicted on medieval misericords, Elaine Block (she has examined more than ten thousand historiated misericords in situ, the length and breadth of Europe and in museums beyond, and photographed them all) informs me that she has found a total of 18 medieval misericord examples of this fable in seven different countries, but none in England. Furthermore, she has found it 'on innumerable other choir-stall carvings: arm-rests, side and dorsal panels' but again none in England. The complete absence of this never-Reynardized fable from medieval England after the emergence of the Beast Epic in its great vernacular forms is strange.

202 *The fable of the fox and the stork who invite each other to a meal. Swavesey Parish Church; either 16th C. or modern. Kenneth Varty.*

203 *The fable of the fox and the stork who invite each other. Chester Cathedral, misericord; 19th C. D.R. Maxted.*

The Fox and the Eagle

Though well known from classical antiquity to and throughout the Middle Ages in most of western and central Europe, but appearing in only one English fable collection (Caxton's), and also not drawn into the *Roman de Renart* or into any other Beast Epic, this fable, or a variant form of it, may be represented twice in medieval English art, once in Poughill and once in Gloucester. One of the oldest versions tells how an eagle and a vixen became friends and decided to live near each other. The eagle made her nest in the top of a very tall tree and there laid her eggs. The vixen made her hole at the foot of that tree and there gave birth to her cubs. When she left them in search of food, the eagle swooped down, snatched up the cubs, and made a meal of them with her brood. When she discovered what had happened, the vixen thought only of revenge, but was unable to get at the eagle and her nestlings. But it chanced before long that the eagle was punished for violating the sanctity of friendship. While some men were sacrificing a goat in a field, the eagle darted down on the altar and carried off a piece of burning offal to her nest. Just then a strong wind sprang up and fanned into a blaze the bits of dry twigs of which the nest was made. As a result, the nestlings, not yet fully fledged, fell to the ground. The vixen seized her chance and gobbled up every one right under the eagle's eyes. In the French *Isopet I* the vixen becomes Reynard (*Renart*), and he manages to rescue a cub before the eagle feeds it to his young. He does this by piling up lots of green twigs against the tree in which the eagle has nested, then sets fire to the twigs and smokes the eagle into submission. Caxton's retelling is much closer to the ancient versions (Bastin 1929, II, 222-4).

In St Olaf's at Poughill in Cornwall, there is a bench-end carving which seems to depict the first part of the old fable when the eagle makes off with a small quadruped [204]. This is probably what the carver intended, but the eagle's victim looks more like a rabbit than a fox cub. The vixen looks on helplessly, from the left. In Gloucester Cathedral there is a misericord carving which shows only the eagle pouncing on a cringing fox cub. The cub does not look particularly fox-like, but a comparison with the way an unmistakable fox is depicted in other misericords (e.g., in the fox-physician scene, [176]) confirms that this is indeed a fox cub.

It is a curious fact that in all these English representations of the fabulists' fox, he is never shown getting the better of his opponent, even when, in the fable, he does so at one stage or another.

It is only in the earliest cycles of woodcut illustrations made, in the first place, for the Beast Epic in Dutch that we definitely see pictures of fables that have become part and parcel of Reynardian matter. Taken in the order they occur in the Wynkyn de Worde cycle, we begin with a picture of a modified form of the fable of the fox who, after eating his fill, is unable to get out of a cave by the narrow passage through which he entered [72] (Perry 1965, fable 107). Here it is the wolf who is trapped after being inveigled by Reynard into the food store of a very rich priest through a narrow hole, a story which forms part of Reynard's confession to Grimbert in Caxton's chapter twelve. This may also be contaminated by the fable about the fox who invites the wolf into a trap (Perry 1965, fable 169). Then there is the modified version of the fable of the fox who persuades a wolf to approach a mule and read what is written on its

204 *The fable of the fox, the eagle and the rabbit. Poughill, St Olaf, bench end; early 16th C. (?). The National Buildings Record.*

hoof [216] (Perry 1965, fable 603). This also becomes a part of a confession, another confession to Grimbert, told in Caxton's chapter 27 about a time when Reynard persuaded Isegrim that the price a mare wanted for her foal might be found underneath a rear hoof. This fable may be contaminated by the one about the wolf who gets kicked in the face after removing a thorn from a donkey's hoof (Perry 1965, fables 159, 593, 699). Next there is the fable about the dragon and the peasant in which the peasant is freed from the dragon's hold by the fox acting as judge [219]. (Perry 1965, fables 560, 650a). Malcolm Jones has identified a marginal scene in the Rutland Psalter (c.1260, reproduced in Randall 1966 at 382) as what must be the earliest English illustration of this fable. Finally, the illustration of an allegedly magic mirror incorporates at least three fables [222]: top left, the ass that tried to ingratiate itself with its master in the same way his dog did (Perry, 1965, fables 91, 167, 438); bottom left, the fable of the cat and the fox out in the country where the fox boasts about the many tricks it knows while the cat knows only one (which, when they find themselves being pursued, proves to be the particularly effective one of being able to climb a tree) (Perry, 1965, fables 542, 605): bottom right, the fable of the wolf and the crane in which the wolf gets the crane to remove a bone from his throat after promising her a reward (which, in the event, turns out to be his refraining from biting off her head while he had the chance to do so) (Perry 1965, fables 115, 201).

It is interesting to note that none of the fables illustrated in this cycle of woodcuts depicts an episode that is part of the mainline narrative. They all illustrate scenes of past misdeeds which are recalled by Reynard either as he confesses his sins to Grimbert or scenes from imagined events as he 'confesses' to Noble. The latter, all in the one fable-rich woodcut of the magic mirror, are told over four pages in Caxton's thirty-third chapter.

Notes

BASIC TEXTS

There are two great scholarly collections of fables: the one edited by Hervieux 1884 and the other by Perry 1965. The latter contains translations into English and a fine index which will quickly lead the reader to the original text and the translation of every Latin fable referred to in this chapter. Important for the *Isopets* is Bastin 1929-30: here are all the French fables referred to in this chapter. A mine of information on the fable, and in particular fables featuring the fox, is Schwarzbaum 1979. Although it is centred on fables in German, and Latin fables kept in Germany or composed by Germanophones, the catalogue by Dicke & Grubmüller is a comprehensive and most useful tool for tracing the whereabouts of editions and translations of hundreds of fables. Other important, relevant editions of fables are those by Ewert & Johnston 1964; and Warnke 1925 (for Marie de France); Jacobs 1985 (for a translation into English of Odo of Cheriton); and Toulmin-Smith & Meyer 1889 (for Nicholas Bozon). Caxton's *Aesop* was edited by Jacobs 1889 and by Lenaghan 1967.

The fox and the crow episode in the *Roman de Renart* is in Dufournet & Méline 1985, 251-261 where the Old French is faced by a translation into modern French; and is translated into English in Owen 1994, 62-67. The fox and the sour grapes (blackberries) is in Martin 1882, I, br.XI, 390-484, lines 256-337, and has not been translated.

CRITICAL STUDIES

For reproductions of the fox and crow scenes in the borders of the Bayeux Tapestry, see, for example, Stenton et al 1965, plates 4, 20, and 31. For a wide-ranging study of the iconography of the fox and stork fable, see Peterson 1981. For comment on the replacement of 'indecent' misericords in Chester Cathedral, see T. Cannon Hughes, 'Misericords in Chester Cathedral' in the *Chester Archaeological Journal*, V, 1 (date and pagination not recorded).

CHAPTER TEN

The Fox's Triumph

The seeds of Reynard's ultimate victory over all the other animal-barons in Noble's kingdom, including Noble himself, were sown early in fable-fiction time. In Aesopian fable, the fox causes his arch-enemy the wolf to suffer humiliating and painful defeat when the wolf publicly accuses him of disloyalty to the sick lion. As a result, the fox causes him to be flayed to provide medicine for the lion and gains in prestige and royal favour (Perry 1965, fables 258, 473 and 698). Other fables tell a similar story substituting the bear for the wolf (ibid. fables 534 and 585). In the *Ysengrimus,* Reinardus's various encounters with Ysengrimus invariably result in the wolf's serious discomfiture, in particular in that epic's version of the sick lion story, at the end of which the King of the Animals is so pleased with his fox-physician and courtier that he asks him to tell him about other occasions on which he has outwitted and put down the unfortunate Ysengrimus. And, of course, he does. Right from the beginning of the *Roman de Renart,* Noble the Lion is portrayed as having a soft spot in his heart for Reynard. When, in Branch Va, Ysengrin complains about Reynard's rape of his wife, Hersent, Noble's first reaction is to hold back a smile. At the end of Branch X, Reynard is made Noble's chief adviser and richly rewarded by the king for curing him of the fever. And, in spite of all his insolence, Reynard's 'death' in Branch XVII is deeply regretted by Noble. In poems and stories derived from the *Roman de Renart* the royal favour shown to the fox, however evil he may appear to all the other animals and to the reader, is developed as part of the satire which characterizes most of these later works. Rutebeuf's poem *Renart le Bestorné* (which Owen 1994 translates 'Reynard the Reprobate'), composed about 1260, begins with the words 'Reynard is dead, Reynard is alive; Reynard is foul, Reynard is vile; yet Reynard reigns.' This marks the beginning of the bitterly satirical fox-literature in which Reynard, symbol of falsity, is depicted as the supreme power in the land. As early as Branch XI, *Renart Empereur* (early thirteenth century), Reynard plays the role of usurper of the throne. Here Reynard is appointed Regent by Noble himself as he goes off to fight distant invaders of his kingdom. In his absence, the fox plunders the royal treasury, 'marries' Fière, the Queen, and has himself declared emperor. However, when the lion returns to his capital and defeats the fox in battle, the rightful king forgives the usurper and lets him go free. Later poems also tell of further usurpations which leave the fox ruling for good, as in *Le Couronnement de Renart,* 1263-70; others tell how Reynard becomes Noble's completely trusted, right-hand man, as in *Renart le Nouvel,* c.1289.

Illustrating the Fox's Triumph

It is possible that two poor and mutilated misericords depict the fox basking in the lion's favour. The first of these, at Knowle in Warwickshire, shows the lion in the centre of the carving, glaring from beneath half-lowered eyelids [205]. To the left of the lion is an unicorn distinguished by his single horn. To the right of him is a proud-looking fox, distinguished by his brush. The unicorn was a symbol of virtue and innocence, the fox one of evil and falsity. Although the unicorn plays no part in Reynardian literature, he does, on rare occasions, in Reynardian iconography and is prominent in two of Wynkyn de Worde's woodcuts ([82 & 218]) where his presence seems to point to the power the lion has to see justice is done, to distinguish between right and wrong. Perhaps it is important that the unicorn stands on the lion's right hand. The second of these two misericords is at Gresford in Denbighshire [206]. It shows a fox, distinguished by the brush on which he sits, between a lion and a lioness. The lion is to the right, as his shaggy mane and male member prove; the lioness (less her head) to the

205 *A fox and a unicorn on either side of a lion. Knowle Parish Church, misericord, early 16th C. (?). J.C.D. Smith.*

206 *A fox embraced by a crowned lion and lioness. Gresford, All Saints, misericord; late 15th C. (?). D.R. Maxted.*

left. One can just make out the worn remains of a crown on the lion's head, and where the crown was on the lioness's. The crowns indicate that these are the animals' king and queen, and the purpose of this picture is probably the public honouring of their favoured subject. (The lioness always had an even softer spot in her heart for the fox than the lion did. When, in Branch I, Reynard obtained mercy from Noble on condition that he went on a pilgrimage to the Holy Land and never returned, Fière gave him her ring as a parting gift. This was obviously meant to remind the reader of courtly romances of Queen Isolda's gift to her lover, Tristram, nephew of her husband, King Mark when he had to leave the royal court. In Branch XVII, it is Fière who has Reynard released from the chessboard to which Ysengrin had nailed him by the testicles, and has him carried to her bed. And in both Branch XI and in *Renart le Nouvel*, she even marries the fox when her husband is falsely reported to be dead.)

But it is in the thirteenth- and fourteenth-century Dutch adaptations of Branch I and in the original additions to it that the fox's triumph is especially well told and, subsequently, illustrated. The composition of the Gresford misericord shows a certain similarity to that of the most important part of the Wynkyn de Worde woodcut where Noble presents Reynard, seated

207 *Reynard's triumph. Copperplate etching by Canton (1852).*

between himself and his queen on a raised platform to his assembled court [85], and annouces to all his subjects (among whom the wolf and bear are prominent) that he has pardoned the fox for his alleged crimes, and that henceforth he is to be held in the highest respect, he and all his family. The fox's savouring of his triumph is depicted in the next cut in this series [86] after which he enjoys a royal and public handshake [88]. Later, after further trouble with both the king and the wolf, Reynard again triumphs, receives another royal handshake [223], defeats Isegrim in a duel [225], and is then depicted with his faithful ally Grimbert at his side [226] listening to the lion declare him victor and, henceforth, his highest ranking officer and right-hand man. The last Wynkyn de Worde cut is of inferior quality and fails to end the series on a visually triumphant note [227]. It shows Reynard bidding farewell to his friends and returning

208 *Reynard's triumph. Copperplate etching by Kaulbach (1846).*

home supposedly in triumph. Visual justice is not done to this vulpine victory by artists in England till the middle of the nineteenth century, and this begins with a German artist, Gustav Canton (invited to, and published in Britain along with so many other talented artists of various kinds while Albert was Prince Consort and Queen Victoria smiled on all things German). Canton illustrated a version of the Beast Epic (in the Germano-Flemish tradition) meant specially for young people [207]. Bearing traces of British experiences in India, this depiction of the most joyous event in Reynardian history is markedly influenced by the parallel illustration in the series made by Kaulbach for Goethe's *Reineke Fuchs* as, indeed, are all Canton's illustrations [208].

Notes

BASIC TEXTS AND SUPPORTING INFORMATION

Details of all the titles mentioned in the first paragraph of this chapter are given in the Bibliography. Canton's illustrations may be seen in Vedder 1852, and Kaulbach's in Goethe 1973.

CHAPTER ELEVEN

The Enduring Fortunes of Wynkyn de Worde's Picture Cycle

Part One: From Wynkyn de Worde (c.1495) to Edward Brewster (1701)

A summary of Caxton's Anglo-Flemish *Hystorie of Reynart the Foxe* (which Wynkyn de Worde took over and had illustrated about 1495) is given in Chapter Three up to the point where the bad faith of the pilgrim-fox has been fully revealed, and both Lapreel the Rabbit and Corbant the Rook have complained to Noble the Lion of the attacks Reynard has made upon them as he began his 'pilgrimmage'. Once more, the angry king vows to bring Reynard to justice. The rest of the story which Wynkyn de Worde's artist illustrated may be summarized thus:

Grymbert the Badger slips away to warn his kinsman of impending danger. He finds Reynard with two young pigeons which had just fallen out of their nest, and tells him what has happened at court. The fox is confident he can still win the day once more with his lying ways, and he invites Grymbert to meet his wife and children and to share with them the two young pigeons. After their meal they return together to court and on the way, recalling an earlier and similar journey, Reynard asks Grymbert to listen to his confession and to shrive him. His catalogue of sins is a familiar one concerning offences chiefly against the bear, the wolf and the lion. However, he comes to tell of one as yet unknown to his confessor (and to the reader!). It is about the time he negotiated with a mare over the sale of her foal to Isegrym. The mare said the price she wanted was written underneath one of her hind hoofs and the wolf should come and read it for himself if the fox could not. (Guessing the mare's intentions, Reynard had said he could not read when the mare had invited him to check the price on the underside of her hoof, then report it to Isegrym). The wolf, proud of his learning (he boasted that he could read French, Latin, Dutch and English, having been to school in Oxford) went forward to read the price tag. All he got, of course, was a terrible hoof-blow to the forehead. Reynard ends his confession with this story, and is shriven. Following a lengthy discussion on the temptations of this world and the rottenness of people in high places and positions of power, they reach Noble's throne where the fox immediately falls down on his knees before the king. Reynard defends himself ably with detailed descriptions of the advice given to him by his uncle Mertyne the Ape whose wisdom, it seems, is much sought and respected in high ecclesiastical circles. So good is the fox's defence that Lapreel and Corbant sneak away and are not there to reiterate their accusations when Noble calls upon them to do so. However, Noble now accuses Reynard of deceiving him personally over his feigned repentance and lying about buried treasure.

At this point, Dame Rukenawe, Reynard's aunt, comes to the rescue. She too, like Mertyne, is clever with words. A judge, she points out, should not pronounce sentence while angry. Noble should remember the Gospel command 'judge not lest you be judged', and should follow Christ's teaching about casting stones. She reminds Noble that Reynard has many friends, and is more loved than many of his courtiers, especially Isegrym and Bruyn who are worse flatterers than the fox. She recalls Reynard's excellent judgment made on Noble's behalf in the case of the farmer who took pity on a serpent which was tied to a tree and dying of hunger. Although the farmer got the serpent to promise not to harm him if he released it, it promptly tried to devour him once released. It agreed to delay devouring him in order to allow others to judge the case. First, Tyselyn the Raven judged in the serpent's favour; then, on appeal, so did Isegrym and Bruyn; then, on a further appeal to Noble, the lion delegated the job to Reynard. The fox said he would be able to judge the case better if they all returned to the scene of the alleged crime and saw how things were in the first place; so they do this, retying the serpent to the tree. Reynard's judgment was that the farmer should now be free to release the serpent in the same way and on the same conditions as before if he so wished. Reminded of Reynard's occasional good service in times past, Noble, now much calmer, allows the fox to plead his case yet again, especially to defend himself against the charge of Cuwaert's murder. Reynard now argues that he did the hare no harm, that he put three rich treasures intended for the king and his queen in the scrip which he gave to Bellyn the Ram to bring to court, implying that Cuwaert's head must have been placed there by the ram and that the treasures must have been stolen by him. He then describes these three fictitious treasures. There was, he says, a colourful ring inscribed with three magic words which protected its wearer from all manner of suffering and evil; an ivory comb engraved with scenes from the story of Paris's judgment of Venus, Juno and Pallas, a comb which had magical healing properties; and finally a mirror which also had healing properties, and allowed its owner to see in it all that was happening within a mile around. On the wood into which this mirror was set was engraved, at each corner, a scene from each of four different stories or fables which Reynard relates. After this account of these 'lost' priceless gifts, Reynard concludes his defence first with a lengthy retelling of the way his father had cured the king of an illness when none of his other courtiers were able to help; and then by an equally lengthy recounting of the way he was so much more generous than Isegrym on more than one occasion when it came to dividing prey between them and the lion. Noble is finally persuaded to let Reynard go free, superficially because there were no witnesses to his alleged murder of Cuwaert, but also, it is hinted, because he hopes the 'lost' treasures may be found and finally reach those for whom they had been intended.

Isegrym, deeply angered at Reynard's release, promptly complains to Noble about the way his wife Dame Erswynde had once been tricked by the fox into fishing with her tail in freezing conditions so that, once frozen into the ice by her tail, he was able to rape her. Reynard denies that this is what had happened. He argues that she got frozen into the ice because she had tried to fish at a spot other than the one he had recommended; and when Isegrym thought he saw him raping her, what he was really doing was trying to push her from behind to get her unstuck. The wolf then accuses the fox of having led him into a dung-encrusted she-ape's den where she was guarding three dung-encrusted offspring, a situation from which he emerged badly wounded. The memory of these insults and injuries together with so many more prove too much for Isegrym. He hurls his gauntlet down before Reynard, and the fox takes it up. A duel must ensue. Bruyn and Tybert agree to act as Isegrym's seconds; Grymbert and Byteluys (a young ape) as Reynard's. Much worried, Reynard turns to Dame Rukenawe for advice. Her main recommendations are that he should have his fur cut short, oil his body well, and drink a lot to ensure a full bladder so that whenever the opportunity presents itself he can urinate into his brush and slap Isegrym in the face with it. And this is what happens. Isegrym has the greatest difficulty in getting a hold on Reynard who, every time he has a chance, slaps his urine-soaked brush across his enemy's eyes and then throws loose earth and dust into them. While Isegrym is thus temporarily rendered blind, Reynard tears skin off his head and knocks an eye out of its socket. Even so, Isegrym manages to pin Reynard down and get one of the fox's forepaws into his jaws. At this point in the duel Isegrym demands that the fox should admit defeat and surrender; otherwise he will kill him.

Reynard decides that discretion is the better part of valour. He apologises for past offences, and offers to become the wolf's liege man. He paints a rosy picture of their future together if they patch up their differences and become friends. Isegrym rejects this offer and explains at some length why he does so, and why he should not spare his arch-enemy. As he speaks, with the one free paw, Reynard finds and grabs Isegrym's testicles. Then he 'wrong them so sore that for woe and pain he [Isegrym] must cry loud and howl...and spat blood and for the great pain beshat himself'. Finally he swoons. Reynard then catches him by the legs and pulls him on his back through the field to demonstrate his total victory. Noble declares him to be the victor and innocent of all the charges brought against him. He then elects the fox to the highest office in his kingdom: 'in all my lands shall you be above all sovereign and my bail'. Doctors attend Isegrym and reassure his wife Dame Erswynde that he will make a full recovery. Meanwhile Reynard takes courteous leave of Noble and his queen, and returns triumphantly with his many friends (more now than ever before!) to his Castle Maleperduys. There he recounts all to his wife Dame Ermelyn and to his children. 'And the fox lived forthon with his wife and children in great joy and gladness.'

THE FIRST ENGLISH PICTURE CYCLE FOR THE HISTORY OF REYNARD THE FOX

(Part II; Wynkyn de Worde's Woodcuts: from Reynard's pilgrimage to his return home)
The first twenty-four woodcuts in Wynkyn de Worde's picture cycle are described in Chapter Three. The twenty-fourth is the one which depicts the beginning of the fox's 'pilgrimage', with the ram-priest bestowing a blessing upon the fox [88]. The series continues as follows: 25. The ram and the hare accompany the fox as far as his home where he says he wishes to bid his wife and children farewell [209]. In the middle ground the fox speaks to the ram at the

The Hystory

his staffe and espied his shoes, she marueiled and said: Deare Reinard how haue ye spead. He sayd I was arested in the court, but the king let me go, I must go on pilgrimage, Bruine the Beare, and Isegrim the Woulfe they be pledge for me, I thancke the kyng he hath

of Reynard the Fox.

hath giuen to vs Kiward here, for to do with him what we will. The king sayd himselfe, that Kiwarde was the first that on vs complained, and by the faith that I owe you, I am right wrothe on Kywarde. Whan Kyward harde these wordes, he was sore afeard, he would haue fledde but he might not, for the Fox stode betwene him and the gate, and he caught him by the neck. Tho cried the Hare helpe Bellin help where be ye, this pilgrim sleyeth me. But that crie was sone done, for ye Fox had anone bitten his throte in two. Than sayd Reynard let vs go eate this good fat Hare, the young whelpes came also. Thus helde they a great feast, for Kyward had a good fatte body, Ermelin eate the flesh and dranke the bloud, she thanked oft the kyng that had made them so mery. The Fox sayd eate as much as ye may, he will paye for it, if we will fetch it. She saide Reinarde I trowe ye mocke, tell me the troth how ye departed thence. Dame I haue so flattered the king & the quene, that I suppose the frendeshippe betwene vs shalbe righte thinne, whan he shall knowe of this, he shalbe angry, & hastely seeke me for to hang me by the necke. Therfore let vs departe and steale awaye into some other forest where we may liue without feare and dreade, And there as we may liue. vii. yeare and more, that none find vs not, there as is plentie of good meate, as Partriges, Wodcocks, and such other wild foule. Dame if ye come with me thither, there bene sweete welles and fayre and clere runninge brokes. Lorde God how sweete ayre is there, there maye we be in peace and ease, and liue in great wealth. For the king

L.iij. hath

209 *The ram and the hare accompany the fox to his den. Wynkyn de Worde woodcut, c.1495. (This, and all the illustrations up to and including 231, are from the Anonymous, c.1560 edition of the History of Reynard the Fox in the possession of Mr Wilfried Grauwels, and reproduced by his kind permission. All are from the c.1495 Wynkyn de Worde cycle).*

entrance to his den. This is probably when he tells the ram to wait outside while he goes in with the hare. In the foreground he is shown seizing the hare by his ears, but in the tale it is inside his den that the fox seizes the hare and, together with his wife and children, devour all but the poor creature's head. 26. In the middle ground the fox puts his pilgrim's scrip round the ram's neck [210] telling him that it contains important letters which he should deliver to the lion post haste. What it really contains is the hare's head. In the foreground he urges the ram on, suggesting that he tell the lion that he was party to the fox's 'message', assuring him that this will bring him a reward from the lion. 27. The ram stands before the lion and the lioness, scrip opened, dead hare's head revealed and held by the cat [211]. This is also witnessed by a leopard (which looks away) and a creature which may be an attempt to depict a beaver. 28. The leopard suggests the release of the now evidently falsely accused and wrongfully imprisoned wolf and bear from their prison, seen in the background [212]. They in fact exchange places with the ram, just visible through the prison bars, and stand at the feet of the lion and the peace-maker leopard. 29. This seems to be a good moment for other victims of

210 *The fox puts his pilgrim's scrip around the ram's neck.*

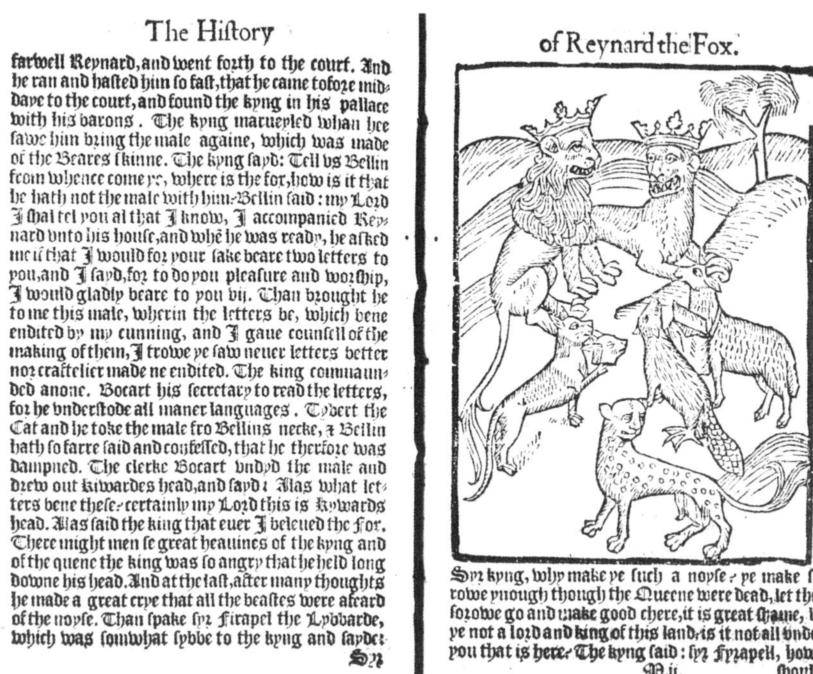

The Hiſtory

farwell Reynard, and went forth to the court. And he ran and haſted him ſo faſt, that he came tofore midday to the court, and found the kyng in his pallace with his barons. The kyng maruepled whan hee ſawe him bring the male againe, which was made of the Beares ſkinne. The kyng ſayd: Tell vs Bellin from whence come ye, where is the fox, how is it that he hath not the male with him? Bellin ſaid: my Lord I ſhal tel you al that I know, I accompanied Reynard vnto his houſe, and whē he was ready, he aſked me if that I would for your ſake beare two letters to you, and I ſayd, for to do you pleaſure and worſhip, I would gladly beare to you vij. Than brought he to me this male, wherin the letters be, which bene endited by my cunning, and I gaue counſell of the making of them, I trowe ye ſaw neuer letters better nor craftelier made ne endited. The king commaunded anone. Bocart his ſecretary to read the letters, for he vnderſtode all maner languages. Tybert the Cat and he toke the male fro Bellins necke, & Bellin hath ſo farre ſaid and confeſſed, that he therfore was dampned. The clerke Bocart vndyd the male and drew out Kiwardes head, and ſayd: Alas what letters bene theſe? certainly my Lord this is Kywards head. Alas ſaid the king that euer I beleued the Fox. There might men ſe great heauines of the kyng and of the quene the king was ſo angry that he held long downe his head. And at the laſt, after many thoughts he made a great crye that all the beaſtes were afeard of the noyſe. Than ſpake ſyr Firapel the Lybbarde, which was ſomwhat ſybbe to the kyng and ſayde:

Syr

of Reynard the Fox.

Syr kyng, why make ye ſuch a noyſe? ye make ſorowe ynough though the Queene were dead, let this ſorowe go and make good chere, it is great ſhame, be ye not a lord and king of this land, is it not all vnder you that is here? The kyng ſaid: ſyr Fyrapell, howe

M.ij. ſhould

211 *The ram delivers the hare's head to the lion and lioness.*

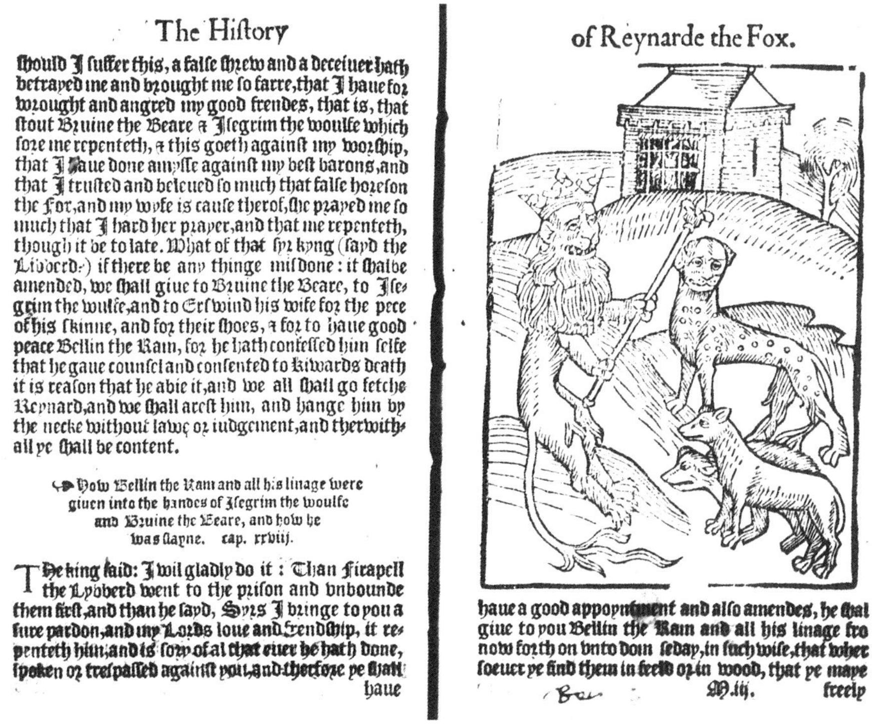

The History of Reynarde the Fox.

should I suffer this, a false shrewe and a deceiuer hath betrayed me and brought me so farre, that I haue for wrought and angred my good frendes, that is, that stout Bruine the Beare & Isegrim the woulfe which sore me repenteth, & this goeth against my worship, that I haue done amysse against my best barons, and that I trusted and beleued so much that false horeson the Fox, and my wyfe is cause therof, she prayed me so much that I hard her prayer, and that me repenteth, though it be to late. What of that syr kyng (sayd the Libberd:) if there be any thinge misdone: it shalbe amended, we shall giue to Bruine the Beare, to Isegrim the woulfe, and to Ersewind his wife for the pece of his skinne, and for their shoes, & for to haue good peace Bellin the Ram, for he hath confessed him selfe that he gaue counsel and consented to Kiwards death it is reason that he abie it, and we all shall go fetche Reynard, and we shall arest him, and hange him by the necke without lawe or iudgement, and therwithall ye shall be content.

How Bellin the Ram and all his linage were giuen into the handes of Isegrim the woulfe and Bruine the Beare, and how he was slayne. cap. xxviij.

The king said: I wil gladly do it: Than Firapell the Lybberd went to the prison and vnbounde them first, and than he sayd, Syrs I bringe to you a sure pardon, and my Lords loue and frendship, it repenteth him, and is sory of al that euer he hath done, spoken or trespassed against you, and therfore ye shall haue

haue a good appoyntment and also amendes, he shal giue to you Bellin the Ram and all his linage fro now forth on vnto doom sday, in such wise, that wher soeuer ye find them in feeld or in wood, that ye maye

M.iij. freely

212 *The wolf and the bear are released from prison.*

213 *The rabbit complains to the lion.*

The History

were playes and pastimes, the feast was full of melodie. One might haue a lust to see such a feast. And as the feast hath endured viij.dayes, about middaye came in Lapreil the Coney tofore the kyng, where he sat at the table with the Queene, and said all heauily that all they that were there hard him: My lord haue pitie on my complaint, which is of great force and murther that Reinard the Fox would haue done to me. Yesterday in the morning as I came running by his borowe at Malepardus, he stode before his dore without like a pilgrim. I supposed to haue passed by him peaceably toward his nest: and when he sawe me come, he came against me saying his beades, I salued him, but he spake not one worde, but caught out his right foote, and dubbed me in the neck, betwene mine eares, that I had wend I should haue lost my head: but thancked be God I was so light that I lept fro his clawes, but it was with much payne. Than hee grined as he had bene angry because he held me no faster, though I escaped from him I lost mine one eare, & had foure great holes in my head of his sharpe nayles, that the bloud ran downe along my checkes, but for the great feare of my life, I lept and ranne so fast from him, that he could not ouer take me. Se my Lord these great woundes hath he made with his sharpe long nayles, I pray you to haue pitie on me, and that ye will punnish this false traytour and murtherer, or els shall their no man go and come ouer the heath in safetie nor in peace, whiles he haunteth this mischeuous and vnhappie rule.

How

of Reynard the Fox.

How Corbant the Rooke complained vpon the Fox for the death of his wyfe. cap. xxx.

Right as the Cony hath made an end of his complaynt: came into the court Corbant the Rooke fleing into the place tofore the kyng and sayd: Deere

N.j. Lord

214 *The rook complains to the lion.*

the fox to complain to the lion. Here it is the turn of the rabbit [213] who describes an attack the fox made on him, badly wounding him. Though he is not mentioned in the text at this point, the badger is shown listening intently from a safe distance. He will shortly slip away and warn his uncle of the trouble that is brewing. 30. Then it is the rook's turn [214]. He tells how the fox pretended to be dead so that he and his wife came close to the 'corpse' which suddenly sprang to life and bit off her head before devouring the rest of her. The committing of the crime is depicted in the background while the two complainants, rook and rabbit, crouch humbly, in the foreground, before the manifestly angry lion. 31. In the background the badger is shown arriving at the fox's den [215] where he discovers the fox with two recently acquired dead pigeons. In the foreground he shares in eating one of these pigeons with the fox while the vixen shares the other with her two cubs. 32. In the background the fox and the badger are shown making their way back to the lion's court [216]. The fox looks towards the foreground where we see a picture which illustrates one of the nasty tricks the fox had played on the wolf and to which he confesses among many others. This is when he got a mare to kick the wolf on the head in the course of some negotiations he was conducting about the possible sale of her foal (depicted behind the mare) to the wolf. 33. The fox and the badger arrive at court and

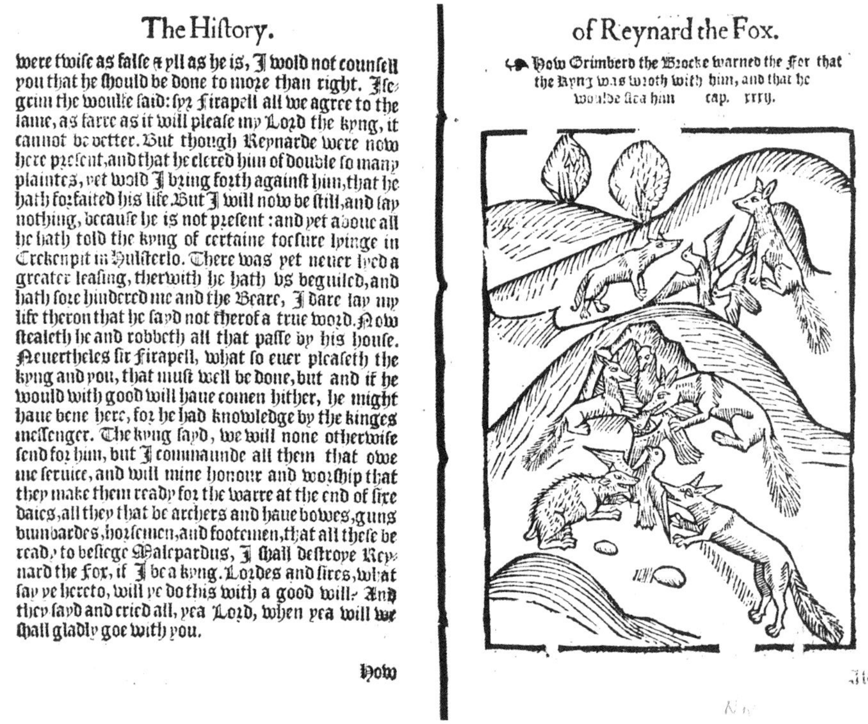

The History.

were twise as false & yll as he is, I wold not counsell you that he should be done to more than right. Isegrim the woulfe said: syr Firapell all we agree to the same, as farre as it will please my Lord the kyng, it cannot be better. But though Reynarde were now here present, and that he clered him of double so many plaintes, yet wold I bring forth against him, that he hath forfaited his life. But I will now be still, and say nothing, because he is not present: and yet aboue all he hath told the kyng of certaine tresure lyinge in Crekenpit in Hulsterlo. There was yet neuer lyed a greater leasing, therwith he hath vs beguiled, and hath sore hindered me and the Beare, I dare lay my life theron that he sayd not therof a true word. Now stealeth he and robbeth all that passe by his house. Neuertheles sir Firapell, what so euer pleaseth the kyng and you, that must well be done, but and if he would with good will haue comen hither, he might haue bene here, for he had knowledge by the kinges messenger. The kyng sayd, we will none otherwise send for him, but I commaunde all them that owe me seruice, and will mine honour and worship that they make them ready for the warre at the end of sixe daies, all they that be archers and haue bowes, guns bumbardes, horsemen, and footemen, that all these be ready to besiege Malepardus, I shall destroye Reynard the Fox, if I be a kyng. Lordes and sires, what say ye hereto, will ye do this with a good will? And they sayd and cried all, yea Lord, when yea will we shall gladly goe with you.

How

of Reynard the Fox.

How Grimberd the Brocke warned the Fox that the kyng was wroth with him, and that he woulde slea him cap. xxxi.

215 *The badger arrives at the fox's den and shares in their meal of pigeons.*

216 *The wolf gets kicked in the head by a mare.*

The Hystory

way saith truth he shal find many lettings in his way. Men may wel lie when it is nede, and after amend it be counsaile. For al maner trespasses there is mercy. There is no man so wise but he dwileth other while. Then sayd Grimberd: well deare Eme, what thing shall let you, ye know all thinges at the narowest, ye should bring me hastely in doting, your reasons passe mine understanding, what nede have ye to shrive you ye should your selfe by right be the priest, and let mee and other shepe come to you for to be shriven, ye know the state of the world, in such wise that no man maye halte tofore you. With such maner of talkinge they came walking to the courte. The Fox sorowed some what in his harte. Neverthelesse he bare it out and went forth through all the folke, till he came to the place where the king him selfe was. And Grimberd was alway by Reinard the fox and sayd. Eme be not afrard, be of good chere, who that is hardy, the adventure helpeth him. Oftentimes one day is better then sometime an hole yere. The Fox sayd: neuew ye say God thanke you, truth, ye comfort me well. And forth he went, & loked grimly here and there, as who saith: what will ye? here come I. He saw there many of his kinne standinge, which wyshed hym but little good, as the Otter, the Bever, and other to the number of tenne whom I shall have afterwarde. And some there were that loved him. The Fox came in and fell downe on his knees tofore the kyng, and began his wordes and sayd.

How

of Reynard the Fox.

How Reynard the Fox excused him selfe before the kyng. cap.xxxvi.

GOd from whom nothinge may be hid, and above al thing is mightie, save my lord the king and my

P.iij. Lady

217 *The fox and the badger arrive at the lion's court.*

stand before the lion [217]. This is when the fox defends himself against the charges which have been made against him and is supported by a large ape, some smaller ones and another little quadruped. (In the story this is when the fox refers at length to the advice given to him by an ape-uncle.) 34. A clearly angry lion accuses the fox (depicted in diminutive form in the immediate foreground) of deceiving him personally [218]. A sad-looking lioness sits at the lion's side. The wolf, cat and bear are prominent in the crowd of onlookers, and the unicorn makes its pictorial reappearance to indicate symbolically that the dispensation of justice is at least in the air. Close by the fox an ape seems to be remonstrating with the lion. (In the story the she-ape aunt of the fox vigorously takes up his defence.) 35. In the background a farmer walks away along a road and into the distance [219]. He looks sideways towards a serpent-like dragon which is tied to a tree, and he makes gestures which suggest that he wants nothing to do with it. In the foreground the lion together with two other animals, probably the bear and the wolf, look towards the serpent-dragon. At a little distance from them, the fox watches what is happening. This is how the artist illustrates the end of the parable of the farmer who delivered a serpent from the threat of death by starvation, and then found himself attacked by the serpent. It is the fox who gets the lion to have the serpent retied to the tree and give the

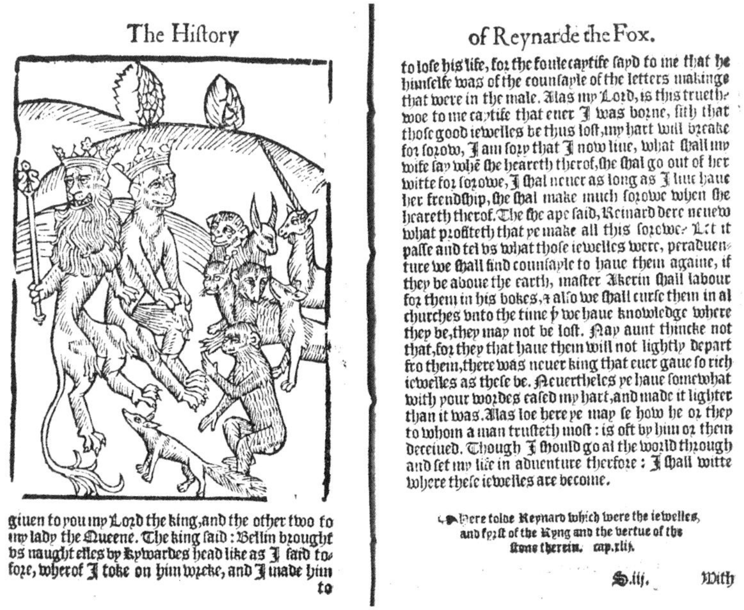

The History

given to you my Lord the king, and the other two to my lady the Queene. The king said: Bellin brought vs naught elles by Kywardes head like as I said tofore, wherof I toke on him wrecke, and I made him to

of Reynarde the Fox.

to lose his life, for the foule captife sayd to me that he himselfe was of the counsayle of the letters makinge that were in the male. Alas my Lord, is this trueth? woe to me captife that euer I was borne, sith that those good iewelles be thus lost, my hart will breake for sorow, I am sory that I now liue, what shall my wife say whẽ she heareth therof, she shal go out of her witte for sorowe, I shal neuer as long as I liue haue her frendship, she shal make much sorowe when she heareth therof. The she ape said, Reinard dere neuew what profiteth that ye make all this sorowe? Let it passe and tel vs what those iewelles were, peraduenture we shall find counsayle to haue them againe, if they be aboue the earth, master Akerin shall labour for them in his bokes, & also we shall curse them in al churches vnto the time þ we haue knowledge where they be, they may not be lost. Nay aunt thincke not that, for they that haue them will not lightly depart fro them, there was neuer king that euer gaue so rich iewelles as these be. Neuertheles ye haue somewhat with your wordes eased my hart, and made it lighter than it was. Alas loe here ye may se how he or they to whom a man trusteth most: is oft by him or them deceiued. Though I should go al the world through and set my life in aduenture therfore: I shall witte where these iewelles are become.

Here tolde Reynard which were the iewelles, and fyrst of the Kyng and the vertue of the stone therein. cap.xlii.

S.iii. With

218 *The lion accuses the fox.*

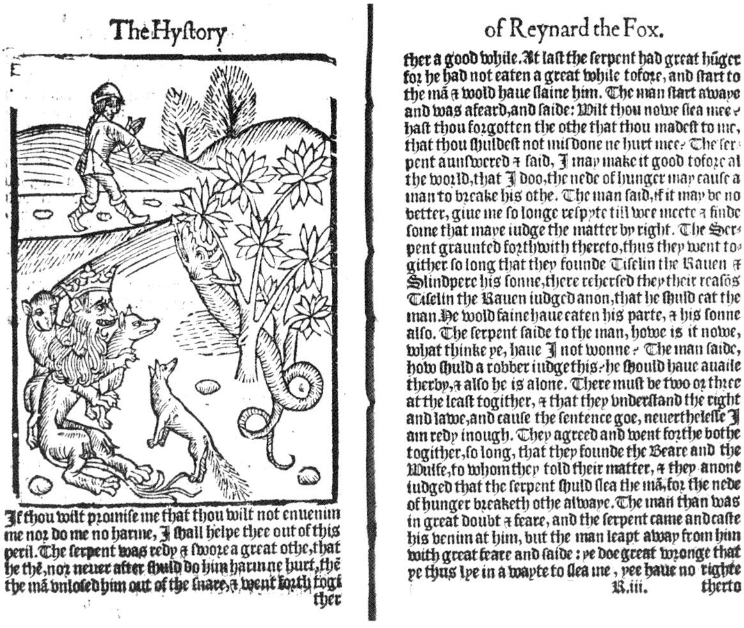

The Hystory

If thou wilt promise me that thou wilt not enuenim me nor do me no harme, I shall helpe thee out of this peril. The serpent was redy & swore a great othe, that he thẽ, nor neuer after shuld do him harm ne hurt, thẽ the mã vnlosed him out of the snare, & went forth togither

of Reynard the Fox.

ther a good while. At last the serpent had great hũger for he had not eaten a great while tofore, and start to the mã & wold haue slaine him. The man start awaye and was afeard, and saide: Wilt thou nowe slea mee? hast thou forgotten the othe that thou madest to me, that thou shuldest not misdone ne hurt mee? The serpent aunswered & said, I may make it good tofore al the world, that I doo, the nede of hunger may cause a man to breake his othe. The man said, if it may be no better, giue me so longe respyte till wee meete & finde some that maye iudge the matter by right. The Serpent graunted forthwith thereto, thus they went togither so long that they founde Tiselin the Rauen & Slindpere his sonne, there rehersed they their reasõs Tiselin the Rauen iudged anon, that he shuld eat the man. He wold faine haue eaten his parte, & his sonne also. The serpent saide to the man, howe is it nowe, what thinke ye, haue I not wonne? The man saide, how shuld a robber iudge this? he should haue auaile therby, & also he is alone. There must be two or three at the least togither, & that they vnderstand the right and lawe, and cause the sentence goe, neuerthelesse I am redy inough. They agreed and went forthe bothe togither, so long, that they founde the Beare and the Wulfe, to whom they told their matter, & they anone iudged that the serpent shuld slea the mã, for the nede of hunger breaketh othe alwaye. The man than was in great doubt & feare, and the serpent came and caste his venim at him, but the man leapt away from him with great feare and saide: ye doe great wronge that ye thus lye in a wayte to slea me, yee haue no righte

R.iii. therto

219 *The parable of the farmer who freed a trapped serpent.*

The Hiſtory

WIth a diſſimuled and a ſorowfull ſpeach: ſayd the Fox, harken ye all my kinne and freendes, I ſhall name to you theſe iewelles what they were, and than may ye ſay that I haue a great loſſe. That one of

of Reynarde the Fox.

of them was a ring of fine gold, and within the ring next the finger were written letters enameled with Sable and Azure, and there were three Hebrew names therin, I could not my ſelfe read ne ſpell them, for I vnderſtode not that language, but maſter Abrion of Trere he is a wiſe man, he vnderſtandeth all maner languages ⁊ the vertue of al maner of herbes, and there is no beaſt ſo fierſe ne ſo ſtronge, but hee can dompe him, for if he ſee him once, he ſhall do as he will, and yet he beleued not in God. He is a Iewe, but he is the wiſeſt in cunning, and ſpecially he knoweth the vertue of ſtones. I ſhewed him once this Ryng, and he ſayd that they were thoſe three names that Seth brought out of Paradice, when he brought to his father Adam the oyle of mercy. And whoſoeuer bereth on him thoſe thre names: he ſhal neuer be hurt by thunder ne lightning, ne no witchcraft ſhall haue power ouer him, ne be tempted to do ſinne, ⁊ alſo he ſhall neuer take harme by colde, though he lay three long winters nightes in the field, though it did ſnow or freeſe neuer ſo ſore, ſo great might haue thoſe three words, witnes of that maſter Abryon, without forth in the Ring ſtode a ſtone of three diuerſe maner of colours, the one part was like red Chriſtall, and ſhone like as fier had ben therin, in ſuch maner of wyſe, that if any would go by night, him behoueth none other light, for the ſhining of that ſame ſtone made and gaue as great a light as though it had bene midday. And that other part of the ſtone was white and clere, as it had ben burniſhed, who ſo had in his eyen any ſmart or ſorenes, or in his body any ſwelling or head ache,

220 *A magic ring.*

farmer another chance to decide whether to release it again in the light of the serpent's broken promise. 36. A picture of an allegedly magic ring [220] ornamented with a large precious stone and engraved with three 'Hebrew' names: Aleernando, Soroabel and Emanuel. 37. A picture of an allegedly magic comb [221] made from panther bone and engraved with scenes from the story of Paris's judgment of Venus, Juno and Pallas. (The text does not explain how Paris comes to be lying down, apparently asleep, by the side of a fountain.) 38. A picture of an allegedly magic mirror set in a wooden frame at each of the four corners of which is engraved a scene from a tale or a fable [222]. Top right, a vain horse which hunts a hart; top left, a jealous ass which tried to show its love for its master in the same way as his pet dog did; bottom left, a clever cat which has escaped from hunters by climbing a tree as it journeyed with a fox; bottom right, a naïvely trusting crane with its head and neck deep inside a wolf's throat. At the centre is the round mirror, evidently convex, reflecting the interior of a room with its beamed ceiling, a window, a kind of sideboard below it, and a cupboard to the left with a pewter (?) plate propped upright on top of it. 39. The lion shakes hands with the fox, declaring him quit of all charges [223]. This is done in the presence of a she-ape who has ably defended him. Two other apes and three other little animals [a badger (?), a marten (?), and a weasel (?)] no doubt represent the many animals who are listed by the she-ape as being among the fox's friends. 40. The wolf challenges the fox to a duel [224]. The fox is shown taking the wolf's gauntlet directly from his hand. In the background the lion and one other animal (a monkey ?)

221 *A magic comb.*

The Hyſtory

had togither was al caruen in the fielde, euery thing by him ſelfe, and the ſtory written.

Here tolde Reynard of the thirde Jewell which was a Myrrour, and of two hiſtories which were written and caruen in the ſame Mirrour. ca. xliiii.

222 *A magic mirror.*

The Hiſtory

lord the king ye ought not to be angry when ye ſit in iudgement,for that beconnneth not your noblenes.A man that ſitteth in iudgemēt ought to put from him all wrath and anger,a Lord ought to haue diſcretion that ſhould ſit in iuſtice.I know better the points of the

223 *The lion congratulates the fox.*

The Hiſtory

YEt thought Reinard the Fox (I haue a good aduauntage, the clawes of his fore feete be of,& his feete ben yet ſore therof,when for my ſake he was vn. ſhod,he ſhalbe ſome what the weaker. Than ſayd the fox,

224 *The wolf challenges the fox.*

The History.

There with she went out of the fielde and let them twayne goe together: The Woulfe trode forth to the Fox in great wrath, and opened his fore feete and supposed to haue taken the Fox in them, but the Fox lept

of Reynard the Fox.

lept from him lightly, for hee was lighter on foote than he. The Woulfe lept after & hunted the Fox sore. Their frends stode without the listes & loked uppon them. The Wolfe strode wider then Reinard did, and oft overtoke him, & lift up his foote and thought to haue smitten him, but the Fox toke heede and smote him with his rough taile in the visage, which he had all to be pissed. Than wend the Woulfe to haue bene starke blinde, the pisse stert so in his eyen. Than must he rest to make cleane his eyne. Reinard thought on his vauntage and stode above the wind scraping and casting the dust with his feete, that it flew in the wolfes eyen. The woulfe was sore blinded therwith in such wise that he must leave ye running after him, for the sand and the pisse cleaued under his eyen, and it smarted so sore that he must nedes rubbe and wash it away. Than came Reinard in a great anger and bote him three great woundes on his head with his teeth, and said: what is that sir woulfe, hath one there bitten you, how is it with you? I will yet all otherwise bite you: I shall bring you some new thinge, ye haue stolen many a lambe, & destroyed many a simple beast, and now falsely haue appealed me and brought me in this trouble, all this shall I now avenge on thee, I am chosen for to reward thee for thine olde sinnes, for God wil no lenger suffer thee in thy great ravine and shrewdnes, I shall now assoyle thee, & that shall be good for thy soule, take paciently this penaunce, for thou shalt live no lenger, hel shalbe thy purgatory thy life is now in my mercy. But and if thou wilte knele downe and aske me forgivenes, & knowledge

225 *The fox and the wolf fight a duel.*

The Hystory

against me, and wold faine haue destroyed me, because they thought that the woulfe was better withholden and greater with you than I was, which am your true subiect. They knewe no other thinge why ne wherfore

of Reynard the Fox.

wherfore, they thought not as wise men be wonte to doe, that is, what at the end may happen. My Lord these be like a great heape of houndes which I sawe once stand at a Lords place upon a dunghil, wheras they awayted that men shoulde bringe them meate. Then sawe they an hound come out of the kitchin and had taken there a faire ribbe of beefe or it was given him, and he ran fast away withall, but the cooke had espied it or he went away, and toke a great boole of scalding water, & cast it upon his hips behinde, wherof he thanked not the cooke, for the heare behind was scalded of, and his skin seemed as it had ben through sodden, nevertheless he escaped away and kept that he had wonne. And whan his fellowes the other houndes sawe him come with this faire ribbe: they called him all and said to him. O howe good a friend is the cooke unto thee, which hath given to thee so good a bone, wheron is so much fleshe. The hounde sayde, ye know nothing therof, ye prayse me like as ye see mee before with the bone: but ye haue not sene me behind take hede and behold me wel behind on my buttocks, and than shall ye know how that I haue deserved it. And when they had loked behind on his hippes how that his skinne and his flesh was all raw & through sodden: than stode they all in dread, and were afraide of that sething water, and wold not of his fellowship, but fled and ran away fro him, & left him there alone. Se (my lord) this right haue these false beastes whan they be made lordes & may get their desire, and whan they be mightie & doubted, then be they extorcioners and pill & pole the people, and eate them lyke as the

Bb.ij.

226 *The lion declares the fox to be the victor.*

The Hiſtory.

Then the court brake vp, and the beaſtes departed & went to their places and homes that they came fro.

How the Fox with his friends and linage departed noblely fro the kyng & went vnto his caſtell Malepardus. cap.lviii.

Reinard

227 *The fox returns home and is greeted by his wife.*

look on. 41. The fox and wolf fight in a five-sided enclosure while other animals look on [225]. These include the crowned lion, the stag (symbolizing justice?), the wolf, the ram who stands immediately behind the leopard-referee holding his staff of office, the bear (?), and the cat. In the foreground is a monkey, a badger, and a weasel (?). The fox is shown striking the wolf across the side of the nose and jaws with his urine-soaked brush. 42. The fox (with his badger friend close beside him) stands before the seated lion and lioness to listen to the lion declare him victor [226] and, henceforth, his highest ranking officer and right-hand man. This is observed, in the foreground, by a large clawed, fierce-looking quadruped and, in the middle ground, to the right, by a cat, ape, hound, and (somewhat illogically since he is supposed to be half-dead somewhere on the battlefield) a wolf. 43. Flanked by the badger and the she-ape, the fox arrives at the entrance to his den where he is greeted by his wife [227]. In the background the badger shakes hands with him as he and other friends bid him farewell.

During the course of reconstructing the original Wynkyn de Worde series of vertical woodcuts, we have had recourse to four of the horizontal series, of which the earliest known surviving set are in the Anonymous edition of between 1560 and 1585. To give a fuller picture of the horizontal series and to show how they repeat the subject matter of the earlier vertical series, we reproduce four of the more interesting of them:

First, the fox disguised as a hermit [228]. Compare with [62]. No castle on the horizon; only one hen pecking at the ground; scarcely any attempt to depict vegetation. Next, the dead hen's funeral service [229]. Compare with illustration [63]. The group of animals in the background appears in outline only and omits the cat; and in the immediate foreground the hooded group of hens is reduced from three to two. Next, the fox at the gallows [230]. Compare with [82]. Apart from the tree on the horizon, this has all the protagonists and paraphernalia of the vertical cut, but is very inferior to it. Last, the magic comb [231]. Compare with [221]. This is about the only cut in this series which is at least as good if not better than its parallel in the vertical series, and this is probably due chiefly to the difference in format. The horizontal shape allows the artist to spread out the detail in his picture, and the scene of the sleeping, dreaming Paris being offered the golden apple is altogether more satisfactory and 'readable'.

228 *The fox, disguised as a hermit, approaches the cock. (This is from the series of horizontal woodcuts which first appear in the Anonymous c.1560 edition of the History of Reynard the Fox, but probably date from the early 16th century, and are based on the c.1495 Wynkyn de Worde series of woodcuts. Also from this edition, courtesy of Mr Grauwels, are illustrations 229-231.).*

229 *The dead hen's funeral service.*

230 *The fox at the gallows.*

231 A magic comb.

THE 1498 LÜBECK SERIES OF WOODCUTS

We have also had recourse to a few examples of the work of the artist who illustrated the earliest complete continental edition of the Reynard story, the 1498 Lübeck Low German *Reynke de Vos*. These measure approximately 8.8 by 8.8 cm and are mostly identical in their subject-matter content to that of the Wynkn de Worde series, but there are occasional differences and even some omissions, the most interesting one being that of the scene in which the cat attacks the naked priest's private parts. To give a fuller picture of the Lübeck series, here are four more examples:

First, the frontispiece picture of the lion presiding over his Whitsuntide open court [232]. Compare with [58]. The German artist's picture seems more crowded (though he omits three animals compared with the English artist's picture), and is altogether 'heavier'. In one interesting respect it is more anthropomorphized, for he gives the lion and the lioness voluminous cloaks. One wonders if he deliberately hides the lion's male member. Next, the first complaints of Reynard's victims [233]. Compare with [59]. The most striking difference is the inclusion in the English artist's picture of the background scene of the fox pouncing on an upturned hare, and the exclusion of this scene from the German artist's picture. Most medieval artists were at a bit of a loss to depict the badger. The English artist usually renders him as a small doggy-like creature, the German as a bigger one, and places him in the bottom left corner,

232 *The lion presides over his Whitsuntide court. Reproduced from the facsimile by T. Sodmann of the 1498 Low German Lübeck edition of Reynke de Vos. This is also the case for illustrations 233-235.*

233 *The first complaints to the lion by some of the fox's victims.*

234 The fox tries to get the cat to enter the priest's barn.

apparently looking (for no good reason) out of the picture and certainly not at the lion (again well cloaked). The wolf, looking more like a dog, has swopped places with him compared with the English artist's picture. While the cat and the little dog or hound keep the same positions, in the text the cat has a difference of opinion with the little dog, and this seems to be reflected in the way it looks at him and raises its left forepaw. The German artist depicts the cat as if he were totally indifferent to what is going on, and he appears to be licking his paw as he turns his back on the lion. Next, the cat being led to the priest's barn [234]. Compare with [69]. The English artist shows the cat already caught in the snare whereas the German artist has the fox point out to the cat where the hole into the priest's barn is to be found, and he makes the snare visible to us, the viewers, but not, presumably, to the cat! The German artist makes the barn more prominent by showing less of other nearby buildings, in particular the priest's quite handsome house and a courtyard well. Last, the fox on the gallows ladder [235]. Compare with [82]. The Lübeck cut is altogether heavier and more crowded than the de Worde cut. Perhaps the most significant difference is the position of the fox on the ladder. The English artist much more successfully conveys the way the fox turns to the members of his audience and makes his cunning confession to them, but the German artist is perhaps better in conveying the cat's determination to get on with the hanging. The spectators are differently grouped: as a result the unicorn's horn and the stag's antlers, both important symbolically, are more prominent in the de Worde cut. A very large hare joins the spectators in Lübeck. This is a nice touch for he is to be the fox's next murder victim.

235 *The fox at the gallows.*

OTHER EARLY USERS OF THE WYNKYN DE WORDE CUTS

We have said that the cuts made for Wynkyn de Worde's edition of the Beast Epic dated 1495 (or a little earlier) were used again and again, taken over by other printers and publishers of the History of Reynard the Fox who may have paid a fee for them or bought them. Sometimes they had to be repaired and eventually they had to be replaced by obvious imitations.

The earliest known use of de Worde's cuts by another printer is by Richard Pynson and may be ascribed to the period 1501 to 1505. The evidence is to be found in two fragments of a History of Reynard the Fox kept at the National Library for Scotland in Edinburgh which acquired them in 1965. Pynson was a contemporary of both Caxton and de Worde, and published an unillustrated *Hiystorye of Reinard the Foxe* somewhere between 1494 and 1500. The illustrated Edinburgh fragments are dated c.1501-1505 on typographical evidence, and they consist of two bifolia, one containing part of Chapter 30 and one part of Chapter 32 in the 43 chapter tradition for the division of the story, a tradition which extended over the period 1481-1550. These fragments are badly damaged. It is in the surviving part of Chapter 32 that almost the whole of Wynkyn de Worde's picture of the fox's magic mirror is to be found. It is clear that Pynson uses exactly the same block as is used in the Anonymous edition for they both show signs of wear and tear in exactly the same places, and a photograph made on thin paper of each of these pictures coincides at every point when superimposed and held up to the light.

THE RE-USE AND REPAIR OF WYNKYN DE WORDE CUTS

A survey of some of the evidence for the re-use and repair of the Wynkyn de Worde cuts may be illustrated by concentrating on the picture of the first complaints made by Reynard's victims [59].

The earliest appearance of this cut is as the frontispiece to Lydgate's poem entitled *The horse, the sheep and the goose* [236] published by Wynkyn de Worde not later than 1495. In fact, it appears twice in this book; first facing Wynkyn de Worde's imprint (formerly Caxton's), then facing the first page of the text. In each case it is beautifully clear, and there is not a flaw in it. It can have been little used, but it will not have been made for this book because it does not

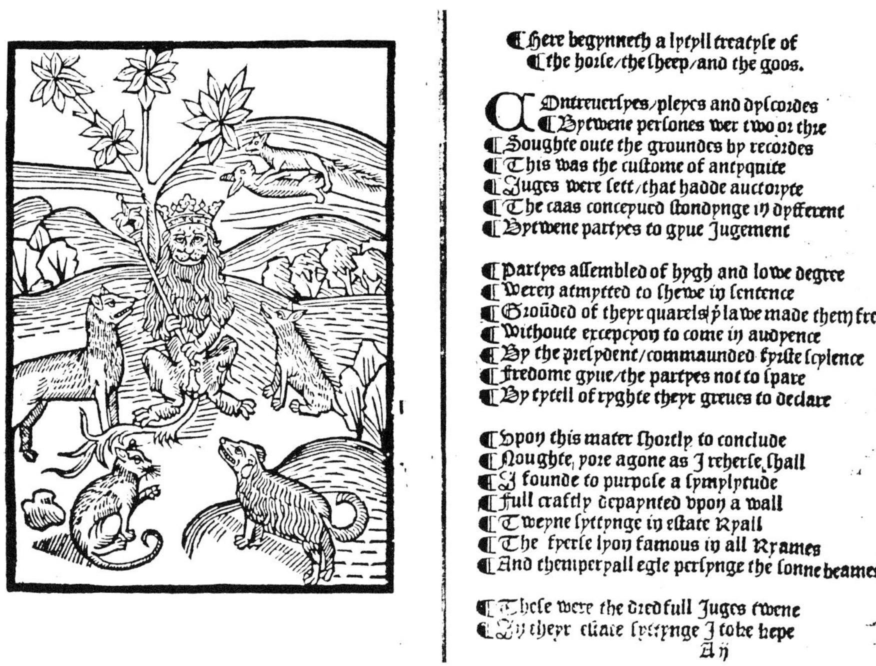

¶ Here begynneth a lytyll treatyse of
¶ the horſe/the ſheep/and the goos.

C Ontreuerſyes/pleyes and dyſcordes
¶ Bytwene perſones wer two or thre
¶ Soughte oute the groundes by recordes
¶ This was the cuſtome of antyquite
¶ Juges were ſett/that hadde auctoryte
¶ The caas conceyued ſtondynge in dyfferent
¶ Bytwene partyes to gyue Jugement

¶ Partyes aſſembled of hygh and lowe degree
¶ Weren atmytted to ſhewe in ſentence
¶ Grouded of theyr quarels/ye lawe made them free
¶ Withoute excepcyon to come in audyence
¶ By the preſydent/commaunded kyſte ſcylence
¶ Fredome gyue/the partyes not to ſpare
¶ By tytell of ryghte theyr greues to declare

¶ Vpon this mater ſhortly to conclude
¶ Noughte, yore agone as J reherſe, ſhall
¶ J founde to purpoſe a ſymplytude
¶ Full craftly depaynted vpon a wall
¶ Tweyne ſyttynge in eſtate Ryall
¶ The fyerſe lyon famous in all Reames
¶ And themperyall egle perſynge the ſonne beames

¶ These were the dredfull Juges twene
¶ In theyr estate syttynge J toke hepe
A ij

236 *The first complaints to the lion by some of the fox's victims. From a facsimile of Lydgate's The horse , the sheep and the goose, Wynkyn de Worde, c.1495, courtesy of Mr Grauwels.*

237 *The first complaints to the lion by some of the fox's victims. From the Allde 1620 edition, courtesy of Mr Grauwels.*

illustrate anything in its text. Clearly, it was in de Worde's possession and belongs to the Reynard the Fox cycle, but is used here as an attractive space-filler. Its next surviving use is in the anonymous edition [59] of sometime between 1560 and 1585. It appears as the first cut in that edition and is used on only that occasion. There is considerable evidence of wear and tear, especially in the thick black border. But it is the same block. When a photograph is made of the two pictures on very thin paper and held up to the light, they superimpose exactly. This picture next appears in Edward Allde's 1620 edition. The first time it is used is on page A iv verso [237], and it looks at first glance as if it is the one used in the Anonymous edition. However, there are differences which may take some spotting and might be due to further wear and tear. It has lost four millimetres from the top, cutting off part of the clusters of leaves on the branches to the left and centre of the tree. From the bottom it has lost only one millimetre so that the rear paws of the animal in the right foreground seem to enter the border of the cut. There are however other subtle differences which suggest that this picture is made from an altogether different block and is not a slightly cut-down version of the Lydgate/Anonymous block. Compare, for example, the stone between the cat's rump and the border. The shape is different. The shadow below the cat covers a different area. The shading in the tree nearest the lion on the right is not the same. Indeed, it is the differences in the shading which prove that this is a very clever, close copy of the Lydgate/Anonymous block. Compare, in particular, the three fat lines which are part of the shading for the ground in the bottom right corner of the Lydgate block, just behind the dog's rear right paw, with the two thin ones here. When a photograph is made on thin paper of this and the Lydgate cut and held up to the light, they do not coincide as they should if the same block were being used. This picture appears for a second time in Allde's 1620 edition, on page Q ii recto [238]. At first glance we seem to have the Wynkyn de Worde orginal. The dimensions are exactly the same as the Lydgate cut, the shading is exactly the same (compare the three heavy lines in the bottom right-hand corner). However, the background detail of the fox pinning down the upside-down hare is not there, nor

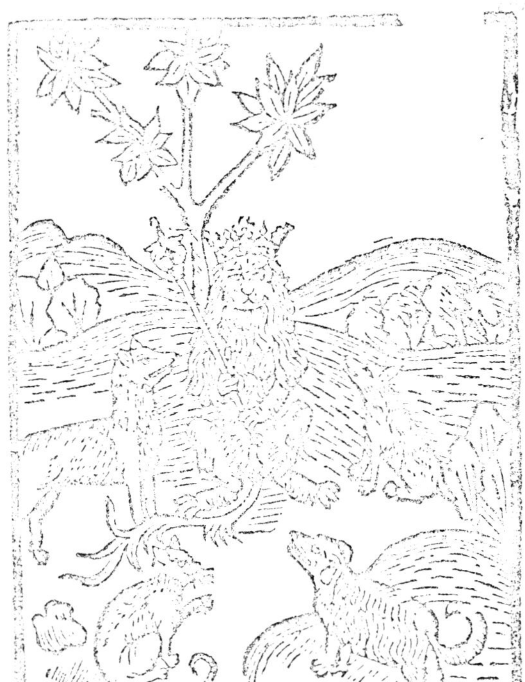

238 *The first complaints to the lion by some of the fox's victims. A damaged version of the cut reproduced as illustration 237, also from the Allde 1620 edition.*

are the lines indicating the distant horizon to both the left and the right. However, superimposed photographs of this and the Lydgate cut show that the same block has been used, but modified, presumably because of considerable wear and tear or damage in the top right area.

From now on, and for quite a long while, the copy [237] and the modified original [238] were to live side by side. For example, in Elisabeth Allde's 1629 edition, the original cut but without the background fox-and-hare scene is used first (at page A iv verso) and the 'new' slightly smaller copy with that scene in the background is used second (at page Q ii recto). In Bell's 1656 edition, a much more worn version of the original Lydgate cut without the fox-and-hare scene is used twice, and the slightly smaller 'new' one with that scene is used once.

Eventually, the Wynkyn de Worde vertical cuts as well as the Anonymous horizontal cuts became too worn to be re-used. When this happened towards the end of the seventeenth century, the publisher whose job it was to have them replaced was careful to have them imitated [239]. This says much for their intrinsic quality, their popularity and their venerable history. It is especially noteworthy that this publisher, Edward Brewster, had both the vertical and the horizontal series copied, but he concentrated on the vertical series. He was so proud of his new

239 *The first complaints to the lion by some of the fox's victims. From the Brewer 1671 edition.*

set of blocks that he had his initials prominently engraved on them. Thus, in 1671, nearly two hundred years after the creation of Wynkyn de Worde's picture cycle, it and the subsidiary sixteenth-century cycle of smaller cuts were given a new and long lease of life.

As we have seen, the earliest evidence we have for the replacement of a de Worde cut is found in Allde's 1620 edition [237]. This was very subtly done. Much less subtle are the occasional replacements in Jane Bell's editions in the 1650s. She replaced some of both the vertical and the horizontal series. Her 1656 picture of the fox and the badger passing the nuns' poultry yard [240] keeps quite close to the original (compare with [74]). The chief differences are in the depiction of the convent church (more obviously a church in the original) and in the conversion of the building beside it from a barn into a house. But Brewster's 1671 copy of this cut [241] is much more faithful to the original. Bell's 1656 copy of the scene at the gallows ladder [242] (compare with illustration [82]) is also similar in content detail, but altogether heavier (contrast the background trees) and slightly more anthropomorphizing in that some of the animals are given more human faces, especially the cat and the lion. Unrealistically, however, Bell's artist has the fox stand with both feet close together on one rung of the ladder [242] while de Worde's realistically uses two rungs (one for each leg) and has the fox prop his back against yet another. Curiously, Brewster's gallows scene [243] closely copies Bell's, but there are slight differences, in particular in the corner where Brewster's initials appear, blotting out a little plant. Here the lion's tail ends in a spear-like shape instead of a four-pronged fork. Perhaps the de Worde original was not available for one reason or another to Brewster's artist, and here we have an example of a copy being made of a copy of one of the most successful of the famous Wynkyn de Worde pictures.

240 *The fox and the badger pass a nuns' poultry yard. From the Bell 1656 edition.*

241 *The fox and the badger pass a nuns' poultry yard. From the Brewster 1671 edition.*

242 *The fox at the gallows ladder. From the Bell 1656 edition.*

243 *The fox at the gallows ladder. From the Brewster 1671 edition.*

THE EARLIEST ILLUSTRATED ENGLISH EDITIONS OF THE HISTORY OF REYNARD THE FOX

From William Caxton's first edition (1481) to Thomas Gaultier's only edition (1550), the story is divided into 43 chapters. This may explain why the Wynkyn de Worde picture cycle contained 43 vertical cuts, though in fact some chapters were not illustrated, and some were illustrated with more than one picture. In the period before the appearance of the Anonymous edition we know, either through tiny fragments or circumstantial evidence, of only three illustrated editions: the one by Wynkyn de Worde sometime before or in 1495 and the other by him c.1515; and the one by Richard Pynson somewhere between 1501 and 1505. In the Anonymous edition (between 1560 and 1585) the story is divided into 58 chapters. This may account for the frequent repetition of the vertical cuts (as space-fillers) and even for the introduction and occasional repetition of the smaller horizontal cuts. For most of the seventeenth century, the story (now short-titled *The Most Delectable History of Reynard the Fox*) is divided into 25 chapters, but this does not result in any noticeable reduction in the number of cuts used of either the vertical or the horizontal kind, nor in the introduction of new illustrative material. In short, the same cuts go on in much the same order (apart from space-filler repetitions) illustrating the same episodes. The first seventeenth-century edition to continue this picture cycle tradition is Edward Allde's (1620) followed by Elizabeth Allde's (1629). It continues in the two editions published in 1640 by Richard Oulton, one for John Slater and the other for John Wright; also in the editions published by Jane Bell in 1650, 1654, and 1656; and in the first edition published by Edward Brewster in 1662. By this date the Wynkyn de Worde blocks had become so worn and damaged that it is not surprising to discover a totally new set closely modelled on them and on the sixteenth-century horizontals, and that this set should appear in an edition made for the publisher who last owned the de Worde blocks; that is, in Edward Brewster's second edition in 1671 of *The most Delectable History of Reynard the Fox. Newly Corrected and purged from all grosness in Phrase and Matter. As also Augmented and Inlarged with sundry excellent Morals and Expositions upon every several Chapter.* The forty different cuts which illustrate this edition all prominently display his initials EB. He published further illustrated editions in 1676, 1681, 1694 and 1701.

THE FIRST MAJOR RENEWAL OF THE REYNARD STORY: A *CONTINUATION... OF THE HISTORY OF REYNARD THE FOX*

In 1671 Brewster gave a new lease of life to the old picture cycle, and in 1672 he grafted new life onto the old story with *A Continuation, Or Second Part Of The Most Pleasant and Delightful History of Reynard the Fox Containing Much Matter of Pleasure and Content Written For the Delight of Young Men, Pleasure of the Aged, and Profit of All.* In due course, this new story about Reynard was to attract new illustrations, but in this volume Brewster makes do with a sprinkling of fifteen cuts from his new cycle bearing the initials EB, and he uses them again in his 1676 edition of the old story (now called Part One) and in his 1681 edition of both Part One and Part Two.

The new story, the *Continuation*, begins with Reynard in his new role as the lion's chief minister. His first move is to form an alliance with the wolf and make him chief prelate. This makes the bear and the cat jealous, so he grants favours to them and wins them over. They all enrich themselves (especially Reynard) and plot against the lion. The leopard and the panther inform the lion of the plot against him, and together they attack Reynard and his allies. After suffering heavy losses, Reynard and his surviving allies retreat to his castle where they are besieged. After a long and fierce resistance, they are taken prisoner. Reynard is put on trial, found guilty of treason, and executed.

THE SHIFTS OF REYNARDINE

In 1684 Brewster marketed a further sequel to this *Continuation*. Since Reynard was dead the chief role in this new story is given to one of his sons, the one called Reynardine. It is entitled *The Shifts of Reynardine The Son of Reynard the Fox, Or a Pleasant History Of His Life and Death. Full of Variety (etc.) And may fitly be applied to the Late Times. Now Published for the Reformation of Mens Manners.* After Brewster's illustrated edition of 1684, further illustrated versions of it were published by W. Onley in 1697, 1702, and 1708; also 'for the Booksellers of London and Westminster', c.1710; for T. Norris in 1723; for A. Bettesworth and C. Hitch in 1735; in Dublin in 1749; in Belfast in 1763; and in Dublin again in 1787.

The Shifts of Reynardine begins by reporting how Reynard, before his execution (at the end of The *Continuation*), gave his vast hidden fortune to his sons Volpus and Reynardine. He instructed them how to hide it safely away for their future use and made them swear to revenge him on his two betrayers, Firapel the Leopard and Sly-Look the Panther. However, the young foxes were quite soon attacked and robbed of their treasure. In the process Volpus got killed, but Reynardine made good his escape and, in a distant land, began a peripatetic series of adventures. He first entered the Kingdom of Zalep, where he made friends with Brocket the Badger. Following the badger's advice, he went on to the monastery of Manton where he was admitted as a novice, but he soon tired of the monastic life and made his escape. Retaining his novice's gown he was able to return to Zalep and make a good living by granting easy shrift to the wicked and by selling indulgences cheaply. He frankly admitted to a shrewd questioner that he was duping the people but insisted they wanted to be duped. Eventually the loss of his gown in a trap put an end to this phase of his life. He returns to Feraria, his native country, meets Zani the ape, teams up with him and, at his suggestion, turns physician. He assumes the title and name of Doctor Pedanto, and quickly gains a large practice among the common people. His reputation is such that when the old leopard Firapel falls ill, he summons him to his bedside. True to the promise he had made to his father shortly before his execution, Reynardine takes advantage of the situation and kills the sick old leopard with an overdose of a sleeping potion. Zani quarrels with Reynardine over the division of the money they had got out of Firapel. Out of spite, the ape denounces Doctor Pedanto as an impostor, but Reynardine manages to leave the country before Noble has a chance to seize him. He then comes into conflict with a mountebank who cuts off his ears and his brush. Unwillingly disguised in this way, Reynardine returns to the royal court where, calling himself Crabron he enters the panther's service only to carry out the oath he had made to his condemned father by poisoning the panther. He feigns grief at Sly-Look's death so successfully that Noble makes him one of his purveyors. In this office he ruthlessly eliminates his enemies but is at last unmasked and, under torture, admits his crimes. Condemned to death he wins a reprieve by telling monstrous lies from the scaffold. Unrepentant, he returns to a life of crime but is caught again and, after a full confession, is executed.

New illustrations for these new English histories of Reynard and his descendants were to follow the ones used for Edward Brewster's editions, though they are almost all powerfully and obviously influenced by the traditional vertical and horizontal series of cuts and contribute little of quality and interest.

Part Two: John Shurley's heroic verses (1681) to the London chapbooks (c.1780)

JOHN SHURLEY

Edward Brewster was not the only late seventeenth-century publisher of the Beast Epic to feel the need to renew it. His contemporary John Shurley (sometimes spelled Shirley) also felt that

244 *The lion's Whitsuntide court. From Shurley's 1681 Most Delightful History.*

need, and in 1681 he published his *Most Delightful History of Reynard the Fox in Heroic Verse*. His iambic pentameters rhyming in couplets are divided into 24 chapters and run to 4,000 lines and 114 pages. Unlike other, earlier renovations of the story, it was never reprinted, perhaps because the verse form was unpopular and because the illustrations were poor and few. There is a moderately good frontispiece, a copperplate etching of the lion's Whitsuntide court gathering [244], and then at considerable intervals a total of eight crude woodcuts of varying sizes. One of these depicts three distinctly different scenes, each within its own frame: the animals' court; the lion listening to complaints from three animals; and the bear trapped in a split log [245]. Another depicts two separately framed scenes: the badger and fox arriving at court; then the moment of the fox's condemnation. Yet another one depicts two separately framed scenes: the fox on the gallows ladder; then the moment when the fox is 'elevated'. Some of the blocks are of the kind which depict two or more scenes within the one frame as when the fox sets off as a pilgrim, decapitates the hare, and sends the hapless ram back to court with the hare's head in a

245 *The lion's court; the animals' complaints; the bear trapped. From Shurley's Most Delightful History.*

scrip. The last block to illustrate this book shows, to one side, an ape advising the fox on how to fight his duel with the wolf (and, oddly enough, seems to be showing him how to handle a sword), and then, to the other side, we see the fox in the duelling enclosure about to strike the wolf with his urine-soaked brush. All these scenes are clearly inspired and heavily influenced by the corresponding cuts in the Wynkyn de Worde cycle.

CHAP-BOOKS

A very different attempt to renew the Reynardian epic and, presumably to respond to its popularity with the less well-off was the slender illustrated chap-book. In this the narrative is considerably abbreviated, being reduced to about 24 small pages (approximately 8.5 cm wide by 15.5 cm high), resulting in a kind of slim pocket-book. Even if aimed at the less well-off, the authors clearly expected their readers to be relatively well-educated to judge by the kind of language they use ('It was when the woods was (*sic*) cloathed with green attire, and the meadows adorned with fragrant flowers; when birds chaunted forth their harmonious songs, the

Lion made a great feast at his palace of Sanden, and issued a proclamation for all the beasts and herds to come thereto without delay, on pain of his contempt...').

There are two kinds of chap-book: those divided into 12 or 13 two-page chapters (like the ones published for J. Conyers in London between 1685 and 1688; by Thomas Saint in Newcastle-upon-Tyne between 1769 and 1788; and by J. Smart in Wolverhampton, c.1780, all called *The Most Pleasant History of Reynard the Fox*), and those divided into 9 two-to-three-page chapters and all called quite simply *The History of Reynard the Fox* (for example, the ones published and sold in Aldermary Church Yard, London, c.1750; in London, c.1775; again in London but c.1780; and in Penrith by A. Soulby, c.1800). It is perhaps worth noting that, with these chap-books, the story is occasionally being marketed outside London. The 12/13-chapter chap-books are not very interesting from our point of view because they contain only title-page illustrations of the lion holding a plenary session of court. In the one in Thomas Saint's Newcastle edition, the presence of the unicorn is rather unusual and betrays familiarity with the Wynkyn de Worde cycle. By contrast, two of the 9-chapter chap-books have a mini-series of woodcuts which, although very crude, owe little to the traditional cycle. Typical is the c.1750 (Aldermary Church Yard) edition which begins with the lion holding court. In fact, it also has two such scenes, of which the one on the title page imitates most closely the de Worde tradition, while the one set into the first page of the first chapter showing the crowned lion perched high upon a gigantic stone throne and a farmer in the distant background leading a heavily laden horse towards his fenced-in farmyard [246] is borrowed from the new Onley

246 *The lion holding court. From the c.1750 chap-book. This and all the illustrations up to and including 251 are from and by the courtesy of Professor H. Menke.*

1708 short cycle of woodcuts specially made for the *Shifts of Reynardine*. The remaining five cuts are either irrelevant or crudely simple.

To sum up; the few chap-book illustrations we have found are mostly of poor quality. They begin to deviate from the Wynkyn de Worde tradition in their content, but they contribute nothing of artistic value to the iconographic history of the Reynard story.

THE EIGHTEENTH-CENTURY HISTORIES OF REYNARD AND OF REYNARDINE

As the seventeenth century drew to its close, W. Onley published (1697) the Reynardian epic in two parts. The first part is in fact the traditional Anglo-Flemish story, and the second part is made up of the *Shifts of Reynardine* which were launched as recently as 1684 by Edward Brewster. Evidently neither the original Wynkyn de Worde series nor the Edward Brewster copies were available to Onley, so he had a new set of woodcuts made, all of the horizontal oblong kind, occupying about half the page and always placed at the beginning of a chapter, following the detailed description of the chapter's contents. There are only five different pictures (frequently repeated), and they depict (in order of appearance) the lion's plenary court, the bear trapped in the split log, the fox on the gallows ladder, the fox beginning his pilgrimage, and the duel of the fox and the wolf. They illustrate both the Reynard and the Reynardine stories, and in the Reynardine part they bear no relationship whatsoever to the story. The only picture showing some artistic originality in its execution is the copperplate frontispiece scene of the lion's plenary court. This particular copperplate is used often in Onley's numerous eighteenth-century editions and in some others that borrow from his.

Just into the eighteenth century (1702), Onley reprinted this two-part form of the epic, and added to it a third but non-Reynardian book centred on a rook called Cawood. To quote the last part of his loquacious title: ...*To Which is added, The History of Cawood the Rook: or, The Assembly of the Birds: With the several speeches they made to the Eagle, in hopes to have the Government in his Absence: How the Rook was banish'd; with the Reason why Crafty Fellows are call'd Rooks. Together with Morals and Expositions on every Chapter*. This joining of the Anglo-Flemish *History of Reynard*, Brewster's *Reynardine*, and Onley's *Cawood* evidently proved successful, for Onley published them again in one volume in 1708; as did Norris in 1723; Bettesworth and Hitch in 1735; J. Blow (?), Dublin in 1749; D. Blow, Belfast in 1763; and Wogan, Dublin in 1787. The two Reynardian parts of these three-part volumes were all illustrated with varying numbers of pictures which are mostly (and obviously) inspired by their counterparts in the traditional vertical and horizontal picture cycles described above in Part I of this chapter. Take, for example, from the 1702 Onley edition, the frontispiece scene of the lion holding court, seated at the foot of a tree [247]. The setting shows a little originality, as does the distribution and mix of the animal-courtiers gathered first beside the lion (lioness to the left, leopard and stag to the right) then before him (cat, fox, bear, wolf). The drawing is also quite competently done but clearly inspired by its model in the de Worde cycle.

The cuts which illustrate the Reynardine part of Onley's 1708 edition are sometimes quite original and contribute something new to our iconographic survey. Part I, the Anglo-Flemish story, uses five different blocks from the Wynkyn de Worde series, but Part II, the Reynardine story, is illustrated with six new woodcuts made specially for it. They are of the horizontal

247 *The lion holding court. From the Onley 1697 edition.*

variety and quite small, measuring about 8.5 cm wide by 4.25 cm high. Some are of the kind that depict several scenes within the one frame. For example, the one at the beginning of Chapter Two [248] shows, in the middle ground, the fox entering a monastery on the advice of the badger who accompanies him to the fortified gateway and bridge over a moat. This leads into a walled and built-up area, most probably the monastery, its chapel, and its outbuildings. When the fox leaves the monastery, he retains his novice's gown and poses as a man in holy orders. One of his misdeeds in this role follows soon after his preaching to geese shown here in the background, on the surface of a pond. We also see him in the foreground dressed as a religious and looking towards an enthroned and crowned lion. Between the two is depicted the same lion on all fours, a crown lying on the ground in front of him. This part of the story is

248 *The fox enters a monastery; preaches to geese; addresses the lion. From Onley's 1708 edition.*

alluded to in the summary of the chapter's contents printed just above the cut: 'How the Lion, upon seeing the Crown, presaged the Ruine of his Family, which so fell out.' This particular picture is reproduced chiefly because it incorporates the motif treated in Chapter Two, The Fox-Preacher and Religious. One wonders if this part of the story, and this illustration, have been inspired by the abundant illustrations of it in English art before the invention of printing and the making of woodcuts. The *Shifts* begins with the execution of Reynard, and this is depicted at the head of the opening chapter [249]. When the story ends with the execution of Reynardine as well, the new cut [250] is based ultimately on the cut made by the Wynkyn de Worde Master for Reynard's near-execution [42], but the more immediate source is probably Bell's or Brewster's version [242, 243]. In the first of these two execution scenes [249], Reynard is shown, in the background, mounting the gallows ladder where he will be hanged; in the foreground he is shown being dragged to his grave, watched over by a large King Noble. This short cycle of six horizontal cuts made for the *Shifts* in 1708 was used again in part in the c.1710 edition (printer unknown, probably Onley) and in full in Norris's 1723 edition. Some were also used in other Onley or Onley-inspired editions.

Often these eighteenth-century editions of the Reynard and Reynardine stories were illustrated with a mixture of cuts from different cycles and by different artists. They would draw on the time-hallowed vertical and horizontal cycles, from the Brewster copies, and Onley's new set of six horizontal cuts. Once in a while, new pictures were specially made for the occasion. For example, the Bettesworth and Hitch edition of 1735 contains twelve different cuts from the earliest cycles, all six of the new horizontal series; four from larger-sized cuts

249 *The fox's execution at the gallows. From the Shifts in Onley's 1708 edition.*

250 *The fox at the gallows. From the Shifts in Onley's 1708 edition.*

251 *The lion holds court; and the fox is hanged. Frontispiece etching from the Dublin, Wogan 1787 edition.*

specially made for this volume, as well as one new full-page cut. Only rarely do any of these new cuts show any originality or offer anything worth pausing over. One such exception is the full-page frontispiece picture illustrating the 1787, Dublin, Wogan edition [251]. This is composed of two pictures, a smaller horizontal-shaped one above and a bigger vertical-shaped one below. The horizontal upper-register picture depicts the fox actually hanging from the gallows and shows a cock and two hens looking on from a foreground position while two large quadrupeds look on from the background. This is of some interest because (as pointed out at the beginning of Chapter Four, The Fox's Death and Resurrection) in spite of all his misdeeds told in all the stories about him from before Brewster's 1672 *Continuation* (with the exception of Henryson's *The Tod*) the fox is never hanged in any of them, even though he is in many a medieval manuscript drawing and painting, in panels of painted glass, in sculpted stone and wood. Iconographically at least, this picture continues an old tradition, but it is the first time the hanged fox is actually depicted in a printed book in English. The vertical lower-register picture below the hanging fox depicts the traditional frontispiece scene of the lion holding plenary court, though the setting and the spectator's viewpoint onto this gathering is unusual in that we see the lion and his courtiers (just as we see the hanged fox) in profile.

The quality of the late fifteenth-century cycle of woodcuts which illustrated the Reynard stories was so good and so much loved for so long a time that it seems to have inhibited significant artistic innovation even after the woodcuts died a natural death. Other episodes which might have been illustrated were not. When new stories were created to continue the old ones they were often such close imitations of their predecessors that it was possible to illustrate them by using the time-hallowed pictures again, or to make new pictures which looked like minor variants of the old ones. It is not until the nineteenth century that artists of real calibre manage to break, and even then not completely, the long-lasting spell cast by Wynkyn de Worde's most talented artist.

Part Three: The Nineteenth and Twentieth Centuries

As the influence of the Wynkyn de Worde Master's picture cycle waned throughout the eighteenth century, so too did the quality of the pictures produced by the diminishing band of his imitators and admirers. This probably had a lot to do with the decline in the appeal of the History of Reynard the Fox and of its various continuations to a relatively cultured adult public, and a feeling that (in spite of frequent attempts to emphasize the moral lessons to be learned) it was no longer proper reading in polite society. Efforts to make it suitable for young people, which had already begun in earnest in the eighteenth century, ran into the difficulties inherent in the adultery, rape, castration, corruption, violence and general bawdiness which characterize its medieval and early post-medieval forms. Yet they are all present both in the text of the literary giant and in the illustrations to that text by the major artist who together were chiefly responsible for the renewal of interest in Reynard which developed in the nineteenth century. As in the Middle Ages, the impetus came from the continental side of the Channel, but this time it came chiefly from Germany.

Goethe's *Reineke Fuchs*, published in 1794, was brilliantly illustrated in 1846 by Wilhelm von Kaulbach. This text, translated into English, and this artist's pictures, published in England, played a major role in the renewal of interest in Reynardian fiction in Britain at both adult and young people's levels. At the beginning of the final stage in this study, it is perhaps worth recalling that both poet and painter had, indirectly, links with that most influential of late medieval and illustrated texts, *Reynaerts Historie*. Goethe's main literary source, through the High German translation of J. C. Gottshed published in 1752, was (via a Wolfenbüttel 1711 reprint) the Lübeck 1498 Low German *Reynke de Vos* which, in its turn, was a translation-adaptation of a version of *Reynaerts Historie*. While Kaulbach's models for his pictures included the seventeenth-century Dutch artist Allart van Everdingen (whose illustrations were published for the first time in Gottshed's 1752 *Reineke Fuchs*), they also included one or more of the several woodcut cycles published in Germany based on the 1498 Low German Lübeck cycle (e.g., Rostock 1517, 1539, 1549; Frankfurt 1550, 1556, etc. Menke 1992, pp. 256-355, gives a comprehensive list of all the illustrated editions in both Low and High German, several of which Kaulbach almost certainly knew).

The earliest translation of Goethe's *Reineke Fuchs* into English seems to have been the one by Soltau in 1803. Others followed in Queen Victoria's reign, probably in part through the influence of Prince Albert who inspired much admiration for German culture, though Goethe's reputation was by then immense. Naylor's translation appeared in 1844; Holloway's in 1852; Arnold's in 1855; Ainslie's in 1886; and Rogers's in 1888. A selection of Kaulbach's Reynardian illustrations first appeared in England as early as 1851 in a rather unusual book which celebrated and commemorated an unusual aspect of the Great Exhibition held in the Crystal Palace in 1850 (inspired by Prince Albert!). This book's title is: *The Comical Creatures from Wurtemberg, Including the Story of Reynard the Fox with Twenty Illustrations Drawn from the Stuffed Animals Contributed by Hermann Ploucquet of Stuttgart to the Great Exhibition* (London: Bogue, 1851). One reads in the Preface that 'the famous painter Kaulbach has recently illustrated Goethe's version [of the story of Reynard] with perhaps the finest series of pictures with which a book was ever adorned'. Ploucquet selected six of Kaulbach's etchings to illustrate the 33-page abbreviated [and censored!] version of *The Story of Reynard the Fox* with which this strange little book (clearly intended for both mature and young people as a kind of souvenir of their visit to the Stuffed Animals Section of the Great Exhibition) concludes. 'Everyone,' says the anonymous author in his Preface, 'from Her Majesty the Queen down to the charity-boys, hastens to see the Stuffed Animals from the Zollverein...' Exaggerated though this claim may seem, it is in part at least supported by the sober Professor J. A. Froude who, in *Fraser's Magasine*, 1852, writing an essay entitled 'Reynard the Fox', says: 'The appearance of the Wurtemberg animals at the Exhibition came fortunately *apropos* to our assistance: a few years ago it was rare to find a person who had read the Fox Epic... but now the charming figures of Reineke himself, and King Lion, and Isegrim, and Bruin... had set all the world asking who and what they were, and the story began to get itself known. The old editions, which had long slept unbound in reams upon the shelves, began to descend and to clothe themselves in green and crimson. Mr Dickens sent a summary of it around the households of England. Everybody began to talk of Reineke...') This is a fascinating tribute to the power of illustration (even if in the form of stuffed animals from Noble's court) to stimulate interest in a story.

Apart from his brilliant draughtsmanship and sense of composition, Kaulbach's great innovation was to push the anthropomorphic qualities of his animals about as far as it is possible without turning them into human beings. Their gestures and facial expressions are immensely and dramatically human. We have had a glimpse of this with his picture of Reynard's triumph [208]. Another typical and telling example of his artistic strength is his depiction of Reynard on the gallows' ladder [252]. This, of course, belongs to the considerable number of subjects he treats which are also treated by both the Wynkyn de Worde and Lübeck Masters; but he often broke away from the old, traditional subject matter to assert his independence, usually with a most impressive sense of humour, as when he shows Noble and his courtiers having a party [253].

252 *The fox makes his confession from the gallows ladder. Kaulbach, etching, 1846.*

253 *The lion and his courtiers have a party. Kaulbach, etching, 1846.*

Although the brilliance of Kaulbach's Reynardian etchings was quickly recognized, they were not immediately used to illustrate English translations of Goethe's *Reineke Fuchs*. Instead, other artists who were clearly much influenced by the new, great master were preferred. Thus, Holloway's 1852 translation, *Reynard the Fox, a Poem in Twelve Cantos*, was illustrated with 37 engravings on steel after designs by the German H. Leutemann [254]. There are a few illustrations by Joseph Wolf, also Kaulbach-influenced, in T. J. Arnold's 1855 *Reynard the Fox: After the German Version of Goethe*. At last, Kaulbach's own etchings appeared in another much finer, folio printing (by T. Stoffer, New York, 1872) of Arnold's translation. Perhaps the last use of them in this context is to be found in the poor copies in Stallybrass's 1924 edition of Caxton's text.

Preceding, then running parallel with the relatively limited interest in Goethe's *Reineke Fuchs* in English was a steady growth in antiquarianism and things medieval. In Britain as elsewhere in the West, a cultured, educated elite sought out the earliest versions of literary masterpieces,

254 *The bear is caught in a half-split log. Leutemann, etching, 1852.*

and attempts were made to edit them in a scholarly way, and even to publish facsimiles. In his Select Bibliography, pp. lxvii-lxviii, Blake (1992) shows that serious editions and translations of Caxton's *Historye of Reynart the Foxe* began in 1844. Others followed in 1878, 1884, 1889, 1892, 1897, 1907, 1924 (Stallybrass's), 1960, and 1970. These statistics suggest that there was something of a revival in the fortunes of the old Beast Epic in the latter half of Victoria's reign, probably accelerated by interest in Goethe's work, and sparked off by a group of stuffed Reynardian animals at the Great Exhibition! But the number of copies printed of both translated versions of Goethe's poem and scholarly editions of Caxton's text was quite limited, as was the fairly cultured and largely learned readership of both. Only a small minority of the Caxton texts was illustrated, and relatively unimaginatively. Sands's 1960 edition reproduces just a few of the 1498 Lübeck woodcuts. There is nothing to compare with the steady production in Belgium, Holland, and France of finely printed and bound copies of the native Beast

Epic which serve chiefly as a vehicle for the illustrations made by an artist of the highest calibre.

But there might have been. In 1896 a wealthy Glasgow textile manufacturer and art collector, T.G. Arthur, commissioned one of Britain's finest young artists, Joseph Crawhall, to make ten drawings to illustrate Caxton's *Historye of Reynart the Foxe*. Though Crawhall made the drawings in 1896-97, Arthur abandoned the idea of the illustrated Caxton, and sold the drawings to a W.A. Coates who had them reproduced in facsimile and offered to the public in 1906 in a limited edition of two hundred copies. Although Crawhall's choice of topics to illustrate sometimes coincided with that made by the Wynkyn de Worde Master, his treatment is always distinctly original. His perspective is invariably different. He often chooses a very low viewpoint, sometimes from the side, sometimes even from the rear. His animals are among the

255 *Tibert is ensnared in the priest's barn. Joseph Crawhall, watercolour, 1896-97. This, and the next two illustrations, are kept at the Burrell Collection in Glasgow and are by the courtesy of the Director of Glasgow's Art Galleries.*

least anthropomorphic of all ever depicted in Beast Epic scenes, and very realistic. Witness the angry snarling cat that is Tibert caught in a snare [255], and Chantecler escaping from Reynard's jaws [256]. One of the more anthropomorphic of his drawings is the one depicting that most frequently drawn of all Reynardian scenes, the complaints made by some of Reynard's victims to Noble at the very beginning of the story [257]. According to the text, this should be Courtois the Hound, but in fact Crawhall whimsically replaces the hound with his own pet dachshund. A frequent spectator at circuses and a traveller to North Africa, Crawhall came to love African animals and the challenge they presented him as an artist, so he replaces most of the complainants in the story and the usual lookers-on with elephant, camel, flamingo, buffalo and zebra. Only two smile-provoking anthropomorphic elements are allowed into the picture: the red carpet for the royal lion to lie on, and a wine-bottle in the crook of the lion's elbow.

256 *Chantecler escapes from Reynard. Joseph Crawhall, watercolour, 1896-97.*

257 *The dog complains to the lion before the assembled court. Joseph Crawhall, watercolour, 1896-97.*

The original drawings have never been used in the way the man who commissioned them intended them to be, and they are kept in Glasgow's Burrell Collection.

The illustration of Caxton's text in modified, simplified, 'purified' form for the younger reader fared rather better. One of the earliest versions intended for the young was Edward Ryland's, published about 1775. He entitled it: *The pleasant and entertaining History of Reynard the Fox Represented in a MORAL Light; Fabulously shewing various Devices which cunning Men pursue, and exciting the Innocent & Ignorant to guard against them; a Work equally humorous and instructive to the YOUNG and to the MATURE; Embellished with 17 Copper Plates elegantly Engraved.* Some of these plates are indeed elegant, in particular the frontispiece [258] which depicts a father and teacher with an open book upon his knees. He seems to be telling three young children about the wicked fox at which he points as it runs off, on the horizon, with a goose flung over its back. While a few of the engravings are of hitherto unillustrated events, as when the fox steals a suckling pig [259] (previously unillustrated perhaps because it did not feature in the Beast Epic), most treat well-known and traditional topics, sometimes rather clumsily, as when Bruin is caught in the half-split log [260], here depicted as a partially split, still-standing tree trunk (how, one wonders, did the woodcutter start this operation?); and when Reynard slaps Isegrim in the face with his urine-soaked brush [261]. Though the title includes adults as well as the young among its intended readership, the condescending tone of the introduction and the size of the children in the frontispiece picture suggest a really young readership was envisaged. 'Attend, ye youths of infant mold, / To what the following sheets unfold!' exclaims the author at the beginning of a

258 *A father teaches his children about Reynard's wicked wiles. Copperplate engraving from Ryland's c.1775 History of Reynard the Fox. This and the next three illustrations are from the same book and by courtesy of Professor H. Menke.*

259 *Reynard steals suckling pigs.*

260 *Bruin is caught in a half-split tree trunk.*

261 *Reynard and Isegrim fight a duel.*

prefatory poem. Nevertheless, the language used in the telling of the tale would often be difficult for the really young, and certainly boring.

Many years pass before the publication of another young person's version of Caxton's *Historye* coupled with extensive and quality illustrations; but the wait is well worthwhile. Summerly's 1843 retelling for children is illustrated by one of the finest of Dutch book illustrators: *The Pleasant History of Reynard the Fox Told by the Pictures of Aldert* (sic) *van Everdingen*. By contrast with Kaulbach's, Everdingen's illustrations are mainly very naturalistic, and as little anthropomorphic as any of the good-quality illustrations produced before the coming of Kaulbach. Another of the earliest, richly illustrated, Victorian young folk's versions is David Vedder's 1852 retelling, *The Story of Reynard the Fox*, but this is not a retelling of Caxton even if the storyline is close to Caxton's. Vedder's text is based on the 1706 English verse version of Hartmann Schopper's 1569 Latin text which, in its turn, is based, via a 1544 High German shortened translation, on that of the 1498 Lübeck Low German, and thence back to the Flemish on which Caxton drew. Vedder's book is splendidly illustrated by the German artist Gustav Canton, who was trained at the same Academy of Art in Munich as was Kaulbach. The two artists knew each other, and Canton, the younger of the two, was clearly much influenced

262 *Reynard on the gallows ladder. Canton, copperplate engraving, 1852.*

in his Reynardian drawings by Kaulbach's. Even so, Canton was capable of many an individual and original touch as when, in his depiction of Reynard at the gallows [262], he makes Noble appear rather like an Indian Rajah in his howdah on top of an elephant. These were, after all, the days when the British admired and were much influenced by certain aspects of Indian culture, and soon Victoria was to be declared Empress of India.

There have been quite a few illustrated children's versions of Caxton's storyline since Summerly's in 1844, but very few have been illustrated by fine artists whose work truly enhances the book and makes it memorable. Two of the better ones in relatively recent times are Roy Brown's *Reynard the Fox* (London, New York, Toronto; Abelard-Schuman, 1969). This is illustrated by John Vernon Lord with numerous black-and-white drawings which sometimes bring the animals close to being cartoon-like creatures, but often convey considerable feeling, as

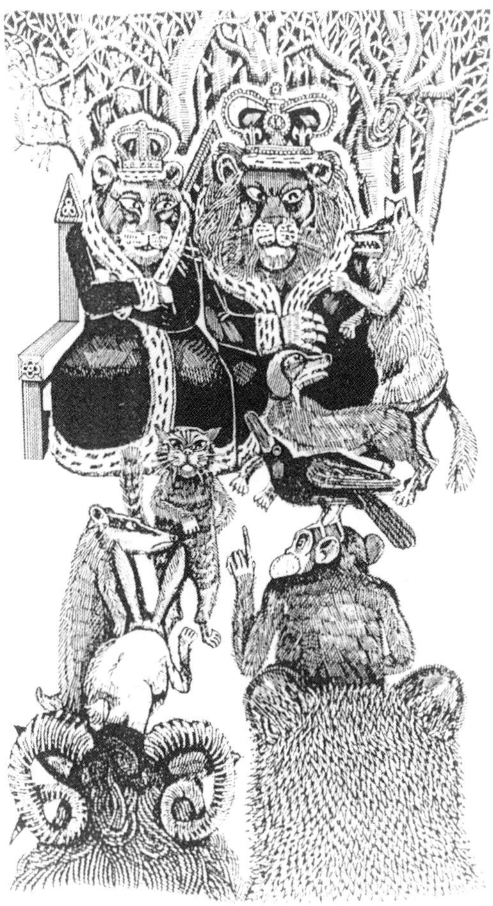

263 *Complaints made against Reynard before Noble's court. John Vernon Lee, drawing, 1967.*

264 *Reynard addresses the crowd from the scaffold. Graham Percy, drawing, 1990.*

when the animals complain to the king about the fox's crimes [263]. More recently, Selina Hastings's *Reynard the Fox* (London: Walker Books Ltd, 1990), abundantly illustrated by Graham Percy (indeed, the space taken up by the pictures is larger than that taken by the text), show considerable independence from the traditional way of depicting significant moments in Reynard's career. So much so, in fact, that, if one could not read the text, one might not realize that this is Reynard speaking from the scaffold to a crowd of courtiers come to see him hanged [264]. The effort to avoid the portrayal of violence and the rather muted colours used may please adults who give this book to children, but the story the pictures tell is a very different one from that told by the Wynkyn de Worde Master, good as they are.

We finish where we began, with the *Roman de Renart*. There are two illustrated versions of substantial parts of the French Beast Epic in English, one for adults, one for children. The former is Patricia Terry's rendering into verse of several of the earliest branches (Berkeley: University of California, 1992). The 28 little black-and-white illustrations which punctuate the text here and there are reproductions from medieval French manuscripts The second of these, the children's version by Anderson, Bradby and Dewar (Oxford University Press, 1986), is of the highest quality in every way. Dewar is the artist, and his 40-odd illustrations, some in colour, some in black and white, are full of action, enlivened by humour, and most expressive. Since most of the branches retold in this book are not the ones on which the medieval Dutch epic is based, there is little room for comparison with the work of other artists who have treated one of the recurring episodes, but when there is narrative overlap, Dewar is very much his own man. Compare, for example, his picture of the fox pretending to be almost immobile [265] lying on the ground after getting the crow to drop his cheese, and now hoping to get the crow to come down from his branch and remove the smelly cheese which is offending Rey-

265 *Reynard feigns immobility as he lies close by a cheese. Bob Dewar, drawing, 1984.*

nard's nostrils. These are some of the best pictures to accompany a Reynardian book of any kind in any age.

Notes

PART ONE

BASIC TEXTS

For Caxton, see Blake 1970; and, in modernized spelling, Sands 1960. To the best of my knowledge, there is no modern edition of either Brewster's 1672 *Continuation*, or of Shurley's 1681 *Most Delightful History*, or of the 1684 *Shifts*, or of any of the chap-books. I have based my summaries and comments on the holdings in a number of libraries, details of which are to be found in Appendix Three (see especially the items numbered 15, 19, 21, 22, 32, 34, 35, and 37-40, and in Menke 1992, 199-250).

CRITICAL STUDIES AND SUPPORTING INFORMATION

Both Blake's and Sands's editions contain many useful comments on Caxton's translation from Dutch, on its immediate source, and on the development of the medieval Beast Epic. Especially relevant to the early history of illustrated English editions of the Reynard story is Varty 1980,

160-95. This concentrates on the 'Anonymous' edition and its two different picture cycles (vertical and horizontal), of which it reproduces every woodcut. There are special sections on the repair and the replacement of the original Wynkyn de Worde cuts; on their similarities with and differences from the 1498 Lübeck cuts; on their source in, and on the work of, the Haarlem Master; and on Richard Pynson's use of the de Worde cuts. For a more detailed study of the 1498 Lübeck cuts, and for comparisons with other continental picture cycles, see Vedder 1980, 196-248. For a detailed description of all extant and hypothetical English editions of the History of Reynard the Fox, both with and without illustrations, see Menke 1992, 195-250.

Until recently, the date ascribed to Wynkyn de Worde's picture cycle has been c.1499; that is, just after the firm date of 1498 for the picture cycle in the Lübeck Low German *Reynke de Vos*. The woodcut which I have numbered two in the description of Wynkyn de Worde's picture cycle occurs in pristine condition in his edition of Lydgate's *The horse, the sheep and the goos*, dated c.1500 by E. Hodnett, *English Woodcuts, 1480-1535* (London, 1935), p. 313, no.1288, and it is on this evidence that the date c.1499 had been reached. (The British Library Catalogue dates this edition of Lydgate's poem c.1499.) However, in the second, revised edition of the *Short Title Catalogue*, the date of c.1495 is now ascribed to *The horse, the sheep and the goose* [STC 17020], so we may conclude that this is now the latest possible date for Wynkyn de Worde's picture cycle, and that it predates the Lübeck cycle. The first person to point out this important consequence was Malcolm H. Jones in his unpublished PhD thesis: *The Misericords of Beverley Minster* for the Polytechnic South West, Faculty of Arts and Design, 1991, p. 275, note 2.

Readers may be interested in two other critical studies relevant to the literary history of Reynard the Fox in England over the first two centuries covered by this chapter, though their authors are concerned with the text and its evolution, not its illustration. Briefly, there seems to have been two textual traditions. The first extended from 1481 to 1550, the second from 1620 and on into the eighteenth century. A simple, fairly adequate description of these two traditions, bringing out the linguistic differences between them, is to be found in Mish 1953-54. A fairly detailed description of some of the linguistic characteristics of the first tradition only is given by Blake 1965, 63-77. Briefly, the text of the first tradition changes only slightly from Caxton in 1481, through Pynson and Wynkyn de Worde to Gaultier in 1550. There is, however, a marked difference between the text of the first tradition and that of the second, first evidenced by the 1620 Allde edition. The first tradition is characterized by a relatively rougher, older English, and by the absence of marginal moralizations which abound in the second tradition with its more modern and elegant English. In the first tradition the story is divided into 43 chapters; in the second, into 25 chapters. The Anonymous edition clearly belongs to the first tradition as far as the language is concerned, and also by the absence of marginal moralizations; but it is unique in that the story is parcelled out into 58 chapters.

PART TWO

BASIC TEXTS

To the best of my knowledge no modern editions have been published of John Shurley's *Most Delightful History of Reynard the Fox in Heroic Verse*, nor of any of the chap-books. I have based my comments on the British Library's copy of Shurley's work, and on its chap-book holdings. For further details, see the relevant entries in Appendix Three or in Menke's Bibliography.

PART THREE

BASIC TEXTS

Goethe's *Reineke Fuchs* has been published together with the whole of Kaulbach's cycle of etchings: see Bibliography, Goethe 1973. Full bibliographical information is given there for the translations into English of Goethe's epic, as well as of modern scholarly editions and translations of Caxton's text, and of the children's Reynardian texts mentioned here.

CRITICAL STUDIES AND SUPPORTING INFORMATION

Froude's essay on *Reineke Fuchs* was reprinted along with other essays by him in Froude 1897.
The family tree of Goethe's *Reineke Fuchs*, starting with the Lübeck 1498 Low German version, together with a brief commentary, is given by Scheidegger 1989, pp. 70-73.
Details of Vedder's *Reynard the Fox* are given in Varty 1995, pp.1075-1085.
A study and reproduction of all of Crawhall's Reynardian pictures is to be found in Hamilton 1990, pp. 114-22.

Conclusions

We can be reasonably sure that the drawings reproduced within Histories of Reynard the Fox depict our villainous hero or other animal-barons subject to King Noble. Or nearly sure, for publishers sometimes incorporated woodcuts made from non-Reynardian books into their Histories of Reynard the Fox, as did the Lübeck publisher of *Reynke de Vos* in 1498. Conversely, woodcuts made for a Reynardian text were sometimes used in a non-Reynardian text as when Wynkyn de Worde illustrated his edition of Lydgate's *The horse, the sheep and the goos* with a picture of Noble listening to complaints about Reynard. In this way Reynard manages to escape from the confines of his History. We have seen him do this in Bristol Cathedral where his escape was not from book to book, but from book to misericord. Most of the pre-1495 drawings and carvings to which reference is made in the preceding chapters could depict Reynard or one of his continental cousins after having escaped from one of several Histories, some of which have survived and some which have not. Without the testimony of words drawn or carved alongside or within these representations, we can never be sure. However, among the earlier drawings and carvings of foxes, those which depict a fox with a cock in his jaws and being chased by a woman wielding a distaff and a man brandishing a stick may be compared with a miniature from a copy of the *Roman de Renart* where this event is similarly depicted. And those of a fox being carried on a bier by other animals and accompanied by other animals to either a funeral service or a place of burial may be compared with another *Renart* miniature which illustrates this moment in Reynardian time. These comparisons leave me feeling reasonably sure that the fox in these chases and in these processions is Reynard on the run, or being carried, outside his History. And this happens in England, whether it be in a French, or Anglo-Norman, or English-speaking society. Similarly, the religious disguises he wears and the religious roles he plays in various Beast Epics, in particular in the *Roman de Renart,* make it possible, even likely, that the many drawings and carvings of the fox in religious habit represent either Reynard or a close relation. But then, it may be argued, the drawings so commonly found in religious manuscripts, and the carvings in so many churches may have been the inspiration for the written accounts of Brother Fox's duping the unwary. Unlikely, for a drawing of an anthropomorphic fox can only be inspired by some kind of story, however brief, such as the one implicit in the proverb 'when the fox preaches, beware your geese'.

Pursuing, as I do in the last chapter, book illustrations which betray something of the influence of the Wynkyn de Worde Master, I have deliberately left aside the information I have gathered about foxes, perhaps escaped Reynards, in non-Reynardian books and pamphlets, in carvings, stained glass and other media of that kind belonging to post-Renaissance times. I have done so chiefly because, for the most part, they belong to one or other of two old and common motifs which may or may not be related to the Beast Epic, namely: the fox-preacher motif, and that of the fox-and-goose, motifs which often overlap. For example, the British Library houses an illustrated broadsheet which is a satire on drunkards and a criticism of drunkenness. Published in 1652, it begins with a drawing which, to the left, depicts a man vomiting copiously; in the middle a fox in a barrel from which it preaches to geese; and to the right, geese dancing to the music of a horn-blowing fox. At the time this was published, it was commonly said of a man who was drunk that he was 'foxed'; and geese, as always, were symbolic of foolish behaviour. The use of a barrel as a pulpit is a nice touch.

There are, however, exceptions to the frequent re-use of these old motifs. One of the most interesting appears in an illustrated broadsheet published on 9th October 1660 and entitled 'The Tryall of Traytors or the Rump in the Pound wherein is presented the Lively Shapes and Bloody Actings of the Chief of those Grand Traytors who subscribed to the horrid Murder of the Blessed Martyr Charles the First of England...' Beneath this title is a drawing of a pound resembling a ten-sided jousting field at the centre of which is a Wheel of Fortune with a map of the world in the middle and above which is engraved a quatrain:

> The World in the Wheele turns round
> Whil'st Haslerig the Fox doth propound
> The Oath of Abjuration to the Speaker,
> Who as an Asse stands shaking like a Quaker.

Haslerig, represented as a fox, stands to the right of the wheel, and the Speaker, represented as an ass, to the left. What is particularly interesting to us, without going into detail about the circumstances of this cartoon and the points it makes, is that most of the Beast Epic's protagonists are here: the Fox, the Ass, the Cat, the Cock, the Bear, the Stag, the Goat, the Ram, the Wolf, and the Boar. There can be little doubt that the artist hoped his viewers would recall the treachery, the intrigue, the duplicity, and the stupidity of the protagonists of the Beast Epic as they pondered this cartoon. The politicians whom the cartoonist had in mind are named: thus 'Oh brave Haselrig' appears below the fox, 'Oh Scobell' below the cat, and so on. This same woodcut was published again on 6 December 1660 on another broadsheet entitled 'The Dragons Forces Totally Routed By The Royal Shepherd'. It has however been altered by giving the figures their animal instead of their human names, ascribing to them a military rank such as colonel or general. And over the wheel there is a different quatrain:

> The subtle old Dragon Saint-like doth appear
> To all other Creatures that you do see here,
> and tells them if they'l enjoy freedom they may
> for the Lion's a tyrant that ore them bears sway.

In addition to the animal roles given to the protagonists in this cartoon, the broadsheet's rambling subtitle contains the odd word or phrase which hints further at its creator's familiarity with the Beast Epic, and his wish to remind his viewers of it: 'Wherein is laid open a horrid bloudy Plot, as it was contrived, fomented and acted against harmless Lambs, with the cruel proceedings of the Dragon and his wicked Councel, viz. General Ram, Col. Bear, Col. Asse,

Col. Wolf, Col Buck, Col. Bore, Col. Cock, Col. Goat and Col Cat, Secr. against their lawful Sovereign King Leonis. Also the manner how they drew in all other beasts...' The 80 lines in rhyming couplets printed below the picture could be mistaken for a watered-down chapter of a Beast Epic in which one of the animals attempts to get King Lion's subjects to rebel and overthrow him. When Mish published his evidence for and arguments about the popularity of the History of Reynard the Fox in the seventeenth century, he did not discuss the role which illustrated editions may have had in achieving that popularity, nor did he bring to bear the part this kind of satirical cartoon may have played.

For similar reasons I have also set aside the many modern images of the fox to be found in buildings, though I have mentioned in passing a few in Chester Cathedral [197, 198, 203].

266 *A cowled, upright fox with a large crozier. Church Stretton Parish Church, Jacobean reredos. Jill and Brian Lucas.*

They, together with other new images, have either replaced earlier, badly deteriorated carvings, or ones that were judged indecent and improper in a holy place, or are simply part of the ornamentation of new furniture and fittings. For example, beginning with the early 1600s, the fox appears in priestly habit holding a bishop's crozier on the reredos at Church Stretton, Shropshire [266]; and running off with a goose flung over his back in a stained-glass roundel at Birtles, Cheshire. This is unusual in several ways, being in glass, and probably of Flemish workmanship. The fox, who looks back at possible pursuers, is set against a bright blue sky in which shines a large, gleaming, gold star. Jumping to more modern times, carved in 1892 on a panel of the choir-stalls in Meavy, Cornwall is the fable of the fox and the sour grapes. From 1915 in Alvington, Devon, is the unusual, indeed unique, bench-end carving of a fox running from its hole on the edge of a cornfield (the ripe corn stands high) towards a tree in which is perched a big bird close by its nest. On a 1954 elbow-rest carved in the choir-stalls at West Barsham, Norfolk, sits a mischievous-looking naturalistic fox. Also carved sometime during this century, we find the fable of the fox and the crow on a bench end in Somerton, Oxfordshire [267]; the Bestiary fox on two misericords in Downham Abbey, Stratton-on-the-Fosse,

267 *A fox (?) approaches a crow on a token branch. Clipsham Parish Church, stained glass; 15th C. Jill and Brian Lucas.*

Somerset; and, in various shades of grey and green, a stained-glass panel depicting a fox with a goose flung over his back in Lynton, Devon. One is struck by the fact that there is not a single modern carving or panel of stained glass representing a scene from the Beast Epic. All we find are moralizing scenes from Aesopian fables or the Bestiary, or, as befits a remote country church, the naturalistic fox. To some extent, this confirms what I say in the Introduction about the disappearance in modern times from English awareness of the fox who was once so well and widely known as Reynard.

In the second edition of his most interesting book *The Lost Literature of Medieval England* (London: 1970), R. M. Wilson pays me the great compliment of arguing, largely from the evidence of my 1967 Leicester University Press study, that there was a medieval English Beast Epic which has been lost. I doubt this, but he may be right. I am more inclined to think that some branches of the *Roman de Renart* (of which we now know manuscript copies were available in fourteenth-century England) were well known, first by the French- and Anglo-Norman-speaking aristocrats, administrators, prelates and their entertainers, then, through modified adaptations (rather than translations), most probably in oral form, in English. Clearly the anonymous *Vox and Wolf* as well as Chaucer's *Nun's Priest's Tale* had their French connections, so it may be that there were other written *Roman-de-Renart*-inspired tales which have been lost. If so, one of the most likely ones will have been a version of the presumed death, funeral service for, and near-burial of our villainous hero.

Evidently, the fox was a popular figure with artists in the late Middle Ages, probably in part because he was a very common nuisance with certain admirable qualities, partly because he had come to symbolize the Devil and many evil characteristics in an age which was much concerned with spiritual values, and partly because he was the central figure in the Beast Epic. One finds in drawings and carvings of the fox, just as one does in the literature about him, a mingling of animal realism, didactic symbolism, and human characterization. The real difficulty is to know which was uppermost in the artist's mind. However, since the majority of the representations date from the late Middle Ages when churches were decorated with imagery which had messages to convey and lessons to teach, we can reasonably guess that most artists had a didactic purpose. Conversely, since the later medieval stories about Reynard were mostly didactic, it is fairly safe to assume that these same artists had Reynard in mind.

The few hundred foxes I have tracked down may represent a minority of the total hiding in these Isles, and a minute fraction of the total that once lived here. If I thought I had unearthed a majority of England's medieval foxes, I would have analysed their distribution carefully to see if one adventure or another appeared to be more popular in one region or another. And if it were possible to date the evidence more accurately I would have attempted to discover if some adventures were more popular in one age than in another. Even so, one is struck by the paucity of foxes in Scotland, Wales and the far north of England, and by the relatively large numbers in parts of Yorkshire, East Anglia, and England south of the Thames and a little distance north of the river. Clearly, in some areas, religious zealots took a heavy toll of church decoration at the Reformation, while accidents, wars and thoughtless restorers further reduced the numbers of Reynard's tribe. Areas less given to fanaticism, far from the tide of battle, and too poor to afford restoration have provided the safest retreats for the fox and some of the happiest hunting grounds for us.

Anyone who knows the many episodes into which Reynard's adventures may be broken must be struck by the failure of medieval artists to depict many more of them, and by the limited choices they sometimes made, like those made by the Bristol Cathedral artist. But it is a fact that, even in the illustrated manuscripts of the *Roman de Renart*, usually only one miniature is given to each branch which belongs to that minority of branches that are illustrated. And that miniature usually captures something of the culminating or most significant event in the branch. From a literary historian's point of view, only a small handful of branches seem to have been represented in medieval and Renaissance English art: the branch which tells of Reynard's trial and some of the events leading up to it, and his subsequent triumph; the Reynard and Chantecler adventure in the oldest of the branches; the branch which tells the story of the sick lion and the way he was cured by Reynard; and the branch which culminates in Reynard's presumed death, and the ceremonies which followed. From an art historian's viewpoint, the literary accounts help to throw light on some of the drawings and carvings which, in their turn, set them in a wider context. There is also considerable iconographic evidence of an alliance between the fox and the ape, an alliance only rarely illustrated or referred to in the *Roman de Renart*, its continuations and derivatives. There is plentiful evidence of Reynard in his various religious roles. And one notes how the Bestiary fox and the fabulists's foxes were Reynardized in art just as they were in literature.

Caxton was nothing if not a good businessman. When he decided to translate the Dutch text into English, he will have been pretty sure that he was making a sound investment. He knew that the stories about Reinaert were a great success in Flanders, and we may guess that he knew enough about popular fox lore in England to calculate that new stories about the fox he called Reynart would thrive here. And they certainly did, especially when illustrated by the Wynkyn de Worde Master. They made an immensely appealing combination, text and picture, one of the greatest success stories in publishing and at the same time one of the greatest tributes one could pay to that Dutch-speaking culture in the midst of which, in the mid-twelfth century, appeared the *Ysengrimus*, and then, in the thirteenth, fourteenth and fifteenth centuries, various versions of the Beast Epic centred on the fox called Reinaert, culminating in the version Caxton translated and the other one which the Haarlem Master so magnificently illustrated and thereby provided the model for the equally fine artist employed by Wynkyn de Worde.

When, after nearly three centuries, the popularity of that extraordinary marriage of text and picture began to wane, Reynard-Reinaert finally gave way to Reynard-Reineke in yet another marriage of translated text and imported picture. But this lasted for less than a century. It is a strange story, the story of Reynard the Fox. He seems always to have been an immigrant. First from France, about 1200, when he came in the wake of the invaders. Although he and his descendants seem to have survived for the best part of three centuries, they kept a low profile and finally disappeared from view. Then from Flanders in 1481, in the company of business-men who saw to it that he flourished. He and his descendants were very popular, and played quite a role in society for another three centuries or thereabouts. Then tentatively in 1823 and more readily in 1850 from Germany, almost, one might say, under the patronage of an immigrant royal family. But he and his descendants disappeared quite a long time ago, unless one of them is the one Beatrix Potter called Mr Tod, and Roald Dahl, along with many another author, called Mr Fox. If so, they have moved into very different circles since they left Noble's kingdom.

APPENDIX ONE

Drawings and Paintings of Foxes in Manuscripts Kept in Britain, together with Some of English Origin Kept Abroad

ABERDEEN, UNIVERSITY LIBRARY

MS 24. 12th C. A Bestiary.

1 f.16. A fox lies on its back while six cubs look out of holes in a green hill below. Four birds perch on top of the fox and four more hover above it.

BALTIMORE, MARYLAND, U.S.A., THE WALTERS ART GALLERY

MS 102, c.1300. A Psalter and Book of Hours.

Contains, in the lower margins of the Service for the Dead, the fox's funeral procession extending over ff.73-81:

2 f.73. A camel rings handbells.
3 f.73v. An elephant-pilgrim blows his own trumpet.
4 f.74. An ox blows a great horn.
5 f.74v. A dappled horse plays a flute and beats a drum
6 f.75. A donkey with a wind instrument and a handbell.
7 f.75v. A dog plays bagpipes.
8 f.76. Four monkeys by the wayside, mourning.
9 f.76v.- f.77. A stag and a cat carry the fox on his bier.
10 f.77v. A cock carries a censer.
11 f.78. A robed wolf-bishop with crozier.
12 f.78v. A striped cat (or tiger) beats a kind of tambourine.
13 f.79. A goat with crucifix.
14 f.79v. A bear (?) plays a large wind instrument.
15 f.80. A ram carries an aspergillum and a holy-water vessel.
16 f.80v. A boar digs a grave.
17 f.81. A hare rings church bells.

BELVOIR CASTLE, LEICESTERSHIRE, DUKE OF RUTLAND COLLECTION

A Psalter. Mid- 13th C.

18 f.98v. A mitred fox preaches to a cock and, at a slight distance from the cock, two birds. (Randall 1966, ill. 202).

BRUSSELS, BIBLIOTHÈQUE ROYALE

MS 9961-2. The Peterborough Psalter. c.1300.

19 f.14 (Beatus page). A fox runs off with a cock held by the neck in its jaws and flung over its back.

20 Also, f.38: a fox steals a goose.

21 Also, f.94: A fox creeps up to a hare which sits upright, a little higher than the fox. The hare seems to be mesmerised by the fox. (Randall 1966, ill. 192).

CAMBRIDGE, CORPUS CHRISTI COLLEGE

MS 4. The Dover Bible. 12th C.

22 f.239. An historiated initial S at the opening of the Second Epistle of St Peter. In the upper part of the S a fox creeps up on a cock. (Dodwell 1954, plate 43).

23 Also, (folio not known, reference given in Dodwell 1954, p.71). The fox and crow fable.

CAMBRIDGE, FITZWILLIAM MUSEUM

MS 2-54. The Bird Psalter. Late 13th C.

24 f.6. A fox steals a goose.

25 Also, f.18. A cowled fox blows a horn.

26 Also, f.56. A fox dressed as a cleric.

27 Also, f.124. A fox dressed as a pilgrim.

28 Also, f.158. An erect fox, robed, cowled, plays a harp. (Randall 1966, ill. 264).

MS 298. The Metz Pontifical. Northern French. 1302-16.

29 f.138v. A man hauls a wolf up from a well in a bucket by means of a rope over a pulley. Nearby a fox, as it dashes off, looks back at the wolf as it emerges over the well wall.

CAMBRIDGE, UNIVERSITY LIBRARY

MS 11.4.26. A Bestiary. 12th C.

30 A fox feigns death and four birds settle on it. (White 1984, ill. p.53).

LONDON, BRITISH LIBRARY

MS Add 15229. The *Roman de Renart,* French. Late 14th or early 15th C.

31 f.1. A fox on a fisherman's cart full of fish, drawn by two men. The fox seizes an eel.

32 f.6. A crowned lion seen in profile presides over a gathering of his court.

33 f.13. A fox seizes a very big white cock by the throat, from behind.

34 f.19v. The farmer Liétart with his cart which has enormous wheels. A horse, a goat (?) and a bear.

35 f.33. A fox looks up at a crow perched in a tree. A cheese falls to earth.

36 f.42. A white-frocked monk draws a wolf up from the bottom of a well. He holds up a stick with which to strike the wolf.

37 f.53. A fox and a big white cat sit facing each other.

38 f.63. Three white monks brandishing sticks chase a fox. Above, against a blue sky, two cocks and a white hen.

39 f.68v. A fox stands before a seated, white monk.

40 f.70v. A fox emerges from a hedge and creeps alongside a brick wall, presumably to attack one of three cocks.

41 f.77v. A fortified house or castle.

42 f.92v. A crowned and enthroned lion, legs crossed, looks down at a fox and a wolf who stand before him.

43 f.103. A fox peeps out of its hole at four animals which are on all fours.

MS Add 38116. Psalter, Lincoln Diocese. c.1275.

44 f.15. A fox stalks a cock which is crowing.

45 Also, f.35. A fox stalks a cock which is crowing.

46 Also, 48. A fox looks back at a lion.

MS Add 42183. The Luttrell Psalter. c.1340.

47 f.31. A fox carries off a goose thrown over its back.

48 Also, f.64. A fox hides in foliage from a man who is about to unleash two hounds.

49 Also, f.64v. A fox makes off with a goose.

50 Also, f.66v. A fox or a wolf hunts a goose. A man holding an axe looks on.

51 Also, f.74. A fox hears the confession of a nun.

MS 49622. The Gorleston Psalter. c.1310-25.

52 f.35, lower margin. In the bottom left corner, a rather static fox makes off with a duck held by the neck and flung over its back. In the bottom right, a creature which is half animal and half woman wields a distaff as if to strike the fox, though she is separated from it by a considerable distance. Above the fox, on a line of decoration, a lion sits on its hindquarters. It smiles across at the animal woman, and seems to applaud her action by clapping its forepaws. Above the woman, looking across at the lion, is a seated ape playing a fiddle. Cf. ff.149v. and 190v. and comments below.

53 Also, f.47, lower margin. A robed and mitred fox holds a crozier in one hand and a duck in the other as he preaches to three ducks which look up at him most intently, necks outstretched and bills wide open.

54 Also, f.49v., lower margin. A robed and mitred fox holds a crozier under his left arm, and a duck by the neck in his left hand. He preaches to two ducks which gaze intently at him with wide-open bills.

55 Also, f.55, upper margin. A peasant archer aims an arrow at a fox which makes off with a duck.

56 Also, f.87v., lower margin. A fox runs off with a duck. A dog, sitting on its hind quarters, looks on and barks.

57 Also, f.96, lower margin. A robed and mitred fox or ape (no brush is visible) holds a crozier under its right arm, and preaches to a small ape. (The preaching animal's pose and garments are very like the fox's on f.49v.)

58 Also, f.103, lower margin. A peasant archer aims an arrow at a fox which makes off with a duck. Very similar to the drawing on f.55. The chief difference is the position of the arrow which, here, is still in the archer's hands.

59 Also, f.128, lower margin. A robed and mitred fox holds a crozier and a duck under his right arm, and preaches to three quacking ducks.

60 Also, f.143v., upper margin. A robed and enthroned fox, holding a crozier, preaches to two quacking geese.

61 Also, f.145v., upper margin. A cleric stands between a duck and a crouching fox. He seems to be shooing the duck away as he points a warning finger at the fox. (Randall 1966, ill. 110).

62 Also, f.149v., lower margin. A fox makes off with a duck and is pursued by an animal-woman. From the waist upward she is a woman, from the waist downwards, a horse or a cow, as on ff.35, but she wields her distaff differently, and has a broad grin on her face. The duck, held by the body in the fox's jaws, says 'quec'. This word is written in the tiniest script between the bird's wide-open bill. See also f.156v. below.

63 Also, f.152v., lower margin. A robed fox rides side-saddle on a large goat. He steadies himself by holding on to one of the goat's horns.

64 Also, f.156v., lower margin. A fox makes off with a duck, held by the neck, and flung over his back. He is chased by a woman who is probably meant to be wielding a distaff, but only the base of the distaff is visible in her clenched hands.

65 Also, f.190v., lower margin. A fox makes off with a duck, held by the body between his jaws, and he looks back at a woman who pursues him and aims a blow at him with her distaff. The woman is half animal, half human, as in the drawings on ff.35 and 149v. The duck says 'queck'. This word is printed in very small letters between the bird's open bill.

MS Add 5000. The Oscott Psalter. c.1275.

66 f.146v. A fox approaches, stalking a cock which sings at a lectern on which is an open book. (Randall 1966, ill. 130).

Cotton Claudius E.v. Probably early 12th C.

67 f.49. A flute-playing fox-dog, rather like the animal in the crypt of Canterbury Cathedral listed in Appendix Two.

Egerton MS 2781. Book of Hours. c.1350.

68 f.53. A fox preaches to a hen.

Harley 6563. Book of Hours. c.1385.
69 ff.14v.-15. A fox preaches to fowl.
70 Also ff.22v.-23. A fox with an aspergillum accompanies a fox singing from a book.
71 Also, f.54. An erect fox, dagger at the waist, leans on a large battle-axe. (Randall 1966, ill. 162).
72 Also, ff.54v.-55. A fox preaching to fowl.
73 Also, ff.60v.-61. A fox stealing geese.

Roy. 2. B. VII. The Queen Mary Psalter. Early 14th C.
74 ff.99v.-100. A fox feigns death. Four birds perch on him, or peck him. He leaps to life and seizes a cock.
75 Also, f.157v. A mitred fox preaches to birds. He holds a crozier.
76 Also, f.157v. A woman brandishes her distaff and pursues a fox making off with a duck.
77 Also, f.158. Two men, one with a club, pursue a fox making off with a goose.
78 Also, p. 202. Warner 1912, two men dig a fox out of its hole. A hound is about to seize the emerging fox.

Roy. 10. E. IV. The Smithfield Decretals (of Pope Gregory IX), written in Italy, illustrated in England, perhaps at St Bartholomew's, Smithfield. c.1335.
79 f.48. A fox runs off with a hare between its jaws and flung over its back. To the left, a richly robed person blows a hunting horn.
80 Also, f.48v. Geese, a cock and a hen hang a fox.
81 Also, f.49. The fox is carried in funeral procession by geese. A cock leads the procession, and a hare brings up the rear. The fox is tended by two weeping nuns.
82 Also, f.49v. Left, a mitred fox preaches to birds. He holds a crozier. Right, a woman brandishes a distaff and pursues the fox making off with a goose.
83 Also, f.53. A fox has gone to earth with a man or a woman hot on his trail. Another person kneels before the fox's hole, holding a net over it.
84 Also, f.53v. The fox is summoned by a hare.
85 Also, f.54. The fox feels a sick animal's pulse.
86 Also, f.54v. The fox takes leave of a prostrate wolf.
87 Also, f.55, upper margin. A fox-pilgrim, staff in hand, scrip at hip. The scrip is marked with a cross.
88 Also, f.55., lower margin. A fox-pilgrim before a lion pilgrim.
89 Also, f.55v. The fox is bound and dragged by the wolf before the lion.
90 Also, f.56. The fox offers a pouch to the lion.
91 Also, f.56v. Two foxes skin a wolf.
92 Also, f.57. Two foxes wrap a wolf-skin round a lion.
93 Also, f.57v. A fox-pilgrim faces a rabbit which aims an arrow at him.
94 Also, f.67. A man releases a greyhound to catch a fleeing, backward-looking fox.
95 Also, f.149. A pedlar is about to fall asleep at the foot of a tree. Two apes approach and seize his pack.
96 Also, f.149v. A pedlar is fast asleep and two apes begin to empty his pack.

97 Also, f.150. Four apes with property stolen from the sleeping pedlar.
98 Also, f.150v. Three apes with stolen property.
99 Also, f.151. Four apes with stolen property.
100 Also, f.158v. A fox examines an urinal before a seated wolf.
101 Also, f.175. A woman brandishes a distaff and pursues a fox making off with a goose.

NEW YORK, PIERPONT MORGAN LIBRARY

MS 812. Registrum Brevium and Statutes of the Realm. English. 13th C.
102 f.35. A fox steals a goose.

OXFORD, ALL SOULS COLLEGE

MS 6. The Amesbury Psalter. 13th C with some added 14th-C drawings on f.13.
103 f.13, lower margin. A woman brandishes her distaff and pursues a fox who makes off with a goose.
104 Also, same lower margin, and in close proximity to the fox-chase, a fox wearing a doctor's cap examines urinal at a lion's bedside.

OXFORD, THE BODLEIAN LIBRARY.

MS Ashmole 1462. Early 13th C.
105 f.45. A fox.
106 Also, f.50v. A fox.

MS Ashmole 1504. 16th C.
107 f.22v. A fox holding a crozier and wearing a priestly gown faces a hen and a cock.
108 Also, f.23v. A fox, wearing a blue cape, plays the bagpipes. An ape plays a morris pipe and beats a tabor. It may therefore be that this procession was connected with morris dancing and mumming of some kind.
109 Also, f.33v. A fox (?) has swallowed the head of a large bird. May be meant to represent the wolf and crane fable.
110 Also, f.34. A fox. Also, a woman brandishing a distaff pursues a fox with prey.
111 Also, f.37v. A fox.

MS Ashmole 1523. 14th C.
112 f.249. A fox.

MS Auct. D. 22. 14th C.
113 f.31. A fox leans on a crutch and two hens look up at him. Around the fox is written 'Pax Vobs'.

MS Bodley 264. The *Roman d'Alexandre*, illuminated by Jehan de Grise, Bruges, 1338-44.
114 f.52. A fox steals a goose.
115 Also, f.79v. The fox's funeral procession.

MS Bodley 546. 15th C.
116 f.2. Foxes look out of holes. They are being attacked by hounds.
117 Also, f.3v. A fox, with other animals, in a park.
118 Also, f.38. A fox.

MS Bodley 602. A Bestiary. 12th C.
119 f.11v. A fox feigns death. Eagles and other birds fly down.

MS Bodley 764. A Bestiary. 13th C.
120 f.26. In the lower half of the picture, a fox feigns death and a bird pecks at his tongue. In the upper half, the fox stands upright and holds a bird by its neck in his jaws. The body of the bird is thrown over the fox's back. Two magpies and other birds are shown watching on.

MS Bodley 912. 14th C.
121 f.5. A fox lies on its back feigning death. Three birds fly down to it.

MS Douce 88. 13th C.
122 f.91v. A fox feigns death.

MS Douce 132, French. 13th C.
123 f.69v. A red fox lies on its back. A bird is perched on its snout, two others on its body, and another looks down from a tree in the background. On the right of the painting is written 'del renard'.

MS Douce 151. A Bestiary. 14th C.
124 f.19. A fox lies on its back feigning death. Some birds fly down to it.

MS Douce 167. A Bestiary. 13th C.
125 f.4v. A fox feigns death.

MS Douce 218. 1160-1200.
126 f.38v. A bleeding fox, lying on its back, is attacked by a vulture.

MS Douce 360. The *Roman de Renart.*, French. 1339.
127 f.1. A crowned, enthroned lion, seen in profile, holds a pleniary session of his court. Before him, a rabbit, fox, ram, wolf, stag, ass, and cock (in a tree). At the foot of the page a fox chases a hare.
128 f.21. A fox is chased and beaten by a woman wielding a distaff. A man brandishing a stave follows her. The cock is depicted above the fox, as if it has just escaped from him.
129 f.29v. A fox looks up at a crow in a tree. A cheese falls to the ground.
130 f.33. A fox stands on top of a horse-drawn cart laden with eels, an eel in his jaws.

131 f.36v. A lion holds court; similar to the miniature on f.1 minus the tree and the cock and the rabbit.
132 f.46. A fox and a wolf at a well.The fox comes up, the wolf descends.
133 f.57v. A fox in the right foreground is chased by a monk on foot accompanied by two dogs, and by two other men, an abbot and a monk, on horseback.
134 f.66v. An outline drawing never completed in colour. A fox is seen from the rear, head in a hen-pen; only its brush and hind quarters are outside. Four monks and a dog approach. One of the monks brandishes a stave.
135 f.72. An erect fox-pilgrim precedes a ram-pilgrim who precedes an ass-pilgrim. Each animal carries a staff and wears a pouch.
136 f.75. In the foreground, to the left, a fox and a peasant face each other; to the right, a bear. In the background, a large, oxen-drawn covered wagon.
137 f.99. A fox and a cat on either side of a tree look up at its branches.
138 f.106. Two men look out over the top of the battlements of a castle.
139 f.120v. A fox (?) enters a castle, chased by a dog.
140 f.131v. The artist seems to have painted three foxes looking up at a tree, but this is probably meant to be Renart embracing Hersent to the left side of a tree trunk, and Ysengrin looking on from the other side.
141 f.152v. Two peasants catch a fox with a net. The fox bites the foot of one of the peasants.
142 f.162. A white monk runs from a tower, pursuing a fox. He brings a stave down on the fox's back. The fox has a man's detached private parts in his jaws. A cock and a hen look on from a tree above the monk's head.

MS Douce 366. The Ormesby Psalter. Early 14th C.
143 f.71v. A woman brandishes a distaff and pursues a fox making off with a cock.
144 Also, f.89. A hooded fox holds a crutch. A hare stares at the fox.

MS Hatton 1. 15th C.
145 f.111v. Foxes stealing fowls.

MS Laud. Misc. 247. A Bestiary. 13th C.
146 f.149. A fox feigns death.

MS Laud. Misc. 302. Early 16th C.
147 f.210. A fox plays the bagpipes (centre right). An ape blows a trumpet and beats a drum. A cat sits down to a meal.
148 Also, f.215. Black foxes.

MS Liturg. 104. 1340 or later.
149 ff.1 and 51v. Fox masks.

OXFORD, ST JOHN'S COLLEGE.

MS 61. 13th C.

150 f.2. A fox.

151 Also, f.20. A fox feigns death.

OXFORD, UNIVERSITY COLLEGE.

MS 120. Late 13th or early 14th C.

152 p.13. A brown fox lies on its back and birds swarm over it. Some fox cubs watch.

Carvings and Paintings of Foxes in Buildings
(including some modern examples)

All have been seen in situ or by photograph except for those followed by an asterisk

A

Alne, Yorkshire. St Mary.
153 South doorway, stone voussoir, 1160-70. A fox feigns death and birds peck him. The carving is inscribed VULPIS.

Alvington, Devon. Parish Church.
154 Bench end, 1915. Two panels. To the left, a large bird perched in a tree near a nest with four eggs in it. To the right, a fox, tail held high, runs by the side of a cornfield towards the tree.*

Ampleforth, Yorkshire. Parish Church.
155 Stone capital, 1924. A fox, one foot raised.*

B

Bakewell, Derbyshire. Parish Church.
156 Misericord, 1881. At the centre is a crowned lion facing a stag (Noble and Brichemer?). On the left supporter is a stag, on the right, a lion, each facing the centre carving.*

Barfreston, Kent. St Nicholas.
157 Doorway medallion. Norman. A fox plays a harp while a man or woman performs a somersault.

Barton-on-the-Heath, Warwickshire. Parish Church.
158 East side of chancel arch, facing altar. Probably 14th C. A fox.*

Barwick, Somerset. St Mary Magdalene.
159 Bench end. A fox runs off dragging a duck by its bill. Two dogs depicted above are probably meant to be giving chase. Higher still are two quacking ducks.

Bayeux, Normandy, France. The former Bishop's Palace, facing the Cathedral .

160 The Bayeux Tapestry, or Tapisserie de la reine Mathilde. Late 11th C. Probably made in the south of England. The fable of the fox, the crow and the cheese is depicted three times. Reproductions are to be found in Stenton 1965, plates 4, 20 and 31.

Beverley Minster.

Misericords and other stall carving, 1520.

161 Upper stalls, south side of the choir, 6. Eight apes steal from a pedlar who is clearly awake.

162 Also, upper stalls, south 19. In the centre a fox, pursued by three dogs, goes to earth while an archer, running up, takes aim at it. On the left supporter, an ape rides a fox. On the right, an ape tends a fox lying in bed.

163 Also, south 20. In the centre, a woman with a distaff chases a fox making off with a goose. Four geese honk in the background. Behind the woman stands a cottage with a child at the door. On the left supporter, two foxes seem to be planning mischief. On the right, a fox stands over a goose.

164 Also, elbow rest, on the north side of the choir, 3. A fox runs off with a goose flung over his back.

165 Also, misericord, north 4. A fox preaches to geese. The fox holds a rosary which may indicate that he is a Dominican. An ape is also depicted with a dead goose hanging from a stick over its shoulder.

166 Also, misericord, north 7. In the centre, a fox is hanged by geese. On the left supporter, an ape removes a noose from around the fox's neck.

167 Also, in stone, north aisle of the nave, on the outer wall, to the right if the Minster is entered by the north door. Probably early 14th C. A fox wearing a kind of smock and carrying a staff leads a duck, hen and cock. There has been some restoration to the fox's head.

Beverley, St Mary.

Misericords, 1445; roof bosses, 1520-25.

168 Misericord, south, 3. Two fox friars seem to be receiving instructions from a Franciscan

169 Also, south 13. A fox, pierced by an arrow, consults an ape.

170 Also, north 12. A fox preaches to a friar and a nun. Two cowled apes (?) sit below.

171 Also, north 14. Two cowled foxes, each of which touches with a forepaw the corner of an open book behind which is a goose, wings wide open, head to one side, recalling the open-winged eagle design of many a lectern. The goose seems to have been given a halo of leaves.

172 Also, Lady Chapel, roof boss. A fox preaches to geese. He has a cock in his cowl.

173 Also, Lady Chapel, roof boss. A fox carries off a goose.

Birtles, Cheshire. Parish Church.

174 Stained and painted glass roundel high up in one of the nave windows. 16th C. A fox, looking back as it runs off against a bright blue sky, holds a goose by the wing over his back. A large, bright gold star shines in the sky. This may be of Flemish origin.

Bishop's Lydeard, Somerset. St Lawrence.
175 A stone capital. A fox seizes a goose.

Blackburn, the Cathedral.
176 Misericord. 1430. Removed from Whalley Abbey. North, 4. An ape-fox preaches to five ducks.

Bloxham, Oxfordshire. St Mary.
177 Tower (outside). 14th C. Frieze at top of tower, north side overlooking nave roof, over clock. A man with a washing beetle and a woman with a distaff chase a fox with a duck or a goose.

Boston, St Botolph.
Choir-stalls woodwork. 1390.
178 Elbow rest, upper stalls, south 7. A fox devours a chicken.
179 Also, misericord, lower stalls, south 17. A woman with a distaff chases a fox with a duck or a goose.
180 Also, misericord, lower stalls, south 25. A seated fox bishop grasps a nearby cock by the neck. An ass-chaplain, holding an open book, stands at the fox's side.
181 Also, elbow rest, lower stalls, south 25. A fox wearing a cape receives, from a hooded ape, water in a vessel like a water jug.
182 Also, misericord, upper stalls, north 19. A fox consults an ape. Another fox leaves the scene.

Bovey Tracey, Devon. Parish Church.
183 Misericord, exact position not known. Probably early 14th C.
A fox carries off a goose over his back. There is a cock on either supporter.

Bramber, Sussex. St Nicholas.
184 Capital, south tower arch. c.1073. Two foxes with prey. Below them, on its side, an animal's head which could be a lion's.

Brant Broughton, near Newark-on-Trent, Lincolnshire. Parish Church.
185 North porch. 15th C. A fox carries off a goose flung over his back.*

Branston, Lincolnshire. All Saints.
Bench ends.
186 Central aisle, south, two from west. A fox observes two women dancing to the music of bagpipes played by a pig.
187 Also, central aisle, north, six from west. A seated fox faces a seated ape.
188 Also, central aisle, north, nine from west. A fox runs off with a goose.

Bray, Berkshire, Parish Church.
189 Brass of Sir John de Foxley and his two wives, 1378. The figures are on a kind of raised platform supported by a column at the base of which is a recumbant fox.

Brent Knoll, Somerset. St Michael.

Bench ends, 14th or 15th C.

190 A fox abbot preaches to birds.

191 Also, the fox abbot is footcuffed and put in the stocks.

192 Also, the fox abbot is hanged by geese.

Bridlington, Yorkshire. The Priory Church.

193 Coffin lid. Probably 11th C. A fox watches a stork feed from a tall vessel. A lion-like creature watches from below.

Bristol Cathedral.

Misericords, 1520; Lady Chapel stonework, c.1200.

194 South 3. Tibert the Cat runs up the naked priest's back.

195 Also, south 10. Bruin the Bear and Isengrin the Wolf dance.

196 Also, north 1. Bruin the Bear is caught in a partially split log.

197 Also, north 2. Tibert the Cat is caught in a snare and attacks the priest's genitals.

198 Also, north 3. Reynard stands on the gallows ladder.

199 Also, north 4. Apes attack and steal from a pedlar who is awake.

200 Also, north 5. A fox preaches to geese from a pulpit. An ape (?) emerges from behind the pulpit. A lion stands in some stylized bushes on the right supporter.

201 Also, north 9. A fox is hanged by geese.

202 Also, stone spandrel, south side of the Lady Chapel. A fox runs off with a goose. This is immediately below a sculpture of a saint fighting a dragon.

Buildwas, Shropshire. Parish Church.

203 Misericord. A fox preaches to geese.

Burlingham, Norfolk (sometimes called South Burlingham). St Edmund.

204 Bench end 15th C (?). A fox makes off with a big, fat goose.*

Burwell, Cambridgeshire. St Mary.

205 A wooden cornice panel, south side of the nave, just below the roof. Late 15th C. Two foxes, each with a goose flung over its back, face each other on either side of a little stylized tree.

Bury St Edmunds. St Mary.

Roof bosses in the nave, 1430.

206 A fox in a pulpit preaches to a cock and a hen. (Cave 1948, plate 52).

207 Also, a fox carries off a goose.

208 Also, two geese hang a fox. (Cave 1948, plate 53).

209 Also, roof beam in the nave, south side, sixth bay, wooden spandrel. Probably 14th C. A fox seizes a goose.

Bury St Edmunds, Moyses Hall Museum.

210 A stained glass fragment from the Abbey. Probably early 15th C. The fox is hanged by geese.

211 Also, misericord, displayed on a wall in the museum. Probably 14th C. A robed fox stands in a pulpit preaching to two geese and a cock which is perched on a branch. Behind the pulpit, left, is another fox carrying off a bird of some kind.

C

Cambridge. Great St Mary.

212 Stone corbel at north-east corner of south gallery. Probably early 14th C. A fox seizes a cock..

Cambridge. King's College Chapel.

213 In a side chapel on the south side of the nave. A panel of stained glass. Probably 16th C. A fox makes off with a goose.

Canon Pyon, Herefordshire. Parish Church.

214 Misericord, north 1, probably 14th C. A fox has seized a goose by the neck and flung it over his back. A duck tries to hide round a corner.

Canterbury Cathedral.

Roof bosses in the cloisters. 15th C.

215 A woman, brandishing a distaff, pursues a fox making off with a goose.

216 Also, four geese hang a fox.

217 Also, stone capital in the crypt. c.1120. A fox-dog plays a flute; to its right, a winged, dog-like creature plays a harp.

218 Also, nave, stone capital. 14th C. A fox with a goose flung over its back

Carlisle Cathedral.

Misericords. 1400.

219 North 7. A fox seizes a goose by the neck. A fleeing fox is depicted on both supporters.

220 Also, south 12. Almost identical with the composition at north 7.

Castle Hedingham, Essex. St Nicholas.

221 Misericord, south 3. Probably 15th C. An erect fox carries a monk or friar dangling upside down from a stick over his shoulder. On the left supporter a fox blows a trumpet.

Chester Cathedral.

Misericords. 1390 (but modern replacements second half of 19th C.).

222 South 19. A fox friar faces a nun beneath a tree.

223 Also, (modern), north 7. Two foxes are portrayed beneath a stylized vine.

224 Also, (modern), north 8. Two foxes beneath a tree in which is perched a crow with a cheese in its beak.

225 Also, (modern), north 10. A fox watches a crane feed from a long-necked vessel.

226 Also, north 14. In the centre, a fox feigns death and birds peck him. To the right, a fox eats a bird. To the left, a lion curls up beneath a tree.

Chichester Cathedral.

227 Misericord, 1330, south 20. A fox plays a harp and sits on a duck. An ape dances in front of him.

Chippenham. Parish Church.

228 Medieval chest, front, bottom left panel. c.1250. A fox holding a crozier preaches to a cock, hens, geese, and storks.

Christchurch Priory.

229 Elbow rest, upper stalls, south, two from east. 1515. A giant, cowled fox preaches from a pulpit to diminutive hens pecking the ground before him. Behind him, a cock.

Church Stretton, Shropshire. Parish Church.

230 Jacobean reredos. An erect, robed fox holds a large crozier in his right hand. [266].

Cley-next-the-Sea, Norfolk. St Margaret.

231 Roof boss, south porch. Probably 15th C. A woman with a distaff chases a fox making off with a cock.

232 Also, bench end poppyhead, south side of the nave. Probably 15th C. A cowled and robed fox holds a staff.

Clipsham, Leicestershire. Parish Church.

233 A stained glass quarry. 15th C. A large bird (probably meant to be a crow), perched on a thick branch, looks down at a relatively small fox. [267].

Cobham, Surrey. Parish Church.

234 A glass panel, modern (1964), depicts a golden-coloured fox poised to pounce, but no prey is shown.*

Combe-in-Teignhead, Devon. Parish Church.

235 Bench end (damaged). A dog chases a fox with a goose slung over his back.

Crief, Perthshire. The Highland Tryst Museum, Burrell Street.

236 In vellum on the outer side of the lid of a small vesta box, dated 17th C. at the museum. A fox in religious's habit approaches a cock with a written message. The box may well be 17th C., but this picture is a very clear copy of Kaulbach's etching of Reynard approaching Chantecler with what he says is the royal proclamation of universal peace, and may be compared with the Wynkyn de Worde woodcut of this scene [62].

D

Downside Abbey, near Stratton-on-the-Fosse.

237 & 238 Misericords, two, modern (1951). One depicts the fox feigning death (237), the other seizing a bird (238).

Dublin. Christ's Church.

239 Medieval paving stones, nave, centre aisle. A series of upright foxes depicted as friars.*

E

East Lyng, Somerset. Parish Church.

240 Bench end. A greyhound chases a fox.*

241 Also, bench end. A fox drags a duck off by its bill.*

Edinburgh. National Museum of Antiquities.

242 A panel from Abbot Panter's house, Montrose. c.1516. Two foxes dressed as friars. One of them holds a goose. In *Scotland's Magazine*, October 1959, there is a photograph of these foxes, and a short commentary.

Ely Cathedral.

243 Misericord, upper stall, north 19. 1338. In the centre, a woman brandishes her distaff and pursues a fox with a cock. On the left supporter, a fox preaches to a cock and two hens. On the right supporter, a man, facing the central scene, waves a stave menacingly.

244 Also, in the Stained Glass Museum situated in the north gallery of the cathedral, on extended loan from Byfield Parish Church in Northamptonshire, a stained-glass roundel, 15th C., depicting a robed fox in a pulpit preaching to two geese. He holds a third by the neck, and has a fourth in his cowl.

Etchingham, Sussex. St Nicholas.

Misericords. 15th C.

245 Misericord, north 1. Ducks flee from a Franciscan fox friar.

246 Also, misericord, north 9. The same as at north 1.

F

Fairford, Gloucestershire. Parish Church.

247 Misericord, north 1. 1490. A fox runs off with a goose slung over his back. Of the two other geese depicted, one pecks at the fox's brush.

Faversham, Kent. Parish Church.

Misericords. 1533.

248 South 4. The fable of the fox and the sour grapes.*

249 Also, south 7. A fox carries off a goose slung over his back. Two other victims lie beneath his forepaws.

Fawsley, Northamptonshire. St Mary.

Pews probably carved mid- 16th C.

250 Panel, south aisle, facing east, 1 from south door. Below a medallion depicting the head and shoulders of a man, a fox (?) fights a cock (?).

251 Also, two panels further north, facing east, 3 from south door. A fox preaches to geese from a pulpit. A dead goose's head lolls from his cowl.

252 Also, panel, north aisle, facing south, 2 from east. A fox-dog plays a viol. Two other similar creatures look on, smiling.

Fenny Bentley, Derbyshire. Parish Church.

253 Chancel screen, north door spandrel. 1519. A fox carries off a goose slung over his back.

G

Galashiels, Old Gala House, now a museum.

254 19th C. ceiling above the first floor landing of the stairway. To the right, a fox with its tongue out vainly tries to reach some fruit high up in a tree. To the left, tongue still hanging out, the fox stalks off.

Garstang, Lancashire. Parish Church.

255 Misericord, probably c.1400, north 6. A fox.

Glasgow. The Burrell Collection, Pollock Park.

256 A small piece of stained and painted glass of English origin (ref. no. 45/64). c.1450. A fox (?); it might just be a wolf) in religious habit, holding a sealed document in his left hand, preaches from a pulpit to a congregation of sheep and lambs.

257 Also, a spandrel in the top right corner of a wooden door on the inside of Burrell's reconstructed Hall. Late 15th C. Four geese look up at a fox in a pulpit. To the left is seated another fox, holding a crozier, and with his legs crossed. A goose dangles down from his neck. Further to the left, a woman brings her distaff down onto the shoulders of the seated fox. Further still to the left, a devil-like mask is linked by a carved line to these scenes.

258 Also, a small tapestry or cushion cover of Swiss origin. 1450-75. A fox preaches from a pulpit to four geese. He has two more in his cowl. A banderole woven into the tapestry says, in Swiss German, 'I am well provided with cunning, enough to fill my stomach.'

259 Also, a small piece of stained and painted glass of English origin (ref. no. 45/102a). c.1500. Two dog-like creatures painted in a foxy red lower another similar creature into a decorated stone tomb. Might just be part of a fox funeral sequence.

260 Also, a richly decorated and ornamented stone portal, probably of Spanish origin (ref. no. 44/86). Early 1500s. At the highest point, a fox seizes a hen or a cock by a wing. Unusual in that the spectator sees this happen as if he were above the fox.

261-270 Also, Crawhall's sequence of ten watercolour paintings for an edition of *The History of Reynard the Fox*, executed in 1896-97, are kept here. (For a brief comment on this, see the fifth paragraph from the end of Chapter Eleven; and for three reproductions, see illustrations 255-257. For a fuller comment and reproductions of all of these pictures, see Hamilton 1990, pp. 114-22.)

Glasgow, The Hunterian Art Gallery of the University of Glasgow.

Houses two more watercolours, late 1890s, by Joseph Crawhall, one of which was almost certainly meant for the unpublished edition of the History of Reynard the Fox.

271 Reynard consults Rukenaw on the eve of his duel with Ysegrim.

272 A fox looks across a river at a number of apprehensive ducks.

Gloucester Cathedral.

Misericords, 1345; and paintings on wood, 1350-75.

273 Misericord, north 19. A fox carries off a goose slung over his back.

274 Also, misericord, north 15. A fox has climbed a tree and two dogs leap up after him. An archer on the left takes aim at him.

275 Also, misericord, north 12. To the left, a sick lion facing a fox who looks away from the lion, and at a urinal. Both animals are carved against a background of foliage.

276-83 Also, in the Dean's Vestry, painted on two panels of wood behind the north row of choir-stalls. Each panel is divided into an upper and a lower register, and each register is made up of two scenes. Starting with the left panel, upper register; continuing with the right panel, upper register; then the left panel, lower register; and lastly, the right panel, lower register:

276 A fox kills a goose.

277 The fox is taken prisoner by a boar, a goat, and a hare.

278 The fox is brought before a seated, red-robed wolf-abbot or judge, and watched by a cock and a hen.

279 Six yoked geese take the fox to a place of execution.

280 The fox is hanged at the gallows.

281 A horse and a stag stand on either side of a lectern on which lies an open book in which one can see notes of music.

282 Animals having what appears to be a fairly riotous time.

282A The fox is lifted off a bier and into a grave, attended by a hare, wolf, bear, ram (or goat) and ape.

283 The crowned lion and lioness are served food and drink at a table.

Godmanchester, Hertfordshire. St Mary the Virgin.

284 Misericord, south 1. Probably 15th C. A fox carries off a goose.

Great Malvern Priory.

285 Lower stalls, elbow rest, north 1. 1480. A cowled fox.*

Gresford, Denbighshire. All Saints.

286 Misericord, south 2. A fox preaches from a pulpit to a cock, hens and ducks.

287 Also, misericord, 2 from the south east. A fox sits between two crowned lions. Badly damaged.

Grimston, Norfolk. Parish Church.

288 Choir-stalls, elbow rest. 15th C. A fox with a goose flung over his back.

H

Haddon Hall, Derbyshire.

An isolated desk end. Probably mid- to late 14th C.

289 On one side of the shoulder, a fox bishop preaches to birds. A banderole issuing from his jaws says 'Pes be here In'. A cock is perched in a tree above them, and a blank banderole issues from its beak. Behind the fox is shown another one running off with a goose in its jaws.

290 Also, on the other side of the shoulder of this desk end, two geese hang the fox. A cock is perched on the gallows crossbeam, and a banderole issues from his beak. Though badly damaged, this can be interpreted to read 'draw now to his damage'.

Hadstock, Essex. St Botolph.

291 Screen separating Lady Chapel from the nave (south transept). 15th C (?). A cowled fox preaches to geese from a pulpit. He has one before him by the neck, while the two behind him seem to sleep.

Hailes, Cheshire. Parish Church.

292 Wall painting. c.1270. Grotesques. Among them, a fox and a rabbit, each holding a shield, fight face to face.*

Halsall, Lancashire. St Cuthbert.

293 Misericord, south 2. 16th C. A fox makes off with a goose flung over his back.

Halton Holegate, Lincolnshire. St Nicholas.

Pews bench ends. 14th or 15th C.

294 Poppyhead. Probably late 14th or 15th C. South aisle of nave, 4 from west. Six apes steal from a sleeping pedlar.

295 Also, poppyhead, south aisle of nave, 5 from west. A fox runs off with a goose flung over his back.

Hargrave, Suffolk. Parish Church.

296 Wooden rood screen. 15th C. A fox, among other animals, including a unicorn, dragons, fish and eagles.

Hereford Cathedral.

Misericords, 1380.

297 Lower stalls, south 2. A fox seizes a goose.

298 Also, upper stalls, south 12. A fox makes off with a goose flung over his back.

Hexham Abbey.

299 On the stone Leschman arcading. Probably late 15th C. A fox preaches from a pulpit to geese.

Holt, Worcestershire. St Martin.

300 Capital, north doorway. Norman. A fox watches a crane feed from a tall vessel.

Honington, Suffolk. Parish Church.

301 Bench end poppyhead. A seated fox holds a goose by the neck.*

I

Ickleton, Cambridgeshire.

302 On the top of the wall surrounding the parish church cemetery. Of uncertain date, but probably 16th C. A fox carries off a goose slung over his back. Eroded, and often covered with mosses.

Ipswich. Old Half Moon Inn at the corner of Lower Brook Street and Foundation Street.

303 Corner post supporting a dragon beam. Probably 16th C. A fox preaches from a pulpit to geese or ducks. To one side he is shown making off with a goose flung over his back.

K

Kelston, Lincolnshire. St Faith.

304 Bench end. A fox meets with a snarling dog.*

Kenton. Parish Church.

305 Wooden screen. 15th-C. On the inside of an upright, about one-and-a-half inches high. A robed fox in a pulpit, an open book in his hands.*

Kirby Wharfe, West Yorkshire. Parish Church.

306 South chancel wall, above some Swiss and German glass of the 16th and 17th C. A small quarry. 16th C. It depicts a white-robed fox in a pulpit. His robes have some golden decoration embroidered on them. His forepaws rest on the edge of the pulpit, and his tongue hangs out.

Knowle, Warwickshire. Parish Church.

Misericords. Probably 16th C.

307 (Position not recorded). An ape wearing a doctor's robe and holding a urinal to which he points, lectures to two foxes.

308 Also (position not recorded). A crowned lion has, to its right, a unicorn; to its left, a fox.

L

Lakenheath, Suffolk. Parish Church.

309 Bench end poppyhead. A fox carries a goose on his back.

Launceston, Cornwall. Parish Church.

Bench ends, all modern: 1894.

310 A fox holds a quacking bird in his jaws.*

311 Also, a fox looks up at two crows on a branch. One crow has its beak wide open.*

312 Also, a fox and a crane face each other.*

Ledbury, Herefordshire. Parish Church.

313 Misericord. A fox faces a goose.*

Leicester Cathedral.

314 Stained and painted glass, now destroyed, but of which a drawing survives in Nichol 1851, vol. 1, plate XLIII. 14th C. A fox preaches to geese from a lectern. A banderole above them bore the words 'Testis est mihi Deus quam cupiam vos omnes visceribus meis'.

Lincoln Cathedral.

Choir-stalls, quatrefoil panels in wood. Late 14th C.

315 South, west block, 1 from west. A fox rides a goose and a goose rides a fox.

316 Also, south, west block, 1 from west. A fox preaches from a pulpit to geese. To the left, a fox has a goose in its jaws.

317 Also, south, central block, 6 from the west. Possibly modern. A fox (?) carries off a lamb. A bear scratches its head to the left, and a lion to the right.

318 Also, south, central block, 6 from the west. Possibly modern. A fox (?) carries off a lamb and is watched by a lion from the right.

319 Also, north, west block, 3 from the west. A fox steals off, among foliage, with a goose.

London. British Museum.

320 In the border decoration of a gittern (ref. no. 1963, 10-2, 1), 14th C. Of English origin. A scene depicting a man carrying a stick behind five dogs which, in their turn, are behind a fox facing another man with a dog.

London. Museum of London.

321 Part of a chest front. c.1410. Noted for three sculpted scenes illustrating Chaucer's *Pardoner's Tale*. In the lower right corner a large fox runs 'off stage'. Said by Chaucerians to be an allusion to the Pardoner, but probably playing his role as a symbol of evil. For a photograph and comments, see Alexander and Binski 1987, 216, entry 710.

322 Also, badge in tin or pewter. Second half of the 13th C. Takes the form of a peacock with a fox standing on its back. Probably a pilgrim souvenir.

323 Also, fragment of a tin or pewter badge. c.1400. Shows four sides of what was probably an octagonal pulpit, on each of which is depicted a goose peering up at the now missing preacher, most probably a fox.

324 Also, a slightly damaged tin or pewter badge. c.1400. An upright fox with two tails stands on the back of a much smaller fox which is on all fours. The three brushes of the two foxes overlap and join each other. The upright fox (whose head is missing) clasps a portative organ to his chest.

London. Westminster Abbey, Henry VII's Chapel.

325 Misericord. 1509. Upper stalls, north 3. On the left supporter, a goose rides a fox; on the right, a fox rides a goose.

London, Tower of London. Chapel of St Peter ad Vincula.

Frieze of the Duke of Exeter's tomb.

326 The fox attacks a goose;

327 throws it over his back;

328 is then dragged off by a goose, a noose around his neck, to the gallows;
329 and finally hanged by a goose.

Ludlow. St Lawrence.
Misericords. 1435.
330 South 9. Probably depicts the fox being hanged by birds, most probably geese. Badly damaged.
331 Also, north 8. A mitred fox preaches to geese from a pulpit.

Lydeard, Somerset. St Lawrence.
332 Stone capital. 14th C. A fox comes round a corner and seizes a goose by its neck.

Lugdvan. Parish Church.
333 Wall painting, now destroyed, but copied by a Dr Borlase about 1750. In 1935 Mr Clive Rouse made a tracing of Borlase's drawing, and gave me a copy of it. Late 15th C. (The church was built in 1446). The painting extended over most of the inside of the west wall. To the east of the door, an enormous St Christopher with the Christ Child on his back. Above the door, a church at the open doorway of which stands a woman with a lantern. To the west of the door, geese hang a fox over a tree branch.

M

Malvern. Council House of Malvern Hill District Council.
334 Stained glass window panels. Modern. A fox sits on its hindquarters by a river bank against a background of tall flowers. He looks down on a frog which offers a small tube of something to him, and he seems to be about to accept it.

Manchester Cathedral.
Misericords. 1508.
335 South 7. In the centre, a woman brandishing her distaff, pursues a fox making off with a duck or a goose. Behind the woman, a cottage and a child at its entrance door. On the left supporter, a fox supervises two small foxes reading a book. On the right, a fox reads a book.
336 Also, south 8. Eight apes steal from a sleeping pedlar.
337 Also, north 9. A fox rides a hound or a wolf through a wood and carries a hare dangling from a staff over his shoulder.

Mansfield Woodhouse, Nottinghamshire. Parish Church.
338 It is reported that there is a poppyhead carving of a fox reaching for acorns.*

Martley, Worcestershire. Parish Church.
339 Mural painting. East wall of the chancel. A fox and a wolf with other animals, possibly a hart, a dragon, and a griffin.*

Marwood, Devon. Parish Church. 15th C.

340 Bench end. Two carved sections, on each of which is carved a shield. On the left is a duck or a goose which walks away from, on the right, a fox which faces away from the goose. The fox's enormous brush is drawn up and over his body, and he appears to be just outside his den.*

Meavy, Devon. Parish Church. Modern: 1892.

341 Choir-stall front. Top, left corner. A fox prowls among stylized grapes.*

Melbourne, Derbyshire. St Michael.

Stone capitals. Norman, betwen 1140 and 1200.

342 At the corner of the north transept, just inside the choir. A man tugs at a fox's brush as it makes off with a goose flung over its back.

343 Also, at the corner of the south transept and choir. A fox watches a crane feed from a tall vessel.

344 Also, at the corner of the south transept. A fox running off with prey and being pursued by a man.

Mere, Wiltshire. St Michael the Archangel.

345 Misericord. South 6. Probably 14th C. Foliage covering a fox.

Minster-in-Thanet, Kent. St Mary.

346 Misericord. North 10. 1410. In the centre, a seated woman with a distaff across her lap. A cat and a dog by her. On the left supporter, a fox carries off a goose. On the right, a man's face.

Mold. St Mary.

On an outside string course. 15th C. Among many kinds of animal, including sheep, goats, lions, pigs, are three foxes. There is

347 a fox and goose; *

348 a fox with another bird;*

349 and a fox alone.

Inside the church, again on a string course, are

350 two more foxes.*

N

Nailsea Court, Somerset.

351 Window of the main staircase. Painted quarry. Early 15th C. A fox with a goose thrown over his back. For a comment and an illustration, see Woodforde, p. 273, plate XLIX.

Nantwich, Cheshire. St Mary.

352 Misericord, south 2. 1390. In the centre, a fox feigns death, and birds peck him. To the right, a fox friar with a bow; to the left, a fox friar with a hare and a goose.

353 Also, a wooden corbel, either c.1400 or 1855. Head and forelegs of a fox in foliage.

Necton, Norfolk. Parish Church.

354 South wall, easternmost arch brace, on the west side of the brace. 14th or 15th C. A crudely carved fox with a goose. The goose's neck is firmly held in the fox's tooth-filled jaws, and is flung over his back.

Newington, Kent. Parish Church.

355 It is reported that there is a poppyhead carving of a fox with a goose.*

Northampton, Abington Manor.

356 Wooden panel. Probably late 15th or early 16th C. A fox preaches from a pulpit to ducks, and then seizes one of them by the neck.

Norwich Cathedral.

357 Misericord. South 30. 1480. A woman brandishes her distaff and pursues a fox making off with a duck or goose.

358 Also, roof boss in the cloisters, north end of north side. Between 1290 and 1340. A dog seizes a fox which seizes a cock.

359 Also, roof boss in the cloisters, but position not recorded. A fox with an ape, and a fox with a lion.

Nottingham, Sneinton. St Stephen.

360 Misericord. North 4. A fox or an ape rides a hound or a wolf and blows a huntsman's horn.*

O

Oakham, Rutland. All Saints.

361 Capital in the nave. 14th C. A woman brandishes her distaff as a fox makes off with a duck. Behind the woman, a fettered ape.

Oddington, Gloucestershire. Parish Church.

362 Mural. A fox preaches with a monk in attendance.*

Ontwell, Norfolk. Parish Church.

363 South window. There was a medieval piece of stained and painted glass depicting a woman in a white robe with a blue mantle on her knees. She sat between four men. At her feet was depicted a fox hanging from a tree, wounded in the neck by two arrows. This glass has been lost.*

Osbournby, Lincolnshire. SS Peter and Paul.

364 Bench end. A fox preaches from a pulpit.*

Oxford, Bodleian Library. Divinity Hall.

365 Roof boss. 14th C. Fourth bay, north end, west fan. A fox carries off a goose.

Oxford, Magdalen College Chapel.

366 Misericord. c.1500. North 4. A fox carries off a goose slung over his back.

P

Padstow, Cornwall. St Petroc.

367 Bench end, now part of the sedilia in the south aisle chapel. A fox preaches from a pulpit to ducks.

Peterborough Cathedral.

368 Misericord. Free standing. Late 15th C. A fox seizes a goose by the neck. A cock on either supporter.

Poughill, near Bude, Cornwall. St Olaf.

369 Pew end, centre aisle, north 8. Probably early 16th C. A fox watches an eagle taking a rabbit (?) in its talons.

Probus, near Truro, Cornwall. SS Probus and Grace.

370 At the base of the tower, on the exterior. Early 16th C. A hound chases a fox which carries a bird. Eroded.

R

Ribbesford, Worcestershire. Parish Church.

371 A panel from an old rood-screen, probably 14th C., is mounted on a modern pulpit. A fox, holding a book, pr eaches from a pulpit to ducks ot geese, a cock and a hen. Theodern woodwork, dated 1858.

Ripon Cathedral.

Misericords, 1490.

372 South 10. In the centre a fox seizes a goose. On the left supporter, a seated woman shoulders a distaff. On the right, a dog barks after the fox.

373 Also, north 11. A fox preaches from a pulpit to a duck and a cock.

374 Also, north 12. A fox runs off with a goose thrown over his back. Another goose, with raised wings, stands before the fox.

375 Also, north 13. A fox is caught by two hounds.

Rothwell, Yorkshire. Parish Church.

Modern woodwork, dated 1858.

376 Stall front, poppyhead. A fox, a hound and a quacking duck in foliage.

377 Also, stall front poppyhead. A fox's head peeps from a hawthorne bush.

S

Saint Alban's Cathedral, Bedfordshire.

378 Watching Chamber, facing south aisle, 4th group from the west. c.1400. A fox in consultation with an ape. The fox holds what may be a barber's bowl close to his chest.

The fox's brush is erect and prominent. This carving (badly damaged) may show the ape clipping the fox's fur and oiling his body. The ape holds what may be an oil can in his right hand. For a short comment and a photograph, see Woolly 1927, p. 246 and plate XII, figure 2.

Saint Austell, Cornwall. Holy Trinity.

379 Pew end, fixed to tower wall. A fox preaches from a pulpit to a kneeling woman.

Saint David's Cathedral, Pembrokeshire.

380 Misericord. South 7. 1470. A hooded fox's head.

Saint Ewe, near Saint Austell, Cornwall. St Ewe.

381 Rood-screen. A fox, together with some other animals, birds and foliage.*

Salisbury Cathedral.

Chapter House, central pillar, frieze around the base of the column. A 19th-C. replica of the medieval sculptures in stone. The much damaged medieval original stands in the south-west corner of the cloisters.

382 On the west side, a fox sits on either side of a stylized vine.

383 To the north-west, a lion. (To the north, a griffin).

384 To the north-east, a fox bites the rear paw of an animal.

385 To the east, a fox (slightly damaged) sits at the foot of a lion's bed. One paw is raised and is broken off. May have held a urinal. The lion lies on its belly, face towards the viewer, head on a pillow, and is covered by a sheet. (To the south-east, a bull.)

386 To the south, a fox is bitten by an animal.

387 To the south-west, a fox sits before a headless creature.

388 Also, on the eighth capital of the second bay, beneath the spandrel carving of Noah in his vineyard, an ape and a fox hide among stylized foliage.

389 Also, in the Lady Chapel. 1220-25. At the base of the most westerly pillar on the north side. A very eroded fox with prey in its jaws is being pursued by a dog (?) which seems to be seizing the fox's brush.

Salisbury, the Salisbury and South Wiltshire Museum.

390 A tin or pewter badge. c.1400. Depicts a strangely robed, almost feathered, fox in a pulpit, holding a staff, and preaching to geese which look up at him. Another goose seems to be perched on the side of the pulpit. Another hangs from the fox's belt. For a sketch and comment on this badge, see Spencer 1990, ill. 303.

Sherborne Abbey, Somerset.

391 Misericord. Probably 1436. Now missing, but a drawing of it may be seen in Wright 1864, 91, figure 56. Four geese hang a fox. On either side of the fox sits a Franciscan friar.

Silk Willoughby, Lincolnshire. St Denis.

392 A fox with a bird in its jaws.*

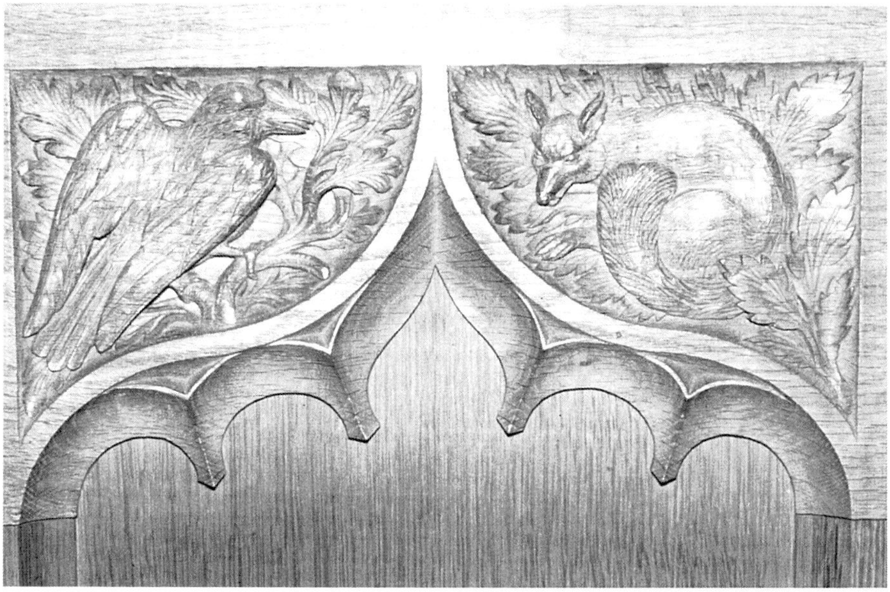

268 *A crow and a fox. Somerton Parish Church, choir-stall bench end; 20th C. Jill and Brian Lucas.*

Somerton, Oxfordshire. Parish Church.

393 Choir-stall bench end. Either 15th C. or modern. A large bird perched on a branch in a tree looks down at a fox. Probably the fable of the fox and the crow. [268].

Stoke-by-Nayland, Suffolk. Parish Church.

394 Capital. Probably 15th C. A fox preaches to geese.*

Stottesdon, Shropshire. Parish church.

395 Font. Some upside down foxes.*

Stowlangtoft, Suffolk. Parish Church.

396 Bench end poppyhead. A seated fox.

397 Also, bench end finial. A fox preaches from a pulpit.

Suffield, Norfolk. Parish Church.

398 Rood-screen. 16th C. Spandrel. A fox lies as if it were dead. An ape inspects a urinal.

Swarkestone, Derbyshire. In the isolated church about a quarter of a mile before reaching the village and the bridge over the Trent, on the Derby side.

399 The Harpur Brass. 1573. Between each word of the inscription is engraved an animal or a flower. Among them is a fox running off with a goose flung over his back. (The other animals in this 'procession' include a bear, a camel, dog, duck, elephant [immediately before the fox and goose], lion, stag, fish, mermaid and unicorn.)

Swavesey, near Cambridge. Parish Church.

400 Bench end poppyhead, priest's prayer desk in the choir. Either 16th C. or modern, probably modern. A fox licks the side of a tall vessel from which a stork or crane feeds. The opposite poppyhead depicts a winged lion-like creature, probably a griffin.

401 Also, pew end poppyhead in the south aisle, south side. Probably 16th C. A fox carries off a goose flung over his back.

402 Also, pew end poppyhead, also in the south aisle, south side. Also probably 16th C. Another representation of the fox making off with a goose over his back.

T

Thanet. See Minster-in-Thanet.

Thornham, Norfolk. All Saints.

403 Bench end poppyhead on the north side, to the front. Probably 15th C. A fox preaches from a pulpit.

404 Also, bench end poppyhead, also on the north side, but at the back. Probably 15th C. A robed fox preaches from a pulpit. Two geese peep out of his thrown-back cowl.

405 Also, on the inside of the wooden door in the south porch. 15th C. The ogee-shaped top is divided into two sections. On the left, a fox preaches from a pulpit to four birds, probably meant to be geese. On the right, he has seized a goose by the neck and is in the process of flinging it over his back.

Tickencote, Rutland. St Peter.

406 Chancel vaulting. Norman. Three heads; one human, and one is probably that of a fox. For a photograph, see Cave 1948, plate 1.

Tideswell, Derbyshire. Parish Church.

407 Stall front. c.1880. A fox standing on its hind legs, its forelegs on a vine, looks at a bunch of grapes.*

408 Also, rood-screen. c.1875. A fox.*

Tilton-on-the-Hill, Leicestershire. St Peter.

409 Capital, north side, 1 from east. 14th C.
Encircling the capital, a crowned lion before which appears a fox with its prey (a goose flung over its back), followed by a badger (?) and a collared, chained monkey.

Topsham, Devon. Parish Church.

410 Font. Early 12th C. A fox seems to pull a goose over its back by the bill. For a photograph, see Stone 1955, plate 32 B.

Tring, near Harrow, Hertfordshire. Parish Church.

411 A medieval carving of a fox and goose is reported to be somewhere in this church.*

Tuttington, Norfolk. Parish Church.

412 Stalls bench end shoulder. Probably 15th C. A woman brings her distaff (broken off) down on to the back of a fox about to take a goose from her basket.

413 Also, choir-stall elbow rest. Probably 15th C. A fox with a goose.*

U

Ufford, Suffolk. Parish Church.

414 Bench end. A fox makes off with a goose.*

Utterby, Lincolnshire. Parish Church.

415 Porch doorway. An eroded fox and goose.*

W

Walpole, Norfolk. St Peter.

416 Roof boss in main entrance porch. A fox carries off a goose thrown over his back.

Wellingborough, Northamptonshire. All Saints.

417 Misericord. South 3 from north. 1385. A fox runs away with a goose thrown over his back.

Wells Cathedral.

Misericords. 1330.

418 Upper stalls, south 16. A fox, leaning on a staff, preaches to four ducks.

419 Also, upper stalls, north 10. An ape either ties or unties a bound fox.

420 Also, capital, north side, 11 from the east, c.1200. A man, holding a mallet over his shoulder and clutching a ball to his chest, watches a fox flinging a goose over his back.

421 Also, on the eastern wall of the passageway leading from the Dining Hall of Vicar's Choral to the stairs leading down to the Chapter house, displayed on a shelf, and apparently upside down: a fragment of carved stone of uncertain provenance. Probably c.1300. A fox lies on his back, jaws slightly open, teeth showing, tongue out, forepaws stetched upwards. A large, long-legged bird with claws (perhaps a crane or a stork) stands in front of the fox's chest. With outstretched neck, it pecks at the fox's tongue.

West Barston, Norfolk. Parish Church.

422 Stall elbow rest. 1954. A seated fox.*

West Keal, Lincolnshire. St Helen.

423 Capital, north aisle, 3 from west. Probably early 14th C. A fox with prey (a goose) is part of an encircling frieze which includes an owl, serpent, monkey and lion.

Weston-on-Trent, Derbyshire. Parish Church.

424 It is reported that there is a medieval stained and painted glass roundel depicting a fox preaching to geese.*

Whalley, Lancashire. St Mary and All Saints.

425 Misericord, removed from Whalley Abbey. North 9. 1435. A fox makes off with a goose, leaving behind a seated and possibly sleeping woman with a distaff. Her dog, in front of her, barks; her cat, behind her, cringes.

Winchester Cathedral.

Misericords, 1305.

426 South 17. A fox emerges from behind a large (cabbage ?) leaf. Two cocks, one on either supporter, fail to see him.

427 Also, upper stalls, south 31. A fox bites his near hind paw.

428 Also, north 19. An ape sits with an owl on its wrist rather like the ape and owl in the York Minster stained-glass panel. Although not now next to the misericord depicting the fox emerging from behind some leaves (upper stalls, south 17), it may have been so.

429 Also, north 29. A fox runs off with a goose.

430 Also, roof boss, 10th bay, south aisle. A hooded fox (?) peers between two monks holding an open book. It places a paw on the book. For a photograph, see Cave 1948, plate 261.

Winchester College Chapel.

431 Misericord. South 1. 1390. A fox runs off with a goose thrown over his back. A hound chases him from the right.

432 Also, roof boss, south side recess, most easterly bay. A fox carries off a goose.

Windsor. St George's Chapel.

Misericords and stall woodwork, 1480.

433 Upper stalls, south 6. On the left supporter, an ape holds up a comb and stands before a fox sitting on a tub and holding a basin.

434 Also, upper stalls, south 8 (4th Garter Stall). A fox preaches from a pulpit to geese. An ape bowman takes aim at one of the geese.

435 Also, lower stalls, south, west block, 1 from the west. Three monks and a fox with a goose in his jaws are shown in a wheelbarrow pushed by the Devil towards Hell's Mouth.

436 Also, lower stalls, south, west block, 2 from west. An ape pours liquid down a fox's (?) throat as it lies on its back. Another ape, hooded, inspects a urinal.

437 Also, lower stalls, south west block, 8 from west. On the left, waterflowers separate a fox from a rabbit. On the right, waterflowers separate a fox from a goose.

438 Also, lower stalls, south, east block, 4 from west. Five apes steal from a sleeping pedlar.

439 Also, upper stalls, north 20. On the left supporter, a fox runs off with a goose.

440 Also, desk front, north, west block, 4 from west. A cat and a rabbit pour something between the jaws of a fox lying on its back. To the left, an ape inspects a urinal.

441 Also, desk front, Choir, north, west block, 9 from west. A fox crouches before a defaced figure against a wooded background.

442 Also, desk front, spandrel, north, west block, 9 from west. To the left, a fox with a heart-shaped pouch hung round its neck, stands on its hind legs before a seated ape.

This ape holds a bowl into which both animals put their forepaws. To the right, a fox with a staff and a hamper on its back stands on its hind legs before a seated ape. They seem to be in a forest.

Woolpit, Suffolk. Parish Church.

443 Bench end poppyhead. A sitting fox holds a goose in his jaws. Its body is half-flung over the fox's back.

Worcester Cathedral.

444 Stone spandrel, north wall, east end of the building. 13th C. A fox looks up at a cock perched in a tree-top.

445 Also, misericord, south 20. 1397. On the right supporter, a fox kneels before an altar with a forepaw resting on the amputated head of a small animal as if blessing it.

446 Also, roof boss in the cloisters, east side, 5th bay from north. Late 14th C. A fox seizes a goose.

447 Also, roof boss in the cloisters, west side, 3rd bay from north. Late 14th C. On one side a fox preaches to geese; on the other, he runs off with a goose.

448 Also, roof boss in the cloisters, west side, 3rd bay from the north. Late 14th C. Geese hang a fox. Close by, the fox preaches to geese.

Wrexham. St Giles.

449 Corbel (in a dark corner). Probably 15th or 16th C., but may be an 1867 imitation. A fox and goose. The goose is twice the size of the fox which lies on its side.

Y

Yarnton, near Oxford. St Bartholomew.

450 Stained and painted glass at the east end of the north wall. Probably 16th C. An owl rings a bell and is depicted as saying 'Ye schal praye for the foxe'.

Yetminster, Dorset. St Andrew.

Capital, south west column. Probably 15th C.

451 Facing east: a fox attacks a goose.

452 Also, facing north: a goose hangs a fox.

York Minster.

453 Stained-glass window, north wall, 5th window from west, bottom border of the central panel (which depicts St Peter). 1310-1320. In the centre, a woman brandishes a distaff and chases a fox running off with a goose. To the left, a man leads a horse out of a stable as if to join in the chase. To the right, a seated ape observes the central scene, and holds an owl on its wrist.

454 Also, same window, bottom border of the left panel. The funeral service of a monkey, laid out on its bier. To the left, at a lectern, a cock and a fox face each other on either side of a lectern as they chant from an open book. The original colouring of the fox has changed with time into a shade of pink.

455 Also, in the Vestibule to the Chapter House, third column of the arcading on the left (as one enters from the transept), a kind of capital with two decorated shoulders. c.1290. On the shoulder facing as one enters (i.e., on the south side), beginning at the wall (i.e., west), a dog, preceded by a web-footed bird, preceded by a lion, all with similar proportions. On the other side, beginning at the wall, a dog, preceded by a fox with a goose over its back, preceded by a lion, also all of similar proportions. The two lions thus come to face each other at the outermost, central, fluted column.

456 Also, it is reported that there is nearby another similar set of figures. These are described as a hare, a hound, the winged bull of St John, a fox carrying a bird, a dog, a pig suckling young, a bird eating an acorn, and an owl.*

457 Also, in the Chapter House, a stone corbel. 1260-85. A fox, a monkey, a squirrel, and a snail.*

458 Also, Screen of the Kings. 1475-1500. In a recently gilded frieze a fox, with a goose flung over his back, peeps out of some foliage.

459 Also, capital of a column at the choir crossing, the westernmost one on the north side of the passageway round the choir. 14th C. A large robed fox leans forward in his pulpit, jaws open wide. His congregation consists of a single grimacing monk who stands facing the viewer and is separated from the pulpit by a small, seated, robed fox holding a large crozier. This little fox looks up at the preaching fox. A goose's head is

269 *A fox preaches from a pulpit, attended by a smaller fox with crozier and a monk. York Minster, capital; 14th C. Jill and Brian Lucas.*

just visible within the preaching fox's cowl. Above and before the fox's right shoulder is an ape, peeping out of some stylized vine foliage ornamented with bunches of grapes. [269].

York. St Margaret.

460 Along the edge of a Norman doorway. The fable of the fox and the crane.

APPENDIX THREE

A Short-Title List of All Extant Illustrated Histories of Reynard the Fox

from Wynkyn de Worde (c.1495) to A. Soulby (c.1800) which are kept in United Kingdom libraries based on H. Menke, *Bibliotheca Reinardiana*

1 *The History of Reinard the Foxe*, fragment (London, R. Pynson, 1494-1500?).
Oxford, Bodleian: Douce V 245. (Menke p. 208).

2 Wynkyn de Worde, title unknown, circumstantial evidence points to London, c.1495. (Menke p.209).

3 Richard Pynson, title unknown, fragmentary evidence points to 1501-1505.
Edinburgh, National Library: RB. s. 250. (Menke p. 209).

4 Wynkyn de Worde, *The History of Reynard the Fox*, fragment, c.1515. Cambridge, UL: Sel. 4. 27. (Menke p. 209).

5 *The Hystory of Reynard the Fox* ('Anonymous', 1560-1585?).
Privately owned by W. Grauwels. (Menke p. 212).

6 *The Most delectable History of Reynard the Fox* (London: Edward Allde for Aldred, 1620).
Oxford, Bodleian: 40 M 36(8) Art. (Menke p. 213).

7 Title as in 6 (London: Elizabeth Allde, 1629).
London, BL: 12410. e. 21.
Oxford, Bodleian, 40 R 21 (3) Art Seld. (Menke p. 214).

8 Title as in 6 (London: Oulton for Slater, 1640).
Oxford, Bodleian: Ashm. 1631 (6). (Menke p. 215).

9 Title as in 6 (London: Oulton for Wright, 1640). (Menke p. 216).

10 Title as in 6 (London: J. Bell, 1650). (Menke p. 217).

11 Title as in 6 (London: J. Bell, 1654).
Cambridge, UL: Syn. 7. 65. 41. (Menke p. 217).

12 Title as in 6 (London: J. Bell, 1656).
London, BL: C. 142. d. 24. (Menke p. 218).

13 Title as in 6 (London: H.B. for Edward Brewster, 1662).
Cambridge, UL / Trinity College: Grylls. 3. 387. (Menke p. 219).

14 Title as in 6. (London: A.M. for Edward Brewster, 1671).
Durham, Cathedral Library: H. IX. 55/1. (Menke p. 221).

15 *A Continuation, Or, Second Part of...Reynard the Fox* (London: A.M. for Edward Brewster, 1672). (Menke p. 222).

16 *The most Delectable History of Reynard the Fox* (London: A.M. for Edward Brewster, 1676).
Leeds, UL.
St Andrews, UL: r 17 PT 5584 E6C7. (Menke p. 223).

17 Title as in 16 (London: A.M. & R.R. for Edward Brewster, 1681).
Aberystwyth, NL.
Cambridge, UL / King's College: M. 17. 19.
Oxford, Bodleian: 70 d. 29. (Menke p. 224).

18 *The Most Pleasant and Delightful History of Reynard the Fox. The Second Part* (London: A.M. & R.R. for Edward Brewster, 1681).
Cambridge, UL.
Cambridge, St John's College Library.
Edinburgh, NL: LC. 3101(2).
Leeds, UL.
London, UL.
London, BL.
London, Victoria and Albert Museum: 60. 2473. (Menke p. 225).

19 John Shurley, *The most delightful History of Reynard the Fox in heroic verse* (London: T. Passinger & C. Passinger, 1681).
Cambridge, UL: SSS. 37. 24.
Edinburgh, UL.
London, BL: C. 39. e. 40.
Oxford, Bodleian: Douce S. 193; and (second copy) 70. d. 29. (Menke p. 230).

20 *The most pleasant History of Reynard the Fox* (London: Conyers for Blare, c.1685-1688).
Oxford, Bodleian: Wood 295(3). (Menke p. 231).

21 *The Shifts of Reynardine...* (London: T.J. for Edward Brewster & Thomas Passenger, 1684).
Aberystwyth, NL.
Cambridge, UL: SSS. 51. 9.
Edinburgh, NL: L.C. 3102. (Menke p. 226).

22 *The Most Delectable History of Reynard the Fox...To which may now be added a Second Part of the said History* (= the Continuation) *also...The Shifts of Reynardine* (London: James for Edward Brewster, 1694).
Aberystwyth, NL: PR 2347 R4c 94.
Cambridge, UL: SSS. 51. 9.
Edinburgh, NL: L.C. 3098.
London, BL: 12410. e. 18. (Menke p. 227).

23 *The Most Pleasing and Delightful History of Reynard the Fox and Reynardine his son...* (London: Onley for Nelme, 1697). (Menke p. 234).

24 *The Most Delectable History of Reynard the Fox...to which may now be added a Second Part* (= the Continuation)*...as also the Shifts of Reynardine...* (London: Ilive for Edward Brewster, 1701).
Cambridge, Christ's College Library: Rouse 5. 4.
Cambridge, King's College Library: S. 64. 38.
Cambridge, St John's College Library: A/G. 27. 60(1).
Cambridge, Trinity College Library: Grylls 3. 387.
Cambridge, UL: Sy. 7. 70. 17.
Edinburgh, NL: L.C. 3101(1).
Edinburgh, UL: De. 6. 91.
London, BL: 1077. f. 16; and (second copy) G.17705.
London, UL.
Oxford, Worcester College Library: LR. 4. 6. (Menke p. 229).

25 *The Most Pleasing and Delightful History of Reynard the Fox and Reynardine his Son...to which is added the History of Cawood the Rook* (London: Onley for Blare & Parker, 1702). (Menke p.235).

26 Title as in 25 (London: no publisher, 1708). (Menke p. 236).

27 *The History of Reynard the Fox and Reynardine his Son...* (London: Onley [?]. c.1710).
London, BL: 12430. a. 8. (Menke p. 237).

28 Title as in 25 (London: Norris, 1723).
London, BL: 1164. a. 23. (Menke p. 238).

29 *The Ancient and Delightful History of Reynard the Fox* (Dublin: Dobson, 1728). (Menke p. 245).

30 *The Most Pleasing and Delightful History of Reynard the Fox, and Reynardine his Son...to which is added The History of Cawood the Rook...* (London: Bettesworth & Hitch, 1735).
Edinburgh, NL: H. 10. G. 2.
London, BL: 11511. a. 24. (Menke p. 239).

31 Title as in 30 (Dublin: Blow [?], 1749). (Menke p. 240).

32 *The History of Reynard the Fox* [chap-book] (London: no publisher, c.1750).
London, BL: 1079. I. 15. (6). (Menke p. 248).

33 *The Most Pleasing and Delightful History of Reynard the Fox, and Reynardine his Son...to which is added The History of Cawood the Rook...*(Belfast: Blow, 1763). (Menke p. 241).

34 *The most pleasant History of Reynard the Fox* (Newcastle-upon-Tyne: Saint, c.1769-88). London, BL: 11621. c. 8. (16). (Menke p. 232).

35 *The History of Reynard the Fox* [chap-book] (London: no publisher, c.1775). London, BL: 1076. L. I. (7). (Menke p. 248).

36 *The pleasant and entertaining History of Reynard the Fox* [schoolbook] (London: Ryland, c.1775). London, BL: Ch. 770/18. (Menke p. 250).

37 *The Most Pleasant History of Reynard the Fox* [chap-book] (Wolverhampton: Smart, c.1780). (Menke p. 233).

38 *The History of Reynard the Fox* [chap-book] (London: no publisher, c.1780). London, BL: 12315. aaa. 7(9). (Menke p. 249).

39 *The most Pleasing and Delightful History of Reynard the Fox and Reynardine his Son* (Dublin: Wogan, 1787). (Menke p. 242).

40 *The History of Reynard the Fox* [chap-book] (Penrith: Soulby, c.1800). London, Victoria and Albert Museum: Forster 1522. 5. 4.to. (Menke p. 249).

Select Bibliography

This bibliography contains only authors, editors, etc., referred to in the text and notes.

Aarne, Annti. *The Types of the Folktale* (Helsinki, 1964). Also, with Stith Thompson, Antti Aarne's Verzeichnis der Märchentypen. FF Communications 3, translated and enlarged (Helsinki, 1973.

Aesop. See Handford; Lenaghan.

Alexander, J. & Binski, P. *Age of Chivalry: Art in Plantagenet England 1200-1400*, (London: Royal Academy of Arts, 1987).

Anderson, M.D. *Animal Carvings in British Churches* (Cambridge: Cambridge University Press, 1938).

Babrius and Phaedrus. See Perry.

Barnouw, A.J. *Reynard the Fox* pp.47-157 in *Reynard the Fox and other Medieval Netherlands Secular Literature*, E. Colledge, editor (Leyden: Sijthoff, 1967).

Bastin, Julia, editor. *Recueil Général des Isopets*, two volumes, (Paris: Société des Anciens Textes Français, 1929-30).

Bedaux, J.B. 'Laatmiddeleeuwse Sexuele Amuletten' in *Annus Quadriga Mundi: opstellen over middeleeuwse kunst opgedragen aan prf. dr. Anna C. Esmeijer.* Ed., ibid. (de Walburg Pers, 1989).

Beer, Jeanette, translator. *Master Richard's Bestiary of Love and Response* (Berkeley, California: University of California Press, 1984).

Bennett, J.A.W. & G.V. Smithers, compilers and editors. *Early Middle English Verse and Prose* (Oxford: University of Oxford Press, 2nd edition, 1968).

Bestiary of Love. See Beer.

Bergner, Heinz. '*The Fox and the Wolf* und die Gattung des Tierepos in der Mittelenglischen Literatur' in *Germanisch-Romanische Monatsschrift*, 54, new series, 1973.

Bianciotto, Gabriel, compiler and translator. *Bestiaires du Moyen Âge* (Paris: Stock + Plus, 1980).

Blake, Norman F. 'English Versions of Reynard the Fox in the Fifteenth and Sixteenth Centuries, *Studies in Philology*, 62, 1965.

Blake, Norman F., editor. *Caxton: The History of Reynard the Fox*, The Early English Text Society (London, New York and Toronto: Oxford University Press, 1973).

Bond, F. *Wood Carvings in English Churches: I, Misericords* (Oxford: Oxford University Press, 1910).

Bonheur, Janie. 'La Vraie Histoire du Corbeau et du Renard' in *Paris Match* No. 763, 23 November, 1963.

Bozon, N. See Toulmin-Smith & Meyer.

Buschinger, Danielle, & Jean-Marc Pastré, translators. *Heinrich der Glichezaere 'Reinhart Fuchs': Traduction Française,* Wiener Arbeiten Zur Germanischen Altertumskunde Und Philologie, 25 (Vienna: Halosar, 1984).

Carlill, James, translator. *The Physiologus* in *The Epic of the Beast*, introduced by William Rose, Broadway Translations (London: Routledge, 1926).

Cave, C.J.P. *Roof Bosses in Medieval Churches: an Aspect of Gothic Sculpture* (Cambridge: Cambridge University Press, 1948).

Chabaille, P. *Le Roman de Renart: Supplément, Variantes et Corrections* (Paris: Silvestre, 1835).

Chaucer. See Coghill 1951; Coghill & Tolkien; 1959; Sisam.

Coghill, Nevill. *The Nun's Priest's Tale,* pp.238-55 in *Chaucer: The Canterbury Tales* (Harmondsworth: Penguin Classics, 1951).

Coghill, Nevill & Christopher Tolkien, editors. *Chaucer: The Nun's Priest's Tale* (London: Harrap, 1959).

Combarieu du Grès, Micheline. '*Faire la morte vieille*: la ruse de la morte feinte dans le *Roman de Renart*' in *Bulletin de Liaison de l'Équipe de Recherche sur la Littérature de l'Imagination du Moyen Âge*, 7, 1991.

Combarieu du Grès, Micheline & Jean Subrenat, editors and translators. *Le Roman de Renart*, Bibliothèque Médiévale series, 10/18, two volumes (Paris: Union Générale des Éditions, 1981; repr. 1985).

Comical Creatures From Wurtemberg, Including The Story Of Reynard The Fox. With Twenty Illlustrations, Drawn From The Stuffed Animals Contributed By Herrmann Ploucquet Of Stuttgart To The Great Exhibition, third edition (London: D. Bogue, 1851).

Curley, Michael J., translator. *The Physiologus* (Austin, Texas, 1979).

Dicke, Gerd & Klaus Grubmüller. *Die Fabeln des Mittelalters und der frühen Neuzeit: ein Katalog der deutschen Versionen und ihrer lateinischen Entsprechungen* (München: Wilhelm Fink, 1987).

Dodwell, C.R. *The Canterbury School of Illumination, 1066-1200* (Cambridge: Cambridge University Press, 1954).

Druce, George Claridge, translator. *The Bestiary of Guillaume Le Clerc* (printed for private circulation by Headley Brothers, Invicta Press, Ashford, Kent, 1936).

Druce, G.C. 'Medieval Bestiaries and their Influence on Ecclesiastical and Decorative Art, *Journal of the British Archaeological Association*, n.s. 25-26, 1919.

Dufournet, Jean, & A. Méline, editors and translators. *Le Roman de Renart*, GF Flammarion 418 (Paris: Flammarion, 1985).

Düwel, Klaus, editor. *Der 'Reinhart Fuchs' des Elsässers Heinrich*, Altdeutsche Textbibliothek, 96 (Tübingen: Niemeyer, 1984).

Ecbasis Cuiusdem Captivi. See Zeydel.

Ewert, Alfred & R.C. Johnston, editors. *Marie de France: Fables*, Blackwell's French Texts (Oxford: Blackwell, 1964).

Field, Richard S. *The Fable of the Sick Lion: a Fifteenth-Century Blockbook* (Middletown, Connecticut: Davison Art Centre, Wesleyan University, 1974).

Flinn, John. *Le Roman de Renart dans la littérature française et dans les littératures étrangères au Moyen Âge*, Romance Series 4 (Toronto: University of Toronto Press, 1963).

Foulet, Lucien. *Le Roman de Renard*, Bibliothèque de l'École des Hautes Études, IVe Section: Sciences Historiques et Philologiques, 211 (Paris: Champion, 1914, repr. 1968).

Froude, James Anthony. 'Reynard the Fox' in his *Short Stories on Great Subjects* (London: Longmans and Green, 1897). Also in his *Essays in Literature and History* in the Everyman's Library Series (London: Dent, no date).

Goethe, Johann Wolfgang von. *Reineke Fuchs: Mit 36 Jllustrationen von Wilhelm von Kaulbach* (Wiesbaden: Hasso Ebeling, 1973).

Goossens, Jan, editor. *Reynaerts Historie, Reinke de Vos: Gegenüberstellung einer Auswahl aus den niederländischen Fassungen und des niederdeutschen Textes von 1498* (Darmstadt: Wissenschaftliche Buchgesellschaft, 1983).

Grossinger, Christa. *The World Upside-Down: English Misericords* (London: Harvey Miller, 1997).

Guillaume Le Clerc. See Druce: 1936.

Hamilton, Vivien. *Joseph Crawhall (1861-1913): One Of The Glasgow Boys* (Glasgow: Glasgow Museums and Art Galleries, 1990).

Handford, S.A., compiler and translator. Penguin Classics, *Fables of Aesop* (Harmondsworth: Penguin, 1954, numerous reprints).

Hassig, Debra: *Medieval Bestiaries: Texts, Images Ideology* (Cambridge: University of Cambridge Press, 1995).

Hervieux, Léopold. *Les Fabulistes latins depuis le siècle d'Auguste jusqu'à la fin du Moyen Âge* (Paris,1884, 2nd edition, five volumes, 1893-99).

Hodnett, E: *English Woodcuts, 1480-1535*.(Oxford, 1935, second edition London, 1975).

Honegger, Thomas. 'A Fox is a Fox is a Fox: *The Fox and the Wolf* Reconsidered', *Reinardus* 9, 1996.

Isopets: See Bastin.

Jacobs, John C., translator. *The Fables of Odo of Cheriton* (Syracuse, New York, U.S.A.: Syracuse University Press, 1985).

Jacobs, Joseph, editor: 1889. *The Fables of Aesop as first printed by William Caxton in 1484 with those of Avian, Alfonso and Poggio*, two volumes (London, 1889).

Janson, H,W. *Apes and Ape Lore in the Middle Ages and the Renaissance*, Studies of the Warburg Institute, 20 (London: The Warburg Institute, 1952).

Jones, Malcolm H.: 1991. *The Misericords of Beverley Minster*, unpublished Ph.D. thesis.(The Polytechnic South West; Faculty of Arts and Design, Plymouth, 1991).

Jones, Malcolm. 'Sex and Sexuality in Late Medieval and Early Modern Art', *Privatisierung der Triebe? Sexualität in der Frühen Neuzeit*, editor Daniela Erlach and others (Frankfurt-am-Main: Peter Lang, 1994) pp.187-301. (This is part of *Frühneuzeit-Studien*, Band I , Institut für die Erforschung der Frühen Neuzeit, Wien.)

Jones, Malcolm & Charles Tracy. 'A Medieval Choirstall Desk-End at Haddon Hall: the Fox-Bishop and the Geese-Hangmen', *Journal of the British Archaeological Association*, 144 (1994) 107-115, and plates XII-XV.

Klingender, F. *Animals in Art and Thought* (London: Routledge & Kegan Paul, 1971).

Köhler, K., editor. *Philippe de Novare: Mémoires (1218-1243)*, (Paris, 1913).

Lenaghan, R.T., editor. *Caxton's Aesop* (Cambridge, Mass., 1967).

Lomazzi, Anna, editor. *Rainaldo e Lesengrino,* Biblioteca dell' Archivum Romanicum, 1, 116 (Florence: Leo S. Olschki, 1972).

Lulofs, Frank, editor. *Van den vos Reynaerde* (Groningen: Wolters-Noordhoff, 1983).

MacQueen, J.& W., editors. *The Tod*, pp.55-85 in *A Choice of Scottish Verse 1470-1570* (London: Faber & Faber, 1972).

Mann, Jill, editor & translator. *Ysengrimus: Text With Translation, Commentary And Introduction*, Mittellateinische Studien Und Texte, Band XII (Leiden: Brill, 1987).

Marie de France. See Ewert & Johnston; Warnke.

Martin, Ernest, editor. *Le Roman de Renart*, three volumes (Strasbourg: Trübner, 1882-87).

McCulloch, Florence. *Medieval Latin and French Bestiaries* (Chapel Hill: University of North Carolina Press, 1960).

McCulloch, Florence: 'The Funeral of Renart the Fox', *The Journal of the Walters Art Gallery*, 25-26 (1962-63), 9-27.

Menke, Hubertus. *Bibliotheca Reinardiana. Teil 1: Die europäischen Reineke-Fuchs-Drucke bis zum Jahr 1800* (Stuttgart: Hauswedell, 1992).

Mish, Charles C. 'Reynard the Fox in the Seventeenth Century', *Huntington Library Quarterly*, 17 (1953-54), 327-44.

Mossé, F. 'Anthroponymie et histoire littéraire: le *Roman de Renart* dans l'Angleterre du Moyen Âge,' in *Les Langues Modernes*, 45 (1951), 70-84.

Neff, Karl, editor. *Die Gedichte des Paulus Diaconus*, Quellen und Untersuchungen zur lateinischen Philologie des Mittelalters 3 (Munich, 1908).

Nichol, J. *The History and Antiquities of the County of Leicester,* two vols (1815).

Nun's Priest's Tale, The. See Coghill 1951; Coghill & Tolkien 1959; Sisam.

Odo of Cheriton. See Jacobs.

Owen, D.D.R., translator. *The Romance of Reynard the Fox* (Oxford: Oxford University Press, 1994).

Pantzer, K.F. et al. The *Short Title Catalogue* (London: British Library).

Paulus Diaconus. See Neff.

Perry, Ben Edwin, editor and translator. *Babrius and Phaedrus* (Cambridge, Mass.: Loeb Classical Library, 1965).

Peterson, P. *Rävens och Tranans gästabad [Fox and Crane Invite Each Other]*, Acta Universitatis Upsaliensis, Studia Ethnologica Upsaliensis 8 (Uppsala: Almqvist & Wiksell International, 1981).

Philippe de Novare. See Köhler.

Philippe de Thaun. See Walberg.

Physiologus, The. See Carlill; Curley.

Rabbi Berechiah Ha-Nakdan. See Schwarzbaum.

Rainaldo e Lesengrino. See Lomazzi.

Randall, Lilian M.C. *Images in the Margins of Gothic Manuscripts,* California Studies in the History of Art (Berkeley and Los Angeles: University of California Press, 1966).

Raynaud, G. & Lemaître, H., editors. *Le Roman de Renart le Contrefait*, two volumes (Paris: Champion, 1914).

Regalado, Nancy Freeman. 'Staging the *Roman de Renart*: Medieval Theater and the Diffusion of Political Concerns into Popular Culture', *Mediaevalia*, 18 (1995 for 1992), 111-141.

Regnart, Le Livre de. See Suomela-Härmä.

Reineke Fuchs. See Goethe.

Reinhart Fuchs. See Buschinger & Pastré; Düwel.

Reinke de Vos. See Goossens.

Reinsch, Robert, editor. *Le Bestiaire: Das Thierbuch des normannischen Dichters Guillaume le Clerc* (Leipzig, 1880, repr. 1967).

Renart le Contrefait, Le Roman de. See Raynaud & Lemaître

Renart le Nouvel. See Roussel.

Renart, Le Roman de. See Chabaille; Combarieu du Grès & Subrenat; Dufournet & Méline; Martin; Owen; Roques; Strubel.

Renert. See Rodange.

Reynaerts Historie. See Goossens.

Reynard the Fox, The History of. See Blake 1965 and 1973; Sands

Rickert, M. *Painting in Britain: the Middle Ages*, Pelican History of Art (Harmondsworth: Penguin, 1954).

Rodange, Michel, editor. *Renert* (Luxembourg: Krippler, 1975).

Rodin, Kerstin. *Räven predikar för Gässen: en studie av ett ordsprak i senmedeltida ikonografi* [The Fox Preaches to the Geese: A Study of a Proverb in Late Medieval Iconography], Acta Universitatis Upsaliensis, Studia Ethnologica Upsaliensia, 11 (Uppsala: Almquist & Wiksell, 1983).

Roques, Mario, editor. *Le Roman de Renart*, Classiques Français du Moyen Âge, 81 (Paris: Champion, 1954).

Rouse, E. Clive & Kenneth Varty: 1976. 'Medieval Paintings of Reynard the Fox in Gloucester Cathedral, and Some Other Related Examples', *The Archaeological Journal*, 133 (1976), 104-17.

Roussel, H., editor. *Renart le Nouvel* (Paris, 1961).

Sands, Donald B., editor. *The History of Reynard the Fox Translated and Printed by William Caxton in 1481* (Cambridge, Massachusetts: Harvard University Press, 1960).

Scheidegger, Jean R. *Le Roman de Renart, ou le texte de la dérision*, Publications Romanes et Françaises, 188 (Geneva: Droz, 1989).

Schouwink, Wilfried. 'The Fox's Funeral in European Art: Transformations of a Literary Motif', *Reinardus*, special volume (1993), 169-79.

Schwarzbaum, Haim. *The 'Mishlé Shu' alim' (Fox Fables) of the Rabbi Berechiah Ha-Nakdan: A Study in Comparative Folklore and Fable Lore* (Kizon: Institute for Jewish and Arab Folklore Research, 1979).

Sisam, Kenneth, editor. *Chaucer's Nun's Priest's Tale* (Oxford: The Clarendon Press, 1927).

Spencer, Brian. *Salisbury and South Wiltshire Museum: Medieval Catalogue, Part 2: Pilgrim Souvenirs and Secular Badges* (Salisbury: Salisbury and South Wiltshire Museum, 1990).

Stenton, Sir Frederick, general editor. *The Bayeux Tapestry: A Comprehensive Survey* (London: Phaidon Press, 1965).

Stone, L. *Sculpture in Britain: the Middle Ages*, Pelican History of Art (Harmondsworth: Penguin, 1955).

Strubel, Armand et al., editors. *Le Roman de Renart*, Bibliothèque de la Pléiade No. 445 (Paris: Éditions Gallimard, 1998).

Suomela-Härmä, Elina, editor. *Le Livre de Regnart*, Bibliothèque du XVe Siècle, LX (Paris: Champion, 1998).

Thordstein, A., editor. *Le Bestiaire d'Amour Rimé*. (1941).

Toulmin-Smith, Lucy & Paul Meyer, editors. *Les Contes moralisés de Nicole Bozon, frère mineur* (Paris, 1889, repr. 1968).

Trachsler, Richard: 1994. *'Si le gita / sor son dos, et si l'en porta (Yvain,* vv.3445-46) ou: comment porter un cerf si vous êtes un lion', *Reinardus* 7 (1994), 183-93.

Tracy, Charles. *English Gothic Choir-Stalls, 1200-1400* (Woodbridge: Boydell and Brewer, 1987).

Tracy, Charles. *English Gothic Choir-Stalls, 1400-1540.* (Woodbridge: Boydell and Brewer, 1990).

Van Daele, Rik, editor. *Van den vos Reynaerde Ontsluierd* (Gent: Kultureel Jaarboek voor de Provincie Oost-Vlanderen, Bijdragen, Nieuwe Reeks - Nr 30, 1989).

Van Daele, Rik & Paul Wackers. 'Nog twee Antwerpse Reynaertmeubelen van omstreeks 1700', *Antiek*, October, 23rd Year (1988), No. 3.

Van den vos Reynaerde. See Lulofs.

Varty, Kenneth. 'Reynard the Fox and the Smithfield Decretals', *Journal of the Warburg and Courtauld Institutes*, 26 (1963), 348-54.

Varty, Kenneth. 'The Death and Resurrection of Reynard in Medieval Literature and Art', *Nottingham Nedieval Studies*, 10 (1966) 70-93.

Varty, Kenneth. *Reynard the Fox: a study of the fox in medieval English art* (Leicester: Unversity of Leicester Press, 1967).

Varty, Kenneth. 'The Earliest Illustrated English Editions of *Reynard the Fox* and Their Links With the Earliest Illustrated Continental Editions' in Niederdeutsche Studien, 27 *Reynaert, Reynard, Reynke: Studien zu einem Mittelalterlichen Tierepos*, ed J. Goossens and T. Sodmann (Cologne and Vienna: Böhlau, 1980).

Varty, Kenneth. 'The Iconography of the Medieval Beast Epic: From Manuscript to Printed Page', in *The Medieval Alexander Legend and Romance Epic: Essays in Honour of David J.A. Ross*, ed. Peter Noble et al (New York: Kraus, 1983), pp.243-58.

Varty, Kenneth: 1991 A. 'Les Funérailles de Renart le goupil' in *À la Recherche du 'Roman de Renart'* Volume II (New Alyth: Lochee Publications, 1991), pp.361-90.

Varty, Kenneth: 1991 B. 'La Représentation visuelle de la *matière de Renart* : les anthologies picturales' in *À la Recherche du 'Roman de Renart'* Volume II (New Alyth: Lochee Publications, 1991), pp.421-444.

Varty, Kenneth. 'A Scottish Victorian Descendant of *Reynke de Vos*' in *Lingua Theodisca: Beiträge zur Sprach- und Literaturwissenschaft. Jan Goossens zum 65. Geburtstag* (two volumes) ed. José Cajot et al, *Niederlande-Studien* 16, No 2 (1995), 1075-85.

Varty, Kenneth. 'On the Comic Qualities of *Vox and Wolf*: and Some Related Predecessors' in *Medieval Heritage: Essays in Honour of Tadahiro Ikegami*, ed. Masahiko Kanno et al, (Tokyo: Yushodo Press, 1997).

Varty, Kenneth. (1998 A). *The 'Roman de Renart': A Guide to Scholarly Work* (Lanham, Md., USA: Scarecrow, 1998).

Varty, Kenneth. (1998 B). 'La Pénétration du *Roman de Renart* en Angleterre au Moyen Âge' in *Mélanges in Memoriam Takeshi Shimmura* (Tokyo: 1998), pp.93-99.

Vedder, David. *The Story of Reynard the Fox* (Edinburgh: Menzies, 1852).

Vedder, Raimund. 'Die Illustrationen in den frühen Drucken des *Reynke de vos*' in Niederdeutsche Studien 27, *Reynaert, Reynard, Reynke: Studien zu einem mittelalterlichen Tierepos*, ed. by J.Goossens and T. Sodmann, (Cologne and Vienna: Böhlau, 1981).

Wackers, Paul & Rik Van Daele. 'Antwerpse Reynaartscribanen van omstreeks 1700', *Antiek*, February, 22nd Year (1988) No. 7.

Walberg, Emmanuel, editor. *Le Bestiaire de Philippe de Thaun* (Lund: Müller, 1930).

Warner, Sir George. *Queen Mary's Psalter* (London, 1912).

Warnke, K., editor. *Die Fabeln der Marie de France* (Halle, 1925).

White, T.H., translator. *The Book of Beasts.* (Sovereign: Sutton, 1954, repr. 1984).

Wolf, J. *Lectionum Memorabilium et Reconditarum*, volume two, 1600.

Woodforde, C. *Stained Glass in Somerset 1250-1830* (Oxford: Oxford University Press, 1947).

Wright, T. *A History of Caricature and Grotesque in Literature and Art* (London, 1864).

Ysengrimus, The. See Mann.

Zeydel, Edwin H., editor and translator. *Ecbasis Cuiusdem Captivi* (New York: AMS, 1966).

Index of Proper Names and Book Titles

Index of Subject Matter

[numbers and text in italics refer to the entries in the Appendixes; plain text numbers refer to pages]